P9-DJA-932

Keys to Prosperity

43648744

Keys to Prosperity

Free Markets, Sound Money, and a Bit of Luck

Rudi Dornbusch

The MIT Press
Cambridge, Massachusetts
London, England

© 2000 Massachusetts Institute of Technology

All rights reserved. No part of this book may be reproduced in any form by any electronic or mechanical means (including photocopying, recording, or information storage and retrieval) without permission in writing from the publisher.

This book was set in Sabon on '3B2' by Asco Typesetters, Hong Kong.
Printed and bound in the United States of America.

Library of Congress Cataloging-in-Publication Data

Dornbusch, Rudiger.
  Keys to prosperity : free markets, sound money, and a bit of luck /
Rudi Dornbusch.
    p.   cm.
  Includes bibliographical references and index.
  ISBN 0-262-04181-2   (hc. : alk. paper)
  1. Economic policy. 2. Economic history—1990– I. Title.
HD87.D69   2000
338.9—dc21   00-035156

Original publication information can be found on the first page of individual chapters.

Contents

Preface

Along with teaching economics, writing economic commentary on issues of the day has increasingly absorbed my attention and enthusiasm. Economics can be understood by anyone who cares to, provided that there is a view expressed. Invariably, I have tried to shy away from the "on one hand and on the other," which, while eclectic, is also dull writing and worse reading. The pieces take a view and most, but not all, have held up well.

The essays focus on issues of economic policy, both domestic and international. They deal with inflation and debt, exchange rates, trade policy, emerging markets, and the intersection of politics and good economics. The underlying economic ideology is unabashedly Chicago, that is, the University of Chicago belief that markets solve problems best and that bureaucrats on balance, even when well-intentioned, are distracted by politics or excessive zeal for perfect solutions. The Chicago view is that complex problems have simple answers. (The MIT retort is that complex problems have easy-to-understand *wrong* answers.) True, those answers are a bit tough at times, but who is to argue that on balance the bureaucrats have had better results? In any event, even if they had, they are always in charge and hence must be challenged all the time to keep them in touch with alternative answers and to limit their ambitions.

The players in charge of policy might sit in a central bank and have problems with prosperity or, on the contrary, make too little of inflation risks. Or they might run international institutions and enjoy seeing themselves in high-noon crisis situations, throwing money at problems that would better be solved by defaults. Or they might be unions that proclaim their provincial and often misunderstood self-interest as a national objective of sound policy. But the focus is not just on central bankers, bureaucrats, unions, or do-gooders. In the firing line are also misgoverning politicians from Brazil to Russia, and Japan and the many other places where the absence of an effective democracy and account-ability has led to scandalous risks and economic disasters.

The material collected here is only a sample of pieces written over the past few years. For a while, I wrote a column for *Business Week* and quite a few pieces are reproduced from that publication. There are also editorials from the *Wall Street Journal*, the *Financial Times*, and a num-ber of foreign papers in which I write regularly. And there are a few longer essays that have appeared, or will, in various books.

This collection of essays was selected from a much larger sample by Kristin Forbes, then a graduate student and now a faculty member of the MIT Sloan School of Management. Many thanks for her efforts and enthusiasm.

I
The Big Picture

1

A Century of Unrivaled Prosperity

On the verge of deflation, Japan bankrupt and Europe moving at near-stalling speed only, the emerging markets battered and the United States beholding a glorious bubble—how can this mark the end of a great century of prosperity? And yet, this has been the best century ever, never mind the Great Depression, and momentary setback from communism and socialism, and two great wars. Humankind today is far and further ahead of where it has ever been, and there are the seeds of innovation from biology to the Internet for better and richer lives even beyond our wildest dreams. One of the great economists of this century, Joseph Schumpeter—Austrian finance minister of the 1920s and Harvard professor after 1932—wrote of creative destruction as the dramatic mechanism of economic progress.

The twenty-first century, and in particular the last three decades, have witnessed just that as the nation state has been dismantled in favor of a global economy, state enterprise and economic repression give way to and free enterprise, and breathtaking innovation and greedy capitalism break down government and corporate bureaucracies. Anyone who says *impossible* finds himself interrupted by someone who just did it. The process is far from complete; innovation and free enterprise spread the mindset, the success, and the acceptance of this model to the horror of status quo politicians and the sheer exuberance of all those who are willing to embrace a can-do attitude. If this century taught anything it is surely this: even daunting setbacks like depression and war are only momentary tragedies—buying opportunities, if you like—in a relentless advance of the standard of living and the scope for enjoying better lives.

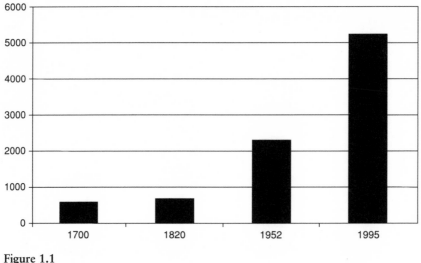

Figure 1.1
World Per Capita GDP

A Century of Unrivaled Growth

For centuries, human progress was limited by low productivity. Estimates of per capita GDP in 1700 that we owe to the creative work of Angus Maddison show every region in the world with much the same income per capita and minimal differences between the United States, China, and India. From 1700 to 1820, almost nothing happened to world per capita GDP. (See figure 1.1.) True, Europe then was somewhat ahead, but less than twenty percent. A century later, by 1820, the differences had widened to give Europe and the United States twice the income per head enjoyed China, Japan, or Russia, where near-stagnation had been the rule. Yet at the time, India and China combined accounted for one half of world GDP! And then comes the first burst of dramatic growth that triples Europe's standard of living in the nineteenth century while quadrupling that in the United States. After centuries of virtually no progress, rapid advances in the standard of living changed both the fact and the aspiration of what could be achieved. The driving forces were capital accumulation and technical innovation, the division of labor, and the spread of skills and capital around the world. (See figure 1.2.)

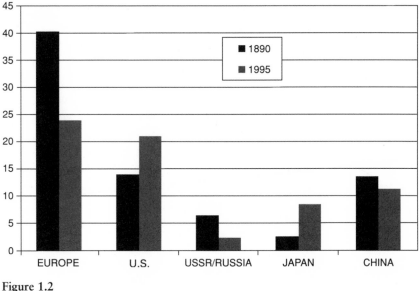

Figure 1.2
Share of World GDP: 1890 and 1995

But what seemed dramatic progress in the nineteenth century does not hold up to the achievements of this century. The twentieth century has seen the most rapid advance in living standards on record, much of it concentrated in the second half. Just since the 1950s, Japan has increased its standard of living eightfold; China has raised more than sevenfold its per capita income in that period. And emerging market Asia has done much the same. An opening world economy, high savings almost every-where (except in the United States), and the implementation of ever bet-ter technologies and economic structures have done much to provide the engine; moreover, a half century of peace (and superpower competition) has helped, not diverted attention from, economic growth. Whether pro-gress is measured by automobiles and TV sets per head, the decline in the cost of phone calls around the world, exploding capacity of an ever smaller computer, the increasing perfection of a CD recording, or the laser sur-gery that yields a new life—by any of these measures, 1900 was the stone age compared to where we stand today. Long-distance learning live and on the screen is a far leap from black-and-white still photography.

The record pace of growth in per capita GDP in the second half of this century naturally invites the question of what is behind it and whether there is a common explanation that is useful everywhere. Economics identifies two elements: first, and quite obviously, a high pace of saving and capital formation in the world. This equips the labor force with increasing amounts of machinery and structures and thus makes labor more productive. No less obvious is the other factor, technological progress, that means that we learn to do things better so that the same amount of labor and machinery produces increasing amounts of output. In the same vein, technical progress also means that over time new ideas and improved technologies are embodied in better machinery and hence improved productivity. And so do better ways of organizing production and institutions that are more conducive to specialization and productivity. Some highlight creative destruction and others view stable accumulation as the trick—have war and ideological clashes held back progress compared to what it might have been without? Or is it possible, on the contrary, that they have been drivers of progress by destroying inherited crusty structures and obsolete technologies? The case has been made by observing Japan's progress and that of Germany after World War II, putting them far ahead of the rest of the crowd. But then why did it not work in France?

Economics Nobel laureate Robert Solow was the first to ask just how much of growth derives from capital formation and how much to attribute to the "residual," aptly named technical progress but really a bag for everything else. His stunning conclusion gave capital formation credit for just one-third of per capita growth and determined technical progress was responsible for the rest. That conclusion remains dramatic because it does suggest that the emphasis on saving and investment—popular among communists, in Japan, and in Europe—is perhaps overdone. After all, the economic game is about consumption, and if it is possible to both consume and get ahead, so much the better. But that is probably the wrong conclusion to draw.

The right one focuses on increased interest in just what makes up the mysterious technical progress. Is it good financial institutions, is it an economic setting that fosters efficient allocation, is it political stability and property rights, and is it Japanese-style obedience training in schools and on the job? Is it copying other countries' best technologies, or is that hard and unrelenting pressure of stock markets to extract yet better cost performance from CEOs and workers? Disappointingly, the empirical evidence does not give us a short list of factors enhancing technical progress; the evidence remains open except in a few respects: instability, inflation, mindless bureaucracies, closed and repressed economies—all these are environments where progress is possible but only by working and saving extra hard. But when it comes to corporate governance, U.S. style versus Japan, or labor-market characteristics with European long-term relations or a U.S.-style high turnover, it is hard to show that one or the other has the better influence on how to get ahead. Japanese governance and the German labor market once seemed to hold out the prospect for much better performance; today, one is identified with the bankruptcy of Japan and the other with the sclerosis of Europe. The search for lasting good answers continues.

Both the nineteenth and twentieth century saw the rapid progress of the advanced countries, so it is no surprise that we identify them with innovation and sustained high rates of capital formation. But the surprise is surely that in just a span of fifty years developing countries have shaken off century-old backwardness. Japan was the first to embark on this path, starting with the reform waves in the last decades of the past century. (See figure 1.3.) But it was in particular the last three decades of this century that witnessed the dramatic performance of emerging economies throughout Asia but also, off and on, in other parts of the world. In this period, India nearly tripled its standard of living. From endemic near-starvation, it moved far in the direction of sustained rates of per capita GDP growth. Singapore came from nowhere to overtake Great Britain, China accomplished a phenomenal sixfold increase in the living standard starting from a situation in 1950 that was no different from what it had been in 1700! There must be no mistake in reading the Asian performance: it does involve very hard work—more hours and more days—and it involves formidable sacrifices of current consumption in favor of capital accumulation and economic advance. There is no indication at all that without equal effort Asia would have made the big leap forward. But yes, it has done so, and Asians have covered the path of centuries elsewhere in just a few decades. Only very authoritarian

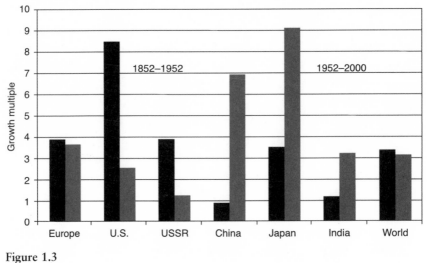

Figure 1.3
Economic Progress

regimes can accomplish such progress since in open societies sacrificing a few generations is not a viable option.

One is tempted to ask which major country is the great winner of this century. Clearly, Russia is not since it has seen more suffering and deprivation and less progress than almost anywhere else. That was not obvious by the mid-1970s when Russian per capita GDP peaked, but it is beyond discussion today and increasingly the case. Europe, Japan, the United States, and China are among the finalists; on the basis of sheer numbers, Japan is the winner, the Great Depression and a drastic defeat notwithstanding. China is next with the awesome growth of the past three decades. Europe and the United States did well enough by historical standards—quintupling income per head in a century had no precedent, but it was just that and not the pace of Japan or China. That is quite in line with what modern growth economics teaches: the ones who come from behind move faster and tend, ultimately, to converge. But that pace of convergence is still very unequal, and its continuation is not even a foregone conclusion: Russia and Africa are moving backward, while India is advancing but not at the gallop pace of emerging Asia. For those who lead the pack, growth tapers off to moderate rates.

Globalization

The late second part of the nineteenth century had seen the steamship, railroads, and telegraph as the major breakthroughs in joining the periphery to the world's center economies. Globalization was the rule in trade, in migration, and in the free flow of capital. The gold standard was but part of what made the open world economy function. The rich countries wrote the rules, they had the gunboats to collect debts, and they had all the interest in keeping open the world economy even as they collected colonies, spreading the benefits of free trade. This was the period in which the United States had risen rapidly to prosperity and Australia and Argentina came to top rank in the world economy. Migration to the New World, and the migration of capital, rapidly developed the world's periphery. If there were concerns about globalization then, they were not important enough to be remembered.

The dramatic event of the next century was the Great Depression—the total collapse of trade flows, belief in open trade, and belief in free market economics. In a handful of years, the lessons of a century were discredited. In just three years, from 1929 to 1932, world trade fell by 70 percent in value terms and 25 percent in real terms. Prices in world trade collapsed, and trade restrictions were mounted around the world, as "beggar-thy-neighbor" policies became the rule. Tariffs were escalated, quantitative restrictions and selected preferences became the rule, and exchange control soon followed. The open economy had given way to protection of national markets and an overwhelming presumption that economics stops at the border. If these were the policies at the center, the periphery responded in kind. Debt default was common, and industrialization behind protective barriers became the rule in those countries where commodity collapses no longer afforded a living. Latin America is a case in point.

But already by 1934, driven by the all-important U.S. Reciprocal Trade Agreements, the attempt to reopen world trade got underway. But it would take decades to gradually break down the fortresses. A key part of that reconstruction was the Marshall Plan, which rewarded European restoration of trade. An attempt at a World Trade Organization failed, but the General Agreement on Tariffs and Trade (GATT) became a pragmatic way of negotiating reciprocal, nondiscriminatory opening of trade. At the end of the 1950s, exchange controls were dismantled gradually, for trade first and increasingly for all cross-border transactions. But all this was only the case for the advanced countries; the world's periphery and Japan had firmly accepted protection and currency controls as the only way to go. For them, opening up had to wait for the 1980s.

By the 1980s, the world was basically back to where it had been before the collapse in the Great Depression. Of course, communications had improved radically and that made for more openness and trade, as did dramatic improvements in transport. But at the time, fully in the midst of an open world economy, it would have been a rarity to find sharp skepticism of globalization. That seems to be an issue of far more recent vintage, fostered predominantly by five factors. First, corporations learned to operate globally in the pursuit of markets and cost reductions. The recipe was easy, capital was mobile, and in no time workers anywhere felt the competition from workers everywhere. Second, because of the mobility of capital, more financial accidents occurred, inevitably or not. Their large fallout costs evidently cast a deep suspicion on globalization that had allowed the money to come in.

The third reason the global economy has a bad name is that competitive pressure forced governments to retreat from their statist policies. That left workers with a reduced sense of protection; standard responses of trade protection were ruled out by international agreements; there was no way to leave the ring. Fourth, with leverage and integrated world capital markets, a disturbance anywhere immediately becomes a problem everywhere. With more volatile economies and markets, no day passes without reminders of the precariously small control people have over their economic lives. Last, the sheer pace of change in technology and finance, innovation, products, and winners and losers outstripped people's ability to cope: their reaction is to opt out simply because things were happening too fast. They see predominantly the threat and very little of the vast benefits. They certainly fail to recognize that when jobs are threatened it is mostly better technology, which in itself is a blessing, rather than cross border competition that puts people out of their jobs.

Globalization is the great challenge of the end of the century because, unlike in 1900, the pace of integration of the world economy has become phenomenally large. Competitors like China can, in a decade or two, move from entry-level technologies well into the middle level, threatening not only emerging markets but even established industries at the center. Workers believe that globalization is responsible for poor real wages and governments feel that their ability to control events, or at least give the appearance of doing so, is sharply diminished by the impact of world shocks on the domestic scene. The wish to opt out, or at least limit the interdependence, is heard all too often.

The openness and interdependence of the world economy is not going to be sacrificed. Nor can we be sure that volatility of financial markets declines or the pace of innovation and implementation of techniques slows down. Globalization will cease to be a concern in a generation or so, when the young who have known no other world and are tuned to less stability come to be representative. But that means globalization will be controversial and will be challenged for quite a while, and with a sympathetic hearing. It puts the burden on policymakers to keep the world economy open and to deal with unnecessary instability in a sound way.

The Fate of Good Money
Throughout the century, major changes in the value of money have been a prime economic and social issue. As the century draws to a close, the circle is complete: we are back to good money and to institutions that promise to keep it just that way. For most of the century we had inflation, interrupted briefly in the interwar period. The post–World War II period in particular raised the issue of intolerably high inflation as the result of irresponsible monetary policy. (See figure 1.4.) The price paid for instability has been steep, both while it lasted and in the aftermath, as good money had to be restored.

The century started with the gold standard: Britain had been there for a century, the United States joined after the Civil War and Germany after the Franco-German war; by 1900 every major country from Japan to Europe and Argentina was on gold. Very few countries were on paper standards, and even fewer were hanging on to silver. The gold standard meant fixed exchange rates around the world, moderate inflation because gold discoveries were not plentiful, and central banks or politicians had not yet discovered the printing press. Public finance was for the most

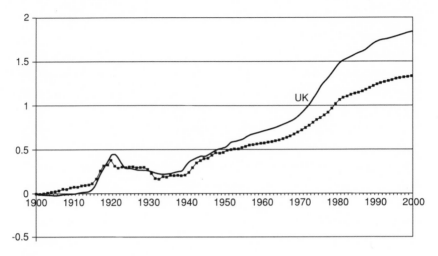

Figure 1.4
Price Level in the United States and the United Kingdom

part conservative and economic horizons were long—British perpetuities yielded 3 percent for much of the second part of the nineteenth century and until World War I. Pax Britannica was a good monetary regime.

World War I ended all that in the most dramatic fashion: along with revolution and social upheaval, good money and the emperor all landed in the garbage dump. Governments that could do virtually nothing could do but one thing, print money. And that is what marked the early 1920s: phenomenal money creation and even more extreme inflation throughout central Europe and Eastern Europe, from Germany to Russia, from Austria to Greece. France, to its own surprise, did not go quite as far; Britain and the United States, not at all.

The hyperinflation of the early 1930s was the first to be witnessed in recorded history. True, the gold discoveries in earlier centuries had led to a trend of rising prices, but ever so moderately. Sporadic episodes of paper money inflation in France had occurred during the period of the assignats, in Russia in the nineteenth century and a bit in Austria, and in Latin America. But they were, after all, insignificant compared to the vast destruction of stability and wealth in the 1920s. Lenin said, "If you want to destroy a country, destroy its money," and that is, of course, what happened. There could be no more convincing and lasting undoing of the established order and the middle class. Hyperinflation was surely the prime reason for the extremism to come.

The brief restoration of hard money in the 1920s did not last. Britain had championed the return to gold around the world and had, in fact, returned at the prewar parity, having locked itself into a desperately uncompetitive situation. From there it was just a few years to the next bout of instability as, following Britain, country after country went off gold; competitive devaluation became the rule, along with exchange control and a collapse of world trade. But going off gold was neither easy nor obvious. It was a deeply countercultural move, going against the grain of everything Britain and the City stood for. In fact, Winston Churchill said at the time, "Nobody told me you could do that"— famous last words for the end of Victorian finance. Whereas in the 1920s hyperinflation was the rule, the Great Depression brought deep deflation, which was just as unsettling to stable finance or public confidence. Those who tried to stay on gold did terribly; those who printed more money and debased their currency most aggressively did best. The world had turned upside down. Internationalism and capitalism were discredited; nationalism and ever more pervasive government took their place.

Postwar monetary reconstruction did not come easy. Huge debts, private and public, had been accumulated everywhere, and many of the assets, including the tax base, had been devastated. Price controls everywhere held off the confrontation between a vast monetary overhang and a shortage of goods; black markets were the rule, from foreign exchange to sausages. Monetary reform and reconstruction, including drastic write-down of private claims and public debts, were the rule throughout Europe. Monetary reform paved the way for price liberalization and the extraordinary resumption of economic activity thought by many impossible. The audacity of reform in Germany, in particular, stands out as notable: U.S. General Lucius Clay told the great reformer Ludwig Erhard, "Mr. Erhard, my advisers tell me your boldness is crazy," and Erhard replied, "General, my advisers say the same." Still, Erhard proved right: without functioning money, economic activity could not possibly start, but with good money it could flourish.

On the domestic front, sound money was restored rapidly almost everywhere. With a brief interruption during the Korean War, inflation was not an issue. But on the external side, it took until the end of the 1950s to restore convertibility and even then it was not general. France had recurrent lapses and Britain got there only in 1980 as one of Mrs. Thatcher's first moves in office. Japan got there almost a decade later, and increasingly the entire world. Among major players, only India and China remain with inconvertibility as a vestige of government control.

The century's monetary history would not be complete without one more attack of instability and the fierce reaction to restore hard money at any price. U.S. overexpansion of the 1960s, oil shocks of the 1970s, and, above all, an unwillingness to confront slow growth or even recession to maintain good money are behind the great inflation of this period. True, by the standards of the 1920s, this was serious inflation, but double-digit rates of price inflation alarmed the electorate and became an even more pressing issue than unemployment. In hindsight, a half-century of inflation has shrunk the purchasing power of money drastically in every advanced country. Germany fared best—of a 1950 deutsche mark, there is almost 25 percent left in real terms; in France, the United Kingdom, or Italy it is only around 5 percent. (See figure 1.5.) Clearly was time to return to stable money, and that was the battle of the past decade. The

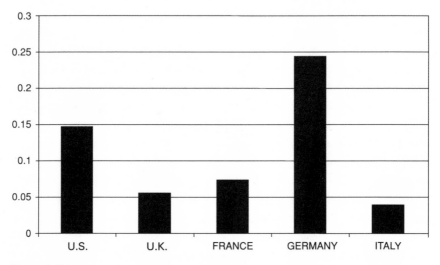

Figure 1.5
What Is Left of 1950 Purchasing Power?

mandate for much better money emerged in a strong fashion and turned central banks deaf to the pleas for accommodation. A new order, dating from the early 1980s, increasingly took hold as inflation was pushed down hard and harder. It took that decade, and another decade, to make it credible and lasting.

Today the world has no more inflation, and if it comes back it will soon hit a concrete wall. Central banks, in Europe and in the United States, are independent and committed to the idea that it needs to be killed at its very inception. Surely that proposition still needs to be tested, surely bond market yields do not quite reflect that lasting regime change yet, but skeptics are sure to be proven wrong.

Thus monetary and financial troubles prevailed basically from World War I to the late 1960s, that is, for half a century. The world we know today is pretty recent even if it is a return to where we were a century ago. The fight for hard money that has marked the past two decades has bought important changes in finance. Governments had to retreat and formally give up their authority over central banks. In Europe, that has gone furthest with the disarmament of central banks in the soft money belt of Europe, from France to Italy and Spain. Debate about whether the European Currency Board is a bit too stingy with interest-rate cuts must not obscure the central achievement: money has been taken out of the hands of politicians who have mismanaged it for the better part of this century. The ECB is a monument to the proposition that money is too serious to be left to politicians: in these matters, there is no such thing as a responsible politician; democratic money is bad money.

The quest for hard money is also taking over the periphery: country after country has suffered the clash between bad central banking and fixed currencies. In the aftermath of defeat and collapse, a simple lesson is becoming quite apparent. Countries with poor political and financial institutions cannot afford their own money. They will do far better with unconditional surrender to the ECB or the Federal Reserve. They should adopt the Euro or the U.S. dollar as the national money, get the benefit of sound money and low interest rates, avoid crises, and thus enjoy a better prospect of economic development. Surely, twenty years from now there will be very few currencies left in the world—just as at the beginning of the century. Perhaps there will be Chinese money in Asia, the dollar for the Americas, and the Euro for everything else. And perhaps the Swiss franc will be a collectors' item. The vast change in public understanding of hard money, and the resulting stability and lengthening of horizons, is a great accomplishment at the tail end of a century of monetary turmoil.

The State

In response to both the trauma of the Great Depression and a deep skepticism of free enterprise, the State has become a dominant part of economic life. At the outset of the century, outside periods of war, the state was minimal and so were levels of taxation, government employment, or public outlays. Whereas before business and finance were substantially unregulated, now the State moved to the center in repressing free enterprise and initiative. Whereas before trade and finance flowed freely across borders, now it became national and regulated. Even in the area of production, state enterprise emerged as a response to bankruptcy or private economic power judged excessive. For some, the rise of the State was an ideological response to a loss of confidence in capitalism; for others, it was a pragmatic answer to a collapse of the world economy and of economic activity.

Whatever justification there may have been for big government in the depression years and wartime, it was clearly gone by the late 1940s. And yet, big government had become the accepted paradigm and growing government the rule. For whatever reason, the State took center place in economic life; in the postwar years, it has been awfully difficult to roll back the large advance the State has made in every dimension. In fact, once the State played a key role in economic life, it was natural to look for ways of expanding its functions and powers to deal with an ever wider range of "problems," substituting government employment, subsidies, or spending for adjustment. The government grew; the private sector shrank in freedom, size, and initiative.

It is interesting to consider just a few numbers marking the case of Germany (see figure 1.6.) By 1960, government employment accounted for 8 percent of the labor force. By 1997, it was 16 percent. And that number does not completely measure the government's largesse since there is in addition the large group of unemployed who are paid not to

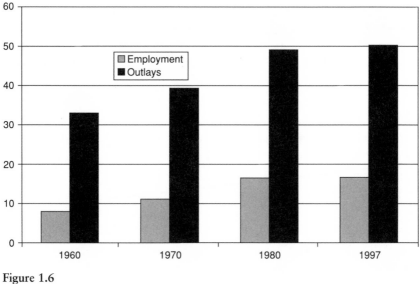

Figure 1.6
Share of Government

work and thus keep the status quo and social peace. Government outlays in 1960 amounted to 33 percent of GDP, and by 1997 they had almost reached 50 percent. Surely it is not exaggerating to say that much of the spending is devoted to stopping people from working and that much of the state apparatus does little but to slow down private initiative and success. Just what was the problem the government was solving that the private sector could not deal with? The answer is obviously that society rejected adjustment and free market responses as a solution—why accept hardship if the government commands purse and power to sustain the status quo? People were paid not to work or firms were subsidized to keep producing as if reality had not changed. Regulation completes the picture in the product market by barring initiative and competition.

The fight to restore stable money was much easier to win, particularly in Germany (see again figure 1.6), than the battle for a more productive and financially responsible economy. The reason is obvious: inflation is an immediate threat to the current generation's assets and their sense of stability. People react immediately and give policymakers a mandate to fight for stable prices. But when it comes to government spending and jobs, the choice runs the other way: borrow from the future and support current waste. Never mind that resources are wasted today and create huge tax burdens for future generations; stick with the status quo. It is unlikely that a major boom will resolve these problems and provide an easy adjustment. Communism has fallen, but capitalism is still not accepted in large parts of the world, notably in Europe, where statism keeps being entertained as a third way. It is not a third way in fact; it simply amounts to shifting burdens to future generations. The reality is that the bad habit of bloated public sectors and bloated unemployment rolls, the lack of individual initiative and responsibility, are a dramatic mortgage on future generations and the next century.

Inequality

Inequality in the world economy is real. It is there across countries, between the rich center and the poor periphery. And it is there within countries where wages are often highly dispersed. Inequality, of course, must not be confused with poverty, even though at the bottom they might feel the same.

The most immediate pass at this issue is to look at the distribution of world income and population. (See figure 1.7.) Not surprisingly, high-income countries have the overwhelming share of world income, nearly 60 percent, but have barely 15 percent of world population. By contrast, the poorest countries in the world have 35 percent of world population but less than 10 percent of world income. And even these averages disguise the more striking differences between the upper-income groups in rich countries and the poorest in poor countries, day and night. Clearly, there is nothing remotely resembling equality, nor is there a trend in that direction.

Within countries, in comparisons of poor and rich, the story is actually more favorable, at least in the past thirty years. (See figure 1.8.) Of course, the poor have a far smaller income share than the rich, but everywhere the discrepancy has declined. In Latin America, where the poor used to have 5 percent of the income of the rich, they are now up to nearly 8 percent. In the far more equal Asian region, the poor have moved from 16 to 22 percent of the incomes accruing to the rich.

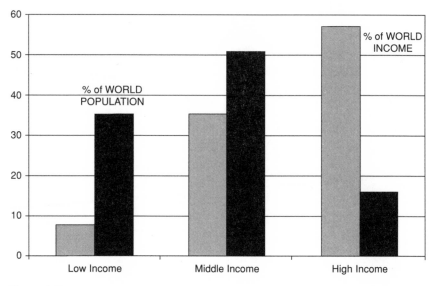

Figure 1.7
Share of World Income and Population

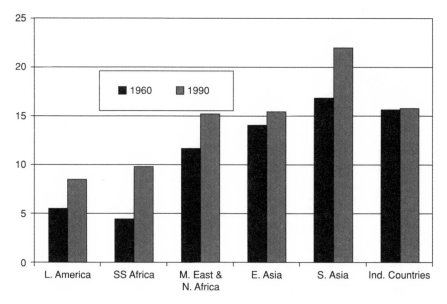

Figure 1.8
Poorest-Richest Income Comparison

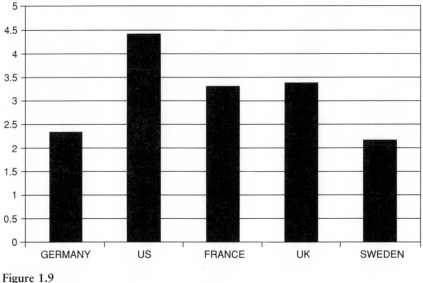

Figure 1.9
Earnings Dispersion: Top to Bottom Decile

And there is a third dimension of inequality, this one on the job. How do the top and bottom groups (deciles) of the labor force compare in earnings? Are wages highly compressed by custom or unions or the fact that one worker is just like any other in skills and motivation or anything else that counts? Or are wages dispersed with stars and losers? (See figure 1.9.) Across industrial countries, we see dramatic differences: as expected, the United States has the largest dispersion, almost twice that of Germany. Not surprisingly, German workers resist the American model because pessimistically they believe that somehow they will wind up at the bottom, even though not everybody can be at the bottom.

What is wrong with inequality? Poverty is bad, but inequality is not. Surely this is one of the battles of the end of the century. In open and competitive markets, wages in any year or for any person may have a large good luck/bad luck component. But surely on average they reflect energy and talent, motivation and investment in human skills. Any society that limits rewards to accomplishment will achieve equality, but it will come on a low common denominator. Rewards to excellence, or inequality if one wants to call it that, are the great driving force of progress.

Public policy should be concerned with giving broad access to strong education and pay less attention to the outcomes of the economic race. Three cheers for inequality; it is good for growth and growth is the best way of rooting out poverty.

The Economist in the Twentieth Century

A century of dramatic economic events can be viewed in terms of its great economic controversies and the leaders that have emerged in the profession. In this perspective, the century started with Victorian calm—everything was known, Alfred Marshall of Cambridge had codified it, and only the details remained to be filled in. Free enterprise, stable money, and an open world economy were the playing ground for prosperity. There was not much in terms of policy other than the gold standard.

The interwar period with growing depression in England, the collapse of financial markets, and the ensuing Great Depression was a dramatic challenge to the profession. This was not supposed to happen, at least not cumulatively and ever for the worse. By 1930, the classics were in the garbage dump, and a new generation brought revolutionary new ideas to cope with the greatest threat to prosperity in memory. They were all rather special: Schumpeter, who as finance minister failed to stop hyperinflation in Austria, ruined a bank, and then became a professor. He said he had three hopes—to be the best horseman in Austria, the greatest lover in Europe, and the best economist in the world—and claimed to have succeeded at two of them. John Maynard Keynes was as much an intellectual and brilliant writer and a financial wizard (he lost two fortunes and made three, mostly in the German hyperinflation) as a deep economist and an acute policymaker. And then there was Irving Fisher of Yale, famous inventor of the Rolodeck, who went bankrupt three times (his own money, Yale's, and that of his wife) in misjudging the stock market and believed the answer to living a healthy life involved sleeping outside, in particular in the winter.

While Keynes comes away as the winner in the context for dramatic and practical ideas, Schumpeter and Fisher left important legacies in the way we think today about business cycles, growth processes, and the interaction of deflation and economic activity. Keynes clearly dominated the scene: his focus on inflexibility of wages and prices and the limits to monetary policy in a depression (now rediscovered in Japan) brought fiscal spending to the foreground. Leave gold and start spending. Governments should pay people to dig holes (never mind that nobody needs the holes), pay them to fill them in again, and the incomes earned will be spent. If done on an ambitious enough scale, the economy can spend itself out of recession or depression. This was radical thinking, both in fiscal terms and in the role of government, and it worked. No surprise that governments for decades bought into Keynesian ideas until public debts had become too high and waste too big to give them further credence.

The next generation of formidable economists was Paul Samuelson and Milton Friedman, the heroes of the 1960s and into the 1970s. Friedman was the free market and hard money advocate, and a brilliantly articulate advocate at that, the very incarnation of the Chicago School. Samuelson of MIT, by contrast, was the modern Keynesian, a Democrat in politics and a formidable thinker about how to formulate a modern and mathematical rendition of economic theory. Both had their victories. Samuelson won in the 1960s when he urged (along with many others) the Kennedy administration to spend its way to prosperity—and they got there. The only rival to that expansion is what is still under way today. But overexpansion gradually built up wage and price inflation, and by the early 1970s, with dollar collapse and oil price shocks, the experiment became largely discredited. Pump priming with monetary accommodation can go some way, but if overdone, will crash. No sooner had inflation emerged when Milton Friedman had his time on the stage. Monetarism was the rage; the quantity theory of money was back in full swing. But his contribution, and that of other scholars at the time, went further: crudely summarized, it said you can fool some people all of the time and some people some of the time, but not all people all of the time. More technically, the public catches up with what governments do, and they (ultimately) have rational expectations. The practical implication was to minimize the scope for government cyclical policy.

Friedman's doctrines became the background for a dramatic period of rethinking economic doctrine: the leadership was provided by Robert Lucas of the University of Chicago. Taking rational expectations to the rigorous extreme, his theories concluded that government should adopt a monetary rule and an unchanging flat tax rate, and be done. In other words, government activism merely confuses, misfires, and distorts; government, get out of the way! Economic agents are rational, they do not leave $100 bills lying on the floor, and the economy does better without activism in policy. Few, at least of my generation, would believe the starkest renditions of this view. But the truth is that our profession by and large views Keynesian economics with deep skepticism, accepts monetarism, and assumes that government has a proclivity to make things worse. The profession has become deeply conservative just as it had been at the beginning of the century. And governments are going that way too, from the care in creating a tamperproof ECB to the Waigel pact, balanced budget amendments, currency boards, and overarching respect for the bond market.

Angst 2000: Who Is in Control?

People of middle age and older around the world perceive that globalization undermines the stability of their lives and that volatility, falsely perceived to be higher than ever, puts them at grave risk. They feel they have lost control, and they perceive the same is true of their governments. They want assurance that security is regained; someone has to do something. Surely these sentiments will get far worse if and when Japan crashes. That is altogether possible since Japan's debt is huge, its budget deficit is mind boggling, its financial institutions are bust, its investments have been bad, its policymakers are unconnected to reality, and the loss of confidence is pervasive.

And there is the potential of a U.S. crash, less likely because monetary and fiscal policy can respond, but never say never. Even with all the U.S. prosperity, the world today has had an overdose of finance, and hence it is far more likely that a serious accident can happen. And if it does, we can be sure the fallout is worldwide, and we must fear that the first instinct is to play the defensive and destructive strategies of the Great Depression.

Citizens want to know who is in charge. The answer is nobody; the United States can't lead Japan, and Europe cannot lead the United States. The United States urges Europe to move to prosperity policies but has no resonance; the United States urges Japan to move out of recession but gets no hearing and surely no success. Europe is critical of the huge U.S. trade deficits and lack of saving, not recognizing that if the United States started saving, the dollar would come down and Europe would lose jobs on a large scale. The Japanese dream of not buying U.S. T-bills, not realizing that the Yen would go through the roof and the Nikkei through the floor.

The world does not need more regulation and agreements to fix this or that; it does need a heavy dose of prosperity policies. Milton Freedman, in commenting on the Great Depression, criticized the Fed for not printing money massively. That is the message to Japan. And to Europe: get deregulation under way so that dynamism in business and employment starts freeing up the fiscal side for emergency use. If Japan and Europe start moving, it is time for the United States to think of a smaller trade deficit; that will come automatically as the rest of the world recovers. The U.S. role today is to assure that stock market problems at home do not become world problems, to make certain that ideas to fix exchange rates get nowhere, and, along with its partners, to insist that the world economy remain open.

2

The Come and Go of the State

A century ago the State, in the economic area, practically did not exist. There was total freedom of trade in goods and services, the work was on gold as a common currency (with a bit of silver in odd places), the welfare state was unheard of, and government production of goods and services, outside defense, just did not exist. The twentieth century brought all that. But just as the century is coming to an end, so is the time of the Economic State, one of the truly bad ideas. A world without boundaries, competition in private markets, and a sharp retreat of the welfare state promise to create a fresh base of prosperity and flexibility to handle the overriding challenges posed by the dramatic arrival of new technologies and billions of people in the world market place. There are some doubts, but the presumption now is that the State is an idea of the past.

The end of the twentieth century takes us back where we were a century ago: enormous confidence in technology, an ever expanding world of opportunity and challenge, and a liberal economic system. During the twentieth century we first departed from that blissful world; statism and protection became the rule, the welfare state made its appearance. Now the world economy is on a bold new course that turns back to where we came from, economic liberalism and individualism, competition and opportunity.

In the late nineteenth century and at the turn of the century the world economy was in a phase of prosperity built on free trade, the free flow of

Originally published in *World Economic Trends* (Trans-National Research Corporation), (August 1997): 20–31. Reprinted with permission.

capital to the periphery, the flow of people toward opportunity and freedom, and the stability of money based on the gold standard. Colonialism took economic advancement and prosperity to the periphery and getting rich was glorious. One country after another joined the system, from Argentina to Japan, from Germany to the United States.

Internationalism was the rule, and the World's Fairs of Chicago in 1889 and Paris in 1893 and 1900 were just one way of showing excitement in a world without borders either in space or technological promise. Internationalism was also obvious in the international conferences to standardize just about anything, from weights and measures to the mail and, of course, achieving a common monetary standard was very much part of the agenda. Peace among the major players and a deep belief in the explosion of technological opportunities created a belief in ever expanding opportunities.

It is clear that today we are back to just such a world; we think it is new, but in fact it just takes us back to where we were a century ago. It is instructive to ask how the sense of an extraordinary future for a wide open world economy was lost and how it was recovered. It will help answer the key question: can this bright new world last?

Two developments were central to the disintegration of the liberal (in the European sense) world: the rise of the nation state and the rise of government as economic actors both in their *welfare state* role and as operators of *public-sector enterprises*. The reversal of tendencies, at least in the economic sphere, is largely responsible for the current prosperity.

The loss of the liberal world was, of course, the result of the Great Wars and of the Great Depression. Whether these were inevitable by the forces of history or just the result of plain stupidity of decadent emperors, militarists, and misguided economic policymakers is left open. The fact is that World War I introduced the deep disillusion about internationalism, the terror of mechanized warfare, and the dramatic challenge to established and outdated authority and weak and unprepared democracy. With income taxes and large public debts, the 1920s brought protection, hyperinflation, and competitive devaluation. The Great Crash and the Great Depression moved government to the center of economic life: exchange control, quotas on trade rather than tariffs, government projects to directly create jobs, regulation of economic life, state operation of key industries—all these became routine, as did the belief that the competitive capitalist economy is at the least unstable and in need of pervasive support and control. Many though went further to say that the public sector had to be at the center of economic life and was essential to stabilizing the private economy.

Not every country went to these extremes, but it is clear that in Europe, outside Germany, that model was dominant. Erhard, Germany's architect of economic reform in the late 1940s, may have taken Germany back to the market, but the "market" was all tangled up in restrictions to the point that it could barely move. The German post-office operated telephone system was a monument to the devastating results of statism, as are the remaining pervasive restrictions on a competitive labor market. Only the United States escaped; in the 1930s it went in the direction of statism, but that went away quite fast. Japan even in the late nineteenth century never quite made it to the open economy: the Meiji restoration was a dramatic start in terms of modernization, but imperial-militaristic government was a counterweight to an open competitive economy. In the interwar period Japan, of course, in a difficult world trade environment found its way to a pervasive role of the state that lasted well into the 1980s. The world's economic periphery that had opened up in the nineteenth century closed down in the 1930s. Latin America went to import substitution and capital controls, pervasive nationalization of business, public sector investments in strategic sectors, and fascist labor market institutions. And what was true of Latin America was also true of Eastern Europe. In fact, that region went straight from statism to communism.

Return to Free Trade

In the mid-1930s the world economy and the liberal economy had been destroyed as thoroughly as we can imagine. Liberalism had barely any defenders and certainly no place on earth that practiced it. Keynesian economics with government activism as the stabilizer and substantial expansion of state economic activity with a deep contraction of trade were characteristic even before the next war got underway. Following the second war, two currents emerged. The first was to reverse gradually the dramatic contraction of trade. That was a long task and it is even incomplete today. The other was the building of the welfare state, which is just now coming into question.

The reopening of trade started quite early on two fronts. Already in 1934 the United States started reversing its extreme protectionism with the Reciprocal Trade Agreements Act, which has been the basis for multilateral trade liberalization ever since. Then, as soon as World War II was over, the United States pushed aggressively for multilateralism and opening up in the European economies. The United States accepted discrimination against itself if only Europe started trading within. The Marshall Plan provided quite explicit carrots and it has worked: the European Union as we see it now is the outcome of those early seeds put in place by the U.S. architects of the postwar international system. Why were policymakers so eager to rebuild world trade? The reasons are two. First, the collapse of trade in the interwar period had been nothing but spectacular. Between 1929 and the bottom year in the early 1930s, in just a few years, the volume of U.S. exports declined to exactly half, and so did the volume of Germany and of almost everybody else. Beggar-thy-neighbor policies had disintegrated any sense of the gains from trade and the notion that trade can only function if it is a two-way street.

As the accompanying figure 2.6 shows, the reopening of world trade has produced a spectacular expansion of trade. In fact, the expansion has proceeded at a far more significant pace than that of the nineteenth century. In just thirty-five years, German trade has increased tenfold and that of Japan almost twenty times. The liberalization of merchandise trade is a well-recognized fact and, with the rare exception of pathetic projectionists, is recognized around the world as a great boon. All countries have participated in it, on a regional and on a world basis. Japan was one of the latecomers, but in the past decade has gone very far in accomplishing an effective liberalization of trade in goods.

Of course, there is more to be done in fully opening the world in trade: China needs to be integrated fully and India as well; services are just at the beginning stage of a real opening. But there is every reason to believe that these extra areas will be covered in the coming decade. The emergence of regional trade agreements, far from breaking up globalism, is in fact a driving force for pushing liberalization ahead on a smaller scale and then widening it around the world. If Asia-Pacific Economic Cooperation holds out for free trade to emerge only in 2000, don't believe it. It is sure to come much earlier, just as the integration of Eastern Europe into the European Union is happening surprisingly fast.

Challenge to Big Government

The reconstruction of a liberal trading order is not the big surprise of the day. The surprise is rather the sharp challenge to statism that has come in the past decade. Thatcher and Reagan were the first, and now it is a common theme around the world. Big, inefficient government had become a dominant characteristic of all advanced economies and even more so in the developing world. It had been the other side of protectionism, in opposition to capitalism and individualism. Those who thought of it as an accomplishment called it the welfare state, those who recognized the impediment to competition and innovation and the waste of resources called it pervasive and stifling government.

Government outlays for consumption and investment, and the very large transfer payments reflecting all social programs from health to unemployment as well as increasingly debt service, are much of the story of big government.

Even more striking is what happened to public-sector employment: the share of the labor force working for the government, outside the United States and Japan, has increased vastly. This was most dramatically the case in Scandinavia, the paradise of the welfare state, where in the end (before the crisis of the past few years) fully a third of the labor force was working for the government!

Table 2.1
Share of Government Outlays in GDP

	1960	1980	1996
United States	24.8	31.4	33.3
Europe	27.4	44.7	49.8
Japan	13.0	32.0	36.2

Source: OECD.

Table 2.2
Government as a Share of Total Employment

	1960	1968	1974	1994
Germany	8.1	10.9	13.0	15.1
France			17.4	24.8
Sweden	12.8	18.4	24.8	32.0
Japan			6.3	6.0
United States	14.7	17.0	16.1	14.5

Source: OECD.

There are a number of reasons government now is under attack and markets are returning to competition and private initiative. First and foremost, big government has become unaffordable. Inefficient state enterprises have become a liability for the productive sector: too little innovation, too high costs, too high taxes to pay for the unproductive use of resources. When firms have to compete, they need a streamlined economic environment, at least as good as their best competitors around in the world. But the overriding reason for smaller government is surely financial: in the past thirty years every government in the world borrowed to share in the broadest fashion the gains from economic growth; subsidies were pervasive, unemployment was treated over-nervously, and there was always money for everything. In a country like Sweden, all net new jobs were in the government sector. Now the debts are large and the future debts in the form of unfunded pension liabilities are huge. The conclusion, popular or not, is that government must shrink.

The State is also under attack in the labor market. In Europe especially, labor markets have traditionally been highly fossilized. Under the pressure of unions, flexibility and competition have been suspended in favor of a high cost and highly restrictive employment system. Of course, that means high unemployment, but what is the problem if the government can pay for it? The government can no longer defend the existing restrictions, and so even labor markets are coming into the range of radical reform. The new idea is that the welfare state and restricted labor markets were a very bad idea. The welfare state is being disbanded, and labor markets are being freed up. That will be the work of a decade, but

Table 2.3
Debt Levels and Unfunded Pension Liabilities (Percent of GDP)

	Deficit	Gross Debt	Unfunded Pensions
Germany	−3.2	65.9	160
France	−3.2	64.3	216
Italy	−3.2	124.1	233
Japan	−3.1	90.8	200
United States	−1.4	63.8	43

Source: OECD and IMF.

at least it has started. Can it work? The U.S. example, the only fully employed economy in the world today, clearly demonstrates that it can be done—there are enough jobs for everybody.

The ways in which the welfare state is being undone are many. In the United States, welfare reform was a dramatic step. Nobody knows how the experiment will work, but the fact is that time on welfare is now limited and soon, who knows how, people who have not worked for years will suddenly have to do so. They need to be integrated into a normal social life—that is, a working life—from which the welfare state in its perversion had given them unlimited leave.

In Europe, where unemployment has been one of the better jobs for many years, replacement of earnings via unemployment compensation reaches (after adjustment for taxes) 70 percent plus. Even after 60 months of unemployment, a couple with two children can get more than 60 percent earnings replacement. Throw in a bit of the informal labor market and you make a good living. By comparison, in the U.S. long-term unemployment does not pay. For those who are insured, the replacement rate falls to 17 percent!

Not surprisingly, incentives have now to be set right. Britain is a good case in point. The government requires unemployment claimants to show up and actually consider job opportunities. Hassling pays off: unemployment has fallen to record low levels! In Germany and France, the attack on the welfare state is particularly hard: the German government is weak and therefore mostly talk, and the French socialists have taken a step back by promising to create more government jobs. It won't last, and in just a few years these key welfare state countries will be on the same track. The reason is that the public debts and deficits just cannot afford to pay the bill for a large number of people to stay away from work while others refuse to pay the taxes that are required to finance the existing scheme. Piling up more debt is impossible, and hence the need for change.

Big government is also under attack in the area of public-sector enterprises. The reason is simple: services are bad and costs are huge. As an approximation that is the right picture. Privatization is the effective response. It is now underway from telecommunications to the railroads, from electricity to airlines. The old idea that the government must control the "commanding heights of capitalism" just looks silly: international competition and the absence of significant barriers to entry do far more for the viability of a firm than government running it.

Even though privatization is being practiced from Moscow and Kiev to Havana and from Tokyo to London, there are places where it remains controversial. France is the obvious one. A socialist government, understanding full well that privatization means increased productivity imposed by the new owners or, in other words, dramatic cuts in jobs, resists. But it can't really hold out long. The swing of the pendulum is against big government. Everybody understands that there are productivity gains of 30 percent or more to be harvested. They are politically controversial, but so is more debt and so are higher taxes. That is why public enterprise is on the chopping block, even if the unions call a general strike.

Is There a Downside?

There are questions about the viability of the attack on the state. Is this just the swing of the pendulum, so that soon we will go back to where we were, perhaps with a bit of dampening and some lessons learned? There is no chance whatsoever that we go back to public sector enterprises. The private market demonstrates by the day that it can finance any scale of operation, that it can design and innovate in a way government is most unlikely to do. Malaysia may get points for spearheading an industrial upgrading and Vice President Gore for talking up the Internet. But don't worry, big government in production is gone.

The return of the nation state, likewise, is not likely. The nation state is no longer the right economic frame of reference. Effective firms play worldwide in their sourcing, production, and sales. They are more interested in market access and deregulation than defending territory against challengers. True, Congressman Gephardt is a protectionist and he may run for the presidency, but don't worry. The United States would be one of the big losers in a retrenchment of the open economy. It just won't happen.

The area where the changes have most political fallout is the abolition of the welfare state. This is being fought street by street, so to speak. One can take encouragement from Clinton's abolishing long-term welfare or Tony Blair's message to European socialists—change or count your days. But one cannot fail to recognize that competition, privatization, and globalization have a dramatic impact on the earnings of relatively unskilled people. In the United States, the shift has already happened, in Europe it is being fought. Low-paid jobs, which is where low skilled labor goes, are plentiful in the United States and are concentrated in trade and services.

Europe and Japan will have to allow a wider dispersion of wages and with that the expansion of low wage employment. That is already the case in all these countries that most low paid workers are in the service sector—67 percent of all low paid workers in France versus 74 percent in the United States. Thus, what is to come is not really new, but there will be more of it.

The coming rise of inequality will be the decisive new development. On one side there are the mega-billionaires who develop technologies that

Table 2.4
Percent of Labor Force in Low-Paid Jobs

	France	Germany	Italy	Japan	United States
Total	13.3	13.3	12.5	15.7	25.0
By Industry					
Manufacturing	11.5	10.6	14.2	20.9	20.9
Services	14.3	16.6	6.6	18.5	24.9
Wholesale/Retail	22.6	22.9	24.2	14.8	40.4

Source: OECD Employment Report.

enhance human productivity, for work and play, dramatically. And on the other hand there are the former middle-class voters who are left out. So far very little of a backlash has come. But most assuredly, as we go into the next century, democracy combining with inequality and economic insecurity almost surely offers a prescription for sparks flying.

Appendix: Data and Forecasts

Table 2A.1
Growth and Inflation

	Growth				Inflation			
	1995	1996	1997	1998	1995	1996	1997	1998
Ind. Countries	2.0	2.2	2.8	2.4	2.4	2.2	2.0	2.4
United States	2.0	2.3	3.5	2.3	2.8	3.0	2.6	3.0
Japan	0.9	3.7	2.0	2.6	−0.1	0.1	1.2	1.1
Europe	2.3	1.5	2.3	2.6	3.0	2.4	1.9	2.3
Germany	1.9	1.4	2.4	2.7	1.8	1.5	1.6	2.0
France	2.2	1.1	2.2	2.8	1.7	2.0	1.4	1.8
Italy	3.0	0.8	0.9	2.1	5.4	3.9	2.0	2.4
UK	2.4	2.4	3.4	2.8	3.4	2.6	2.7	3.2
Spain	3.0	2.1	2.8	3.0	2.2	3.6	2.1	2.5

Source: Economist Consensus forecast.

Table 2A.2
Taxation in OECD Countries (Percent of GDP)

	Tax Change: 80–95	Effective Rate 80		Effective Rate 94	
		Capital	Labor	Capital	Labor
United States	0.7	.46	.41	.21	.23
Germany	0.9	.31	.24	.35	.38
Japan	2.4	.34	.40	.17	.21
France	2.8	.26	.24	.37	.45
Italy	11.6	.18	.30	.26	.35
OECD	2.5	.39	.36	.25	.28

Source: OECD Economic Outlook.

Figure 2.1
European Real Effective Exchange Rates

Figure 2.2
United Kingdom: Real Effective Exchange Rate

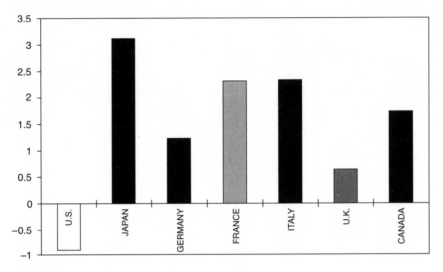

Figure 2.3
1997 Output Gap

Figure 2.4
Brazil: Real Effective Exchange Rate

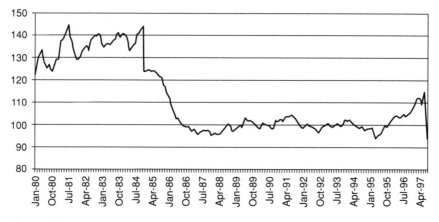

Figure 2.5
Thailand: Real Effective Exchange Rate

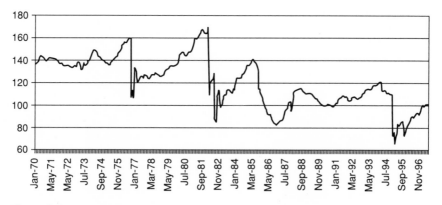

Figure 2.6
Mexico: Real Effective Exchange Rate

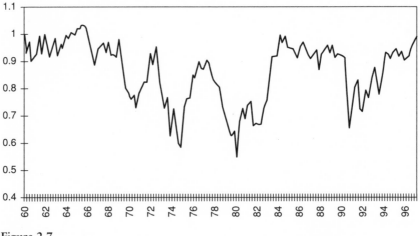

Figure 2.7
Consumer Confidence

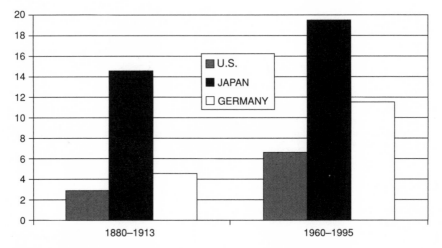

Figure 2.8
Export Volume Increase

II

Macroeconomic Ingredients for Growth and Prosperity

3

Long-Run Growth in Emerging Countries

There is any number of books about what makes for a successful company or a successful CEO—*The Six Habits of Successful Leaders*, *What Makes Attila Special*, etc. What makes countries perform has always been an elusive question, with answers tending to be more a matter of belief rather than proof with hard research. A substantial body of research is now available; nothing surprising emerges, but it is worth knowing too that clichés do not win hands down.

Over the past decade, thanks to an important cross country data set assembled by a team at the University of Pennsylvania (Summers, Heston, and the late Irving Kravis), we know a lot about the time series of various macroeconomic aggregates for more than a hundred countries and more than thirty years. Moreover, that data set is increasingly complemented by political and socioeconomic data. Robert Barro at Harvard has taken much of that initiative, which is reported in his book *Economic Growth*, published by the MIT Press. This has become a goldmine for empirical research and hypotheses regarding the determinants of economic success. We have not seen the end of the research by any means, but it is useful to take stock of where we stand. The most recent IMF Economic Outlook facilitates the task by bringing together convenient tabulations.

The basic hypothesis of growth economics is that progress is made up of two factors: growth in factor inputs (capital and labor weighted by their shares in output) and growth in total factor productivity (TFP

Originally published in *World Economic Trends* (Trans-National Research Corporation), (June–July 1997): 16–20. Reprinted with permission.

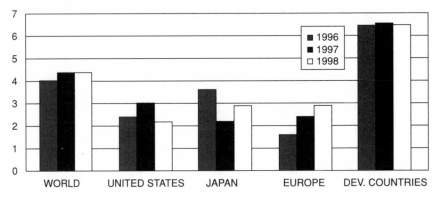

Figure 3.1
IMF World Growth Outlook

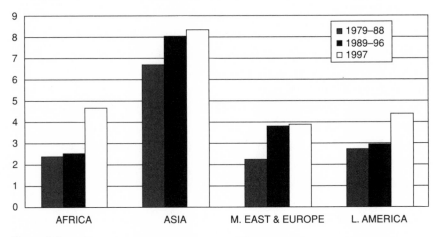

Figure 3.2
Growth Trends in Developing Countries

growth). The former means working more (more hours, more members of the family, etc.) or saving and investing and hence foregoing current consumption. The latter, TFP growth, by contrast, means that the same stock of productive factors produces a higher rate of output, and hence represents an advance that seemingly does not carry with it effort or sacrifice, and thus is highly desirable.

In emerging economies, the TFP growth issue is very prominent for a number of reasons. From a policy perspective, the key question is what are the determinants of TFP growth—are there ways of running the economy that translate into higher TFP growth? Second, following the challenge by Paul Krugman, who argued that Asia was mostly like Russia—mindless and unproductive capital accumulation, no productivity growth, postponing consumption to inch ahead with Stalinist accumulation—there is the simple question of fact: has Asia in fact had so little productivity growth? The answer is still under investigation, but the preliminary indication is that about 30–40 percent of growth is accounted for by education and total factor productivity growth. That undermines the challenge to Asian growth policies quite a bit.

One of the interesting central hypotheses about growth is that of catching up: countries that are behind in terms of per capita GDP will grow faster and, as a result, get nearly to where advanced countries are. That idea seemed tempting and appeared to work when applied to small groups of countries in the 1980s. Today, stated in an unqualified way, it is simply not the case. In the full sample of 100+ countries, there is no evidence of catching up. True, the Asian success stories have been catching up, but many poor countries have fallen behind rather than getting relatively ahead.

The key focus therefore is on conditional catching up, that is, making allowance for all those factors that matter for growth other than merely being behind. This is where research has concentrated, to explore an endless list of potential factors from democracy to property rights, from inflation to trade policy, from the budget to education and the share of government in GDP.

Dividing the sample of 100+ countries into three groups—per capita GDP growth of less than 0.5 percent, 0.5 to 2.9 percent, and 2.9 percent plus—the following results emerge: high growth countries have the

Table 3.1
Characteristics of Developing Countries: 1985–95 (Percent per Year)

	Low Growth	Medium Growth	High Growth
Schooling	3.3	3.8	5.4
Investment	19.4	21.1	31.9
Budget Deficit	−5.6	−3.3	−2.4
Inflation	14.1	11.1	7.8
Private Bank Credit	25.4	31.0	63.1
Curr. Acc't	−2.6	−1.4	0.3

Notes: Schooling = Years of schooling for population 5 years and over; Investment, Budget, Current Account, and Private Bank Credit = Percent of GDP; Inflation = Median of the group.
Source: IMF.

Table 3.2
Developing Country Growth and Characteristics (Percent of Countries in the Sample)

	Per Capita GDP Growth		
	High (>2.9%)	Medium (0.5 to 2.9%)	Low (<0.5%)
Total Sample	28	28	44
High Openness	41	19	41
High Macro Stability	41	32	27
Small Gov't.	30	33	37
Two and a Half +s	57	19	24

Source: IMF.

expected characteristics (more schooling, more investment, less inflation, smaller deficits, more financial intermediation favoring the private sector). Just as your mother told you.

The next question is whether it takes all the various known growth factors or whether just having a number of them is enough. Table 3.2 lists three key summary characteristics: openness, macro stability, and small government. It shows the distribution of countries by growth performance and also shows how the sample lines up on the various char-

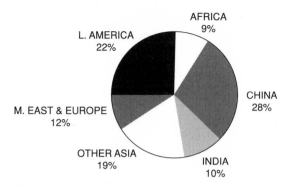

Figure 3.3
GDP of Developing Countries

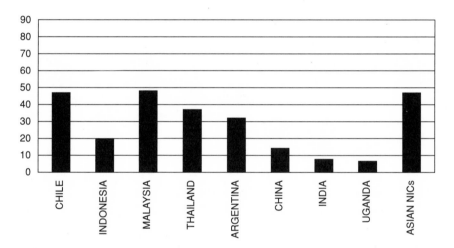

Figure 3.4
PPP-GDP of Developing Countries Relative to the Group of Advanced Economics

acteristics. For example, both high and low growth countries are open, so the question is just how important is openness. The preliminary evidence is that there is no single piece that is uniquely critical; it's the package that matters. When we look at countries that get two out of three right and do at least moderately well on the third, we see a very high incidence of high growth experience. Thus, a lot of things matter, and the more of them we get right (and the fewer very wrong), the more likely that we wind up with high growth. Not surprising, but well worth documenting in two ways: one, we should not be hung up about a single factor. Second, most things have to go right, just as common sense suggests.

There is no prospect whatsoever that the world will converge to narrow differences in per capita income. China may become the largest economy, but it will take forever to catch up with advanced countries on a per capita basis. The accompanying figure 3.4 (using IMF data) shows examples of where various countries stand in their PPP-GDP relative to the group of advanced economies. On that basis China stands at 13.3 percent and Uganda or Bangladesh at less than 7 percent, versus Malaysia at almost 50 percent. At recent growth rates, how long will it take Malaysia to close half the gap? The answer is just eight years. For China it is sixteen years, but that of course still leaves a huge gap with a century of catching up. However that is where, in Asia, the Krugman point comes in—at some stage consumption will rear its ugly head, and that means investment and growth will taper off and so will the pace of catching up.

So far that has not happened, but surely over the next decade or two it will. In Latin America, by contrast, the idea of saving is brand new and coming. Privatized social security goes in that direction, as does plain macroeconomic stability, which raises saving and reduces capital flight. Here catching up speeds will pick up.

4

Containing High Inflation

Inflation is a dramatic problem. All available evidence supports the view that it undermines growth and social stability at the very roots. Containing inflation, therefore, is an utmost priority. But the recognition that inflation is destructive leaves still a host of important questions as to how best to deal with this problem. Importantly, the question is here to draw the line and start thinking about tradeoffs.

Evidence reported in a large number of studies demonstrates that high inflation lowers a country's average growth performance. There is a divergence of views on exactly where "high" starts. Work at the World Bank, for example, draws the line at 40 percent—anything more is demonstrably counterproductive and anything less may be a growth problem, although that is harder to show. Other studies move much further down in setting the threshold for counterproductive inflation. In fact, a recent IMF study finds support for the view that adverse growth effects emerge at inflation rates of only 8 percent. Even more ambitious work looks for counterproductive effects in the range of 0 to 3 percent and comes out in favor of a zero-inflation target as the only growth-friendly strategy.

There is one common thread to all this discussion: nobody has claimed inflation is good for growth, at any level. That contention, if it ever existed, is just gone. The overwhelming presumption today is that inflation is no help at all and that it is totally undesirable. The remaining issue is to know whether there is a temporary cost in bringing down inflation,

Originally published in *World Economic Trends* (Trans-National Research Corporation), (October–November 1996): 10–18. Reprinted with permission.

how high these costs might be, if any, and accordingly what is the range of inflation rates where inflation is the number one policy issue. Interestingly, the World Bank study referred to above has one answer: reducing inflation that is above 40 percent increases growth. At lower rates of inflation the issue becomes less clear cut, as we will see in a moment. Before getting to that topic it is helpful to dispose of one easy issue: extreme inflation.

How to Get Out of Extreme Inflation?

It is not controversial anymore to assert that extreme inflation is impossible without sustained money creation. True, the rise in velocity driven by the extravagant cost of holding money—the flight from money—is part of the inflation process. But extreme inflation does not happen just by chance. The source is always and everywhere, as Friedman has long claimed, extreme money creation that in turn is linked to the financing of budget deficits. If anything above 40 percent inflation (per year) hurts growth, extreme inflation—20, 30, 40 percent per month—certainly takes its toll in full measure. There is no question that stabilization is a sine qua non for growth.

That leaves two important questions. One is *when* to stabilize and the other is *how*. There is a school of thought that claims waiting is a good idea: the longer and more extremely inflation runs its course, the more disorienting the process for the public. In the end, the public will come to endorse whatever is necessary to stop inflation. Starting too early just means failed sterilizations and a loss of credibility.

That view is wrong for two reasons. First, stabilizations almost everywhere are not made of a single, decisive package that overnight abolishes the problem. On the contrary, it is rather a process of a protracted search for the countless things that have to be done in the public sector to reduce the deficit and increase competition and accountability. At the outset none of them is enough. But looking back from a successful stabilization invariably reveals a long history of efforts that ultimately adds up to enough. Waiting merely advances destruction on the economy's immune system and its social structure. These are very hard to put back together. That was the case in Germany, Austria, and Hungary in the

1920s; it may yet be the case in Russia or the Ukraine today. Sometimes it may be desirable to destroy the existing social structure, but that surely goes far beyond the agenda of inflation control, and it is definitely not a technical issue in optimal stabilization.

The next question then is how to stop an extreme inflation process. There is no doubt that *a regime change* must occur. The term is much abused in the literature, but in this context it is appropriate and decisive. The fiscal regime must be changed so that budgets no longer need to be financed by the central bank. Almost invariably that means balancing the budget; possibly the goal may be less ambitious if there is plausible financing from the capital market. One way or the other, the central bank has to be out of the business of printing money to finance the government. Moreover, this needs to be institutionalized in a way that goes beyond mere promises. These have been broken already far too often in the past, and something better is needed to show what is new. Here is the point where institutional arrangements matter—currency boards, constitutional amendments, and the like.

In a situation of extreme inflation, an economy becomes spontaneously dollarized. If dollar deposits are allowed, dollar deposits become the rule. If they are not allowed, dollar holdings in the form of currency and offshore deposits via capital flight will take the role of local currency deposits. That process can be documented for any high inflation country. The implication of this almost complete domestic demonetization and the corresponding dollarization is quite central. If the economy is already near-fully dollarized, going there all the way is only a small step. It merely amounts to recognizing that everyone is already on board and it is just the government that is not. Nothing more definitive is necessary in terms of regime change than taking this extra step. That was true in the 1920s with a restoration of the gold standard in the demonetized economies of Germany or Austria, and it is true today from Argentina to Russia.

There are three ways to take advantage of the fact that foreign exchange will have become central in a hyperinflation. The smallest and least definitive move is to just peg the local, stabilized currency to the dollar or the next best stable money in the region. That is good for a start, but it won't last as a credible anchor; it throws most of the weight of the regime change to the money supply process and the budget. Since nothing very institutional has happened, relapse into the old pattern of inflation can happen easily.

A far stronger move is the drift to a currency board system such as Argentina practices. The rules of central banking are changed in a dramatic fashion, and irreversibly. Money creation is tied to foreign exchange inflows and outflows; a hard line is drawn between the central bank and the treasury. True, all that could be reversed, but only by an act of Congress, which means a financial collapse before the debate even gets underway. But there might be a debate about softening the system and latent fears about the implications of overvaluation. This leads to advocacy of an even stronger system—moving outright and fully on the dollar.

Even this system comes in two ways, 100 percent dollarization with absolutely no domestic money creation—monetary teetotaling—or leaving room for a home money (and local heroes on the coins and bills) in small denominations. It is tempting to leave some room for local heroes, but a second thought is appropriate: who would want to be the dignitary or hero depicted on a debased currency? Surely history books are better places.

Two points reinforce the view that *full* dollarization is preferred to a currency board. First, as long as there is some local money, residual uncertainty about reversal of the hard policy and devaluation is always present. This is apparent in Argentina, for example, where after four years of a currency board, there remain interest differentials between peso and dollar deposits of the same maturity at the same financial institutions. The discussion never stops, particularly outside the country, where the belief in a "permanent and irreversible" regime change is always taken with a grain of salt. Second, an anecdote from Poland in the 1920s makes the point that poor public finance always finds a way to the printing press. A new central bank had been created (by Edwin Kemmerer, the money doctor of the 1920s) with full gold standard and complete independence. But coinage was left to the treasury. For a brief period, inflationary coinage by the treasury resulted in one more bout of inflation. Of course, it could not go very far, since coins are harder to produce and physically cumbersome. This must be one of the strangest inflation episodes in history.

The basic inference is that countries that have plain and simply failed to control their money have reached the most complete debauchery of their monetary system and should spend a few decades on the dollar or the Deutsch Mark. Their history shows that having a national money is a threat to growth and international standing, and is a lesson for us to get rid of it. Arguments about seigniorage are misplaced when the attempt to collect 1 percent of GDP costs 2, 3, or more percent in growth.

There is another way to make the story palatable. Why should a country like Hungary or Poland cultivate its own money and run precarious disinflation attempts with overvaluation in the wings? All of Europe, which they are desperately trying to join, is moving ahead to the recognition that a Europe-wide money gives them more stability and better economic performance. The soft currency countries of Eastern Europe should be in the forefront since they need the extra stability more than anyone else. The IMF should routinely advise, as part of the move from hyperinflation to stability, moving on the dollar, the DM, or the Euro.

The political argument against this strategy, voiced all too often in countries where money has been debased as completely as can be done, speaks for itself: our national currency is like the flag. These people surely would think twice before doing to their flag what they have done to their money!

The currency arrangements are only one part of successful action. At least as important is a shift on the fiscal side. The stabilizing government needs to balance the budget, no less. And that must be accomplished in a lasting and productive fashion. Emergency taxation is a poor way of going about the task; restructuring government spending, privatization, and closing loopholes have to be nine-tenths of the action.

The more waste there is in government, the better the scope for strong fiscal sanitation and hence support for monetary stability—the government is not bankrupt, it is just mismanaged. The more extreme the willingness to adopt monetary institutions or the dollar, the more firm the ground on which reconstruction takes place.

Destroying a money is not easy. It takes years and years of dedicated work. Not surprisingly, reconstructing monetary stability is not an issue of a year or two. It takes a decade or more. Countries that have gone all the way into destruction and have then rebuilt are rightly hypersensitive about the institutions that guard the new stability and about any compromises that might renew their bad experiences in however minor a way. They are right to be uncompromising.

Moderate Inflation

Countries with 15 percent inflation per *month* must stabilize with urgent priority; nothing is likely to be more important. On the other hand, countries with 15 percent inflation per *year* certainly should not belittle inflation. They definitely should attempt, on average, to bring inflation down. But they must see this as one of a number of priorities, and they should view it as a process of five or even more years. Accepting the right perspective on moderate inflation is important, because otherwise severe recession, super high real interest rates, with resulting banking problems, and currency overvaluation, with the risk of a collapse, might be the result rather than the dramatic success hoped for on the inflation front.

To appreciate the point, it is useful to look at an inflation representation in a formal way: inflation this year is what it was last year (this is the indexation effect) except for the influence of real appreciation, which tends to lower inflation or to slow down public-sector inflation (at the cost of bigger deficits) or recession.

$$\pi_t = \pi_{t-1} + \alpha(e - \pi_t) + \beta(p - \pi_t) + \phi y,$$

where π is the current rate of inflation, e the rate of depreciation, p the rate of increase of public-sector prices, and y the output gap. The equation summarizes the proposition that inflation today is what it was yesterday—via formal or implicit indexation or "inertia" as it is often called—except for the accelerating influence of real depreciation, increasing real public sector prices, or overheating. Disinflation then requires real appreciation of the exchange rate (with resulting trade deficit risks), reduced inflation in the public sector prices (with resulting budget deficit risks), old-fashioned recession, or the always suspect *incomes policy* that can never be a substitute for financial discipline, but may help coordinate the disinflation. Something has to give: inflation reduction does not come from ceremonious incantations of the central bank or a spontaneous outbreak of credibility.

Chile, for example, has had an average inflation over the past ten years of 17 percent. At the outset it was 30 percent, in the early 1990s it was still double digit, and today, ten years later, it is down to 7 percent. The average growth rate for the ten-year period was 7 percent.

At the outset a deep recession with near 30 percent unemployment set the tone for sharply lower rates of price increases. From there, productivity growth, not outrun by wage increases, and careful footwork by the central bank have gradually done their work. Chile's approach has been exemplary, particularly in the past few years, as the Central Bank has refused to overreach and squeeze inflation down to the fashionable 2 percent of the industrialized countries. Chile's policymakers recognize that strong growth, modernization, and integration in the world economy are not held back by 6, 10, or even 15 percent inflation, but could be seriously hampered if overambitious disinflation created a macroeconomic problem.

Mexico's experience in the 1990s is the opposite, where there was exaggerated emphasis put on inflation, exaggerated urgency to get to 2 percent, and dangerous imperviousness to overvaluation. The intransigent wish to bring down inflation in the context of an incomes policy, which allowed significant wage increases, led year after year to mounting real appreciation. However, in a country where trade had been liberalized and deregulation led to the shedding of labor in many sectors, real *de*preciation was called for. The cumulative real appreciation in the end amounted to more than 40 percent! The Mexican currency crisis was not surprising; in fact, it is what had long been predicted. The surprise was the extent of the meltdown.

One would have thought that the severity of the recent experience might have taught Mexican policymakers a lesson—stay far, far away from an exchange rate-based stabilization. Yet, precisely that same strategy is being pursued again. Of the huge real depreciation of 1995, much less than half is left. Even in the face of more than 20 percent inflation, monetary policy supports a peso that is flat rather than

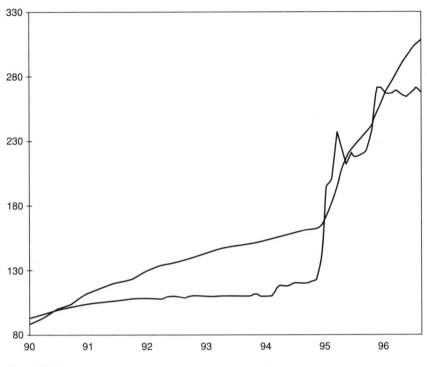

Figure 4.1
Mexico: Exchange Rate and Prices

depreciating at the pace of inflation. It is said to be a "flexible" rate but in between interest rate and aggregate policies it manages to keep the peso, keep the capital coming, and risk preparing yet another instance of overvaluation. (See figures 4.1 and 4.2.) It is early to express that concern, but this is the appropriate time since correction of the course remains easy. Once a large overvaluation has built up—as in Mexico in 1994 or presently in Brazil—it is difficult to expect that inflation can fall sufficiently below world trends to bring a remedy. A vast empirical review of the experience with real appreciation reported by Goldfajn and Valdes shows clearly that large overvaluations have little chance of a mild end.

The central lesson in stabilizing moderate inflation is that it is very perilous, indeed, to use the exchange rate for anything but a very transi-

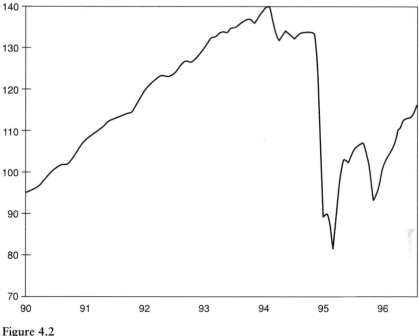

Figure 4.2
Mexico Price Level in U.S.$

tory, initial consolidation effort. The exchange rate cannot carry most or even much of the burden of stabilization. Nor can monetary policy do the job all by itself. Fiscal policy and competition must do a very substantial portion of the work.

The concern for inflation is altogether appropriate, but single-mindedness is not. In the face of moderate inflation, growth also must be part of the discussion. It is not correct to argue that there can be no growth in the presence of inflation, nor is it right to state that even moderate inflation is a detriment to growth. It is hard to find any evidence of a relationship between moderate inflation and growth. In the absence of a cost in terms of growth foregone, that suggests a more gradual disinflation strategy is acceptable.

Of course, it might be argued that the only stable inflation is zero inflation. That is the kind of dogmatic posture which has no empirical foundation. For the past decade or more, countries have been at work reducing inflation or at least containing it. Countries with moderate inflation rates, such as Chile, have perfectly well managed to achieve *gradual* reductions without either compromising the credibility of that strategy or sacrificing growth. On the contrary, the fact that inflation was steadily—over twelve years—falling but growth was strong throughout made the program a textbook case of successful inflation-fighting. Mexico's case, by contrast, is a series of failures and blunders as a result of half-baked ideas about credibility, inflation kills, and the like. Chile today is a low inflation country, Mexico is once again back to intolerably high inflation. The right message is that inflation must come down and that there is never room for complacency; that is not the same as inflation reduction first, growth later.

5

Free Markets Work Best—But They Need a Little Tweaking

In the broad swing of the ideological pendulum, free-market economics has become the antidote to a half-century of failed statism. It's become clear that competition, self-reliance, and profits are the driving engines of prosperity. There is no choice. Moreover, the uncovering of vast corruption in statist economies—France, Italy, Japan—makes the case stronger. Wherever government gets a say in the market, officials can routinely expect big-time payoffs.

Still, many doubt the promise of free markets. Transition, restructuring, and reform all too often seem to create inequality, wipe out an established middle class, or produce windfall fortunes. In Russia, anti-market forces stand a good chance in the upcoming elections; in Eastern Europe, retreaded communists win at the polls; in Latin America, skeptics of the neoliberal experiment command a growing audience. In Western Europe, there is much talk of free markets but not "the American way"—that is, all-out competition, let the chips fall where they may.

But at this critical juncture, there is no third way. Statism has had its time on the stage. Pervasive regulation, public-sector enterprises, a bloated welfare state with crushing tax burdens for those who work—and absurd levels of subsidies for those who don't—have failed as effective alternatives to decentralized decision-making and the hard edge of incentives, private choices, and their consequences.

Originally published in *Business Week* (18 December 1995): 26. Reprinted with permission.

No Special Favors

The transition to free markets is controversial because the broad spread of prosperity often takes a long time to come about. In the meantime, the redistribution of opportunities, income, and wealth is the most visible result. Statist economies focus on creating jobs for everybody. As a result, employment is high, and productivity is low. Shifting to free markets involves job losses and wage cuts for many. True, new opportunities open up, but for every winner there are plenty of losers.

Moreover, the move to free markets wipes out the privileged position of businesses, workers, and politicians who benefited from government intervention in the economy. In the great reshuffling, those who relied on protection and favors from the government are out in the cold, while innovators who spot new opportunities walk away with huge returns. The public sees the windfall gains but doesn't see the risk-taking—and certainly doesn't appreciate the proposition that without rewards, progress will stall. Of course, the redistribution of wealth is often only from one pocket to another: Ukraine's communist bosses got rich in capturing the meatiest assets in a self-administered privatization.

"I am from the government, I am here to help you" rings hollow today. Economics leaves no doubt on the basic proposition: private initiative with a minimum of government interference is the surest way to create the biggest pie. There is no reason to wait, go slow, or be selective.

Social Cohesion

The wholehearted adoption of the free market will leave many with mixed feelings. How can we make a rough transition come about more easily? You don't have to feel good about the market—just recognize the bankruptcy of all forms of statism. Next, avoid making a difficult step even worse: Successful reform needs an environment of prosperity and opportunity. Labor markets must be flexible; otherwise, restructuring just translates into mass unemployment.

At the same time, free markets must be judiciously supplemented. There is a need to regulate so as to avoid market failures, from finance to anticompetitive practices. Moreover, the market-determined distribution of income and wealth may pull society apart. Creating opportunities by education and by removing obstacles to competition imposed by governments or unions is important, as is some fiscal redistribution that stops short of being a disincentive. The aspiration of striking a balance between market forces and social cohesion seems a good idea even if in practice it has culminated in too much "social" and too little "market." In the United States, the rush to abolish welfare should also include jobs, childcare, and education vouchers to help rebuild the social cohesion essential for a functioning market economy.

Finally, the worst enemy of the transition to a free market is a central bank staging fights against inflation or unduly concerned with maintaining a hard currency. Stable and moderate inflation is important for economic performance, but there is a time and place for everything. In Europe today, overdoing inflation fighting and playing desperate currency games do more to harm the cause of free-market reform than all the ideological debates put together.

6

And You Thought Social Security Was in Trouble ...

This fall, Congress will try to ax budget deficits that loom as far as the eye can see. Without such action, the Congressional Budget Office projects that rising medical expenses and a shrinking social security surplus will, by 2005, widen the deficit to 4.1 percent of gross domestic product and the ratio of debt to GDP will climb to 60 percent. Balancing the budget would make room for more investment and reduce the chances that financial markets will have to shoulder the burden of heavy deficit financing. What's more, balancing the budget need not create a slump or a recession. True, the government will spend less, but interest rates will fall, and private spending will take up the slack.

America's fiscal problems sound ominous, but there is a surprise: with respect to its finances, the United States is one of the healthiest economies. Many other major industrial countries face a far greater challenge in meeting future pension and social security obligations two decades or so hence. There is widespread concern about the size and growth of the U.S. debt, but until recently, little attention has been paid to "off the books" debts of other nations.

Invisible Cloud

These hidden debts arise from retirement obligations in countries that have rapidly aging populations. When a large cohort of the population is relatively young, more people pay into government retirement systems

Originally published in *Business Week* (28 August 1995): 20. Reprinted with permission.

than withdraw funds. But when that group starts to age, cash flow eventually turns negative. Calculating the net present value of these future liabilities requires many assumptions, but it can be done. Recent estimates from the Organization for Economic Cooperation & Development show an astounding problem on the horizon for many industrialized nations.

Here are some conservative estimates: in Canada, the ratio of public debt to GDP is near 100 percent; net future pension liabilities amount to another 100 percent. Italy's already huge debt ratio is overshadowed by pension liabilities of an additional 113 percent of GDP. Finally, in Japan, where the debt ratio is moderate, public pensions coming due account for 110 percent of GDP. In the United States, the corresponding liabilities amount to only 31 percent of GDP.

The problem can be traced to a number of factors. First, the active labor force that contributes taxes for future pensions will decline relative to beneficiaries. This effect will come into play between 2010 and 2030, first in Japan, where aging will occur soonest, then in Europe. The second factor is that longevity has risen around the world, but people aren't working longer years in most countries. Hence, their withdrawals from public pension accounts have risen even though their contributions have not. Declining birth rates in industrial countries are also slowing the retirement revenue stream. Last, legislatures were overly generous when the pension schemes ran surpluses over the past thirty years.

Private Pool

With future liabilities so mind-bogglingly large, some people argue that these pensions will never be paid. That's not likely to happen, though, since an aging society also means an aging electorate. So how might the obligations be met? Taxes could be raised on future generations, but tax levels are already high—and hiking taxes is unpopular and unproductive. Another possibility is to find a way to phase in later retirement. Still another option for the industrialized nations is to turn toward their less developed neighbors and borrow from them: Brazil, China, Mexico, and other countries with young populations will have high savings that could be invested in the paper of industrialized nations. Yet while such efforts might ameliorate the problem, they won't solve it.

Two things must be done. First, the accumulation of ever-growing liabilities must be contained. Second, savings in these industrialized nations must be increased sharply—not only by cutting government spending but also by raising private savings. The best way to accomplish this is via mandatory private-savings schemes, such as those in Chile and Singapore, where households must set aside a significant portion of their income for retirement and disability. But rather than paying it to the government in taxes, these savings should be placed in qualified accounts under private management. Thus, private saving is not automatically diverted to finance budget deficits.

Without a buildup in public and private savings, expect a crunch in world capital markets. Major governments will be forced to borrow huge amounts to finance pensions, and interest rates will be driven sky-high. Fortunately, there is enough time for policymakers to figure out how to avoid such a scary encounter with capital shortage.

7

Growth Forever

A stumbling stock market, a poor second quarter, and the prospect of negative numbers for the third quarter raise the question of whether the "new economy" has suddenly become old. Though it is not yet clear just how the long expansion might end, there are three likely possibilities. First, it might run out of steam as demand fizzles. Second, the Asian depression might overwhelm earnings prospects, stock market values, and hence household confidence. Finally, Federal Reserve Chairman Alan Greenspan might, in time-honored fashion, murder the expansion before it gets a chance to die of old age.

But each of these possibilities is remote. The U.S. economy likely will not see a recession for years to come. We don't want one, we don't need one, and, as we have the tools to keep the current expansion going, we won't have one. This expansion will run forever.

Superficially Attractive

The notion that all expansions come to an end and give way to recession is superficially attractive. It has biological overtones and, of course, is a sheer fact of history. This is already the tenth expansion in the postwar period and, by the law of averages, it should already be over. Only one expansion, from February 1961 to December 1969, has lasted longer. Yet none of the postwar expansions died of natural causes—they were all murdered by the Fed over the issue of inflation. Once an expansion

Originally published in the *Wall Street Journal* (30 July 1998): A18. Reprinted with permission.

got under way and unemployment came down, wage and price inflation would pick up. Then the Fed, like a matron at a sock hop, would, as the recently deceased Fed Chairman William McChesney Martin observed, "take away the punch bowl just when the party gets going."

The situation today, amid what is now the second-longest expansion, is quite different in two key respects. First, there is no inflation. Second, the government's coffers are overflowing with budget surpluses. Thus, only natural causes, and not the Fed, can bring the economy to a standstill. Fortunately, we have the monetary and fiscal resources to keep that from happening, as well as a policy team that won't hesitate to use them for continued expansion.

Suppose a drop in the stock market undercuts consumer confidence and spending, or Asian distress undermines exports and hence growth. What comes next? If budget deficits stood in the way of tax cuts, or inflationary pressure kept the Fed from cutting interest rates, that would mean the end of the expansion. The drop in demand would lead to production cuts, resulting in lower incomes and decreased consumer spending, which in turn would produce a recession. Policymakers would stand by while bemoaning the limits on fiscal policy, and the Fed might privately applaud the recession for affording a badly needed cooling-off. Some would talk foolishly about the benefits of creative destruction.

But this scenario is clearly not relevant today. Inflation is at a record low while we have full employment. Granted, we do not know why this is so, and we suspect that it is too good to be true. But whether the explanation lies with the "new economy" or the Asian crisis or some other factor, the point is that inflation figures give the Fed absolutely no excuse not to prop up the expansion should it need encouragement. True, when last heard, Mr. Greenspan tried to restrain the markets by holding out the risk of inflation, as well as the unhealthy valuations of assets. But that is all for the good. The chairman's job is not to prescribe steroids for the Dow Jones Industrial Average, but to keep full-employment growth on track.

The Fed is a keenly political institution simply because that is the only way it can maintain the independence necessary to make good policy. Just as it won't raise rates to tumble the stock market in the absence of inflation, it will very certainly cut rates, sharply if necessary, if growth withers at a time when there is no inflation. That is the situation today. Of course, rate cutting is not quite enough. Because there can be lags of a year from the time of the rate cut to the impact on demand, the Fed must act promptly. But fortunately bond markets have learned to simulate the Fed and thus move the term structure ahead of Federal Open Market Committee decisions. That has become a built-in stabilizer.

The leeway the Fed enjoys on the inflation front is particularly important in case of a stock market disaster. A minor correction surely won't lead the Fed to cut rates—the three hawks on the board won't stand for it, nor will the chairman. But if a massacre gets underway, just as in 1987, Mr. Greenspan is sure to act very quickly. This ensures that markets won't melt down, which in turn rules out one potent source of recession, namely a precipitous unbounded loss of confidence.

Still, if the effectiveness of monetary policy is unduly hampered by long time lags, then the levers of fiscal policy can always be put to use. There is a budget surplus waiting to be raided. Tax cuts burn holes in pockets as households rush out to spend and firms add to the capital stock. And fiscal policy works fast, since it can always be made retroactive. In fact, there is a race between President Clinton and the Republicans in Congress to see who will offer antirecession tax cuts first. Though they will surely squabble about who gets the money—businesses or households, the middle class or the poor—there is more than enough to go around. For policymakers living with budget surpluses and without inflation, a recession would be an unforgivable mistake.

Policy Levers

Just-in-time policy levers give the present expansion years of life. The payoff from a competitive and fully employed economy is low inflation and budget surpluses—double-barreled antirecession weaponry. They in turn carry the potential of a virtuous circle, in that monetary and fiscal policy are free to keep the economy from being accidentally derailed. That feeds back to longer horizons, deeper confidence, higher valuation, and better performance.

8

Germany's Economic Future

In its economy, Germany has two faces. One is that of an immensely successful country, near the top in living standards in the world, so rich and stable that even the momentary appearance on the scene of a Lafontaine could not do much more than make a momentary dent in the stock market. The other view is that of a country that is plain stuck: mass unemployment, slow growth, and no idea of what to do about it and even less courage to try. Not try, at least outside the established boundaries of consensus and don't rock the boat. That was true for Kohl, who basically did nothing (other, of course, than unification, for which he deserves a big place in history). And it is even truer of Schroeder, who looks the wrong way every time he gets a chance.

What is left are plenty of initiatives where Beamte of all stripes try to teach business how to get ahead and where experts look at the myriad distortions to make shopping lists of a grand agenda. Predictably that leads nowhere. And why would it: Germany is rich, most things in everyday life go right, and small changes in the right direction help rationalize why much more is not only impossible but perhaps even inessential. There is no crisis, there won't be a crisis anytime soon, and without one, why expect that anything will change?

Not the Worst

To start with, here is a benchmark. Germany is by no stretch of the imagination the worst—not in living standards among the richest economies, not in hourly compensation, and surely not in sheer effort expanded on working life. Far from it.

Germany ranks among the top in the world when it comes to hourly compensation: workers are paid more (and the government piles costs on top) than in virtually any other place in the world. And as to hours worked, those Germans who do work spend fully 25 percent less time on the job than do Americans or the Japanese. How does all this translate into living standards? Not so well! GDP per head, adjusted for purchasing power parity and on a scale that places the United States at 100, Germany stands at 75 percent, that is, far less successful in terms of the living standard. In fact, Germany runs behind France or Belgium, Canada, and Scandinavia, and only marginally ahead of Italy. Yes, the wages are high, but the purchasing power is low, and the combination takes much away from what would seem a super-rich country. Of course, we can debate how the numbers are made, but by World Bank measures, that is what comes out. That surely is also part of the quality of life.

Of course, these are all measures of accumulated success, a payoff on the efforts and creativity of the past decades. A more current reading, particularly from a business perspective, comes from the World Economic Forum *Competitiveness Report*. Here Germany is thoroughly uninteresting, placed number 24, far behind the Anglo-Saxon economies and those of Singapore, Ireland, or Switzerland. It is right there with France, Sweden, and Spain, who share a disdain for free market economics. What is the high standard of living to workers looks like a serious lack of competitiveness to firms. True, when Germans work, they do work! But they work fewer hours, they cost a fortune, and each worker has six Beamte and ten trade unionists walking behind him to make sure work does not get out of hand.

Another perspective on how Germany ranks comes from the stock market. Consider the relative value of the German and the U.S. stock markets. For years, the relative value of Germany has fallen. Investors don't see what good news lies ahead. And they are right. Companies are moving in slow motion on things that elsewhere happen at a hot pace. Investors are a sideshow; they get what is left after trade unions and the government, and regulations and inefficiency, and lack of competition have taken their toll.

Figure 8.1
Germany-United States Relative Stock Prices

True, the U.S. stock market will tumble one day, and that will change the picture. But if and when it does, will the German market go, too? And even if it does not, with say a 30 percent drop in the U.S. market, holders of stocks in U.S. business are still way ahead of those who have put their bet on German firms. The stock market is forward looking; it asks what lies ahead. Of German stocks it says, "Not much, sorry."

The overall picture is mixed: accumulated success, comfortable living standards if not the best. But surely it is not the place people talk about when they look for a business opportunity. But if they do not, who will pay the upkeep? Unemployment is huge, the welfare state is generous, debts are high, and unfunded pensions are huge. True, there is no crisis, but is there a reality that is being denied? Not even that; there is sheer and patent discomfort already. Reality is not altogether denied; it is merely resisted. Everybody knows that all the jobs-summit talk notwithstanding, unemployment will not fall. Everybody knows there won't be a boom that solves all problems; everybody knows that there is a mountain of public debt that won't go away. But in the absence of a perfect answer, namely, an answer that everybody can accept, no answer is the best that can be expected. In the meantime, tax reform is good topic, but it surely is an insignificant part of any solution strategy and merely diverts attention from essentials.

Hopes of the Euro

It is as well to dispense with any thought that the Euro, or more broadly the European Union, provides answers that make the status quo more viable. The Euro has already lost quite a lot of its glamor—it was supposed to carve out a major place in world finance, push the dollar aside, and soar in currency markets. Not quite, at least for the time being. In fact, just now there are risks of there being too much disdain for the Euro. After all, it will have some beneficial impacts for European growth, albeit small benefits, and they won't come fast either. To start, we must denounce a claim that surely is exaggerated.

• The Euro will not lead to great gains in competition and transparency: exchange rates have been fixed in Europe for more than a decade (discounting Italy's momentary departure). Everybody can divide by the exchange rate, and any repeat purchaser surely will. Price discrepancies in Europe reflect two facts: first, all prices (like all politics) are local. There are price discrepancies within and across U.S. cities, from wholesale to retail and across service add-ons. No surprise in this, and it has nothing to do with one or many monies. Second, price discrepancies do have a lot to do with the limited competition at the retail level and above all with a long tradition of anticompetitive practices. But that leaves us still with plenty of good points.

• One great payoff of the Euro is the financial disarmament of the periphery—Italy, Spain, and even France. The common money has made these regions safe for investors, and that in turn is reflected in lower interest rates and higher growth; risk premia have been sharply compressed because they no longer have central banks or exchange rates to play with. Waigel pact restrictions have further helped by stabilizing sovereign risk, adding on to the benefits of lower interest rates. Macroeconomics is gone as far as local initiative is concerned, and that is a good thing in a world where whenever the Banca d'Italia practices "independent monetary policy," investors can't run fast enough. In this respect, the Euro is a thoroughly modern institution, well adapted to a highly integrated and trigger-happy world capital market.

• In the medium term, the Euro reinforces financial deregulation (national and cross-border) in Europe to create a broad and deep capital market. Europe comes from a very dinky and segmented national and bank-based financial structure. It is on the way to a U.S.-style capital market where households hold funds and companies issue paper and stocks; intermediation margins are small and governance significant. European companies will benefit from the transformation, and it is likely to be the most significant supply-side influence we will now see.

• There is no prospect of the Euro changing deeply or quickly the world capital market in the sense that portfolio shifts will favor the Euro despite some alleged dollar privilege—remember General de Gaulle speaking of the *exorbitant privilege*, always a French obsession. The Euro will not, per se, appreciate on the dollar just because it is the new kid on the block. In the labor market, Europe cannot afford a steep appreciation and that, for one, is why it won't happen. Central banks are well equipped to avoid the appreciation by offsetting open-market operations, and treasuries can reinforce it with their funding policies.

In sum, the Euro, complementing a lot of other deregulation measures and the force of new financial technology, will help Europe have a better capital market. That is very good; it does not unfortunately mean that growth will double. The benefits are measured by perhaps one tenth of 1 percent extra growth. Nice, but not on the scale of solving big problems.

Hope on the Domestic Front?

If the rest of the world does not solve the German problems, perhaps the cure can come on the homefront. Not so, because two major obstacles stand in the way of a major upturn in growth and a virtuous cycle of mobilizing energies for growth and prosperity. The first is a deep-seated proclivity for consensus.

Historically that is easily understood. Coming out of the Nazi years and with communism next door, a very inclusive economic regime was the obvious strategy for consolidating politics. Government, unions, and business all crawled into the same bed and never came out. "Social Partners" is the euphemism for the corporatist arrangement, which of course stifles competition and initiative, not to mention reform and dramatic deregulation. First, growth was high enough not to raise issues of structural rigidities. Next, when the rigidities did start to come to the fore, the government simply borrowed for two decades to paper over the frictions. By now there is not much growth, and there is far too much debt. The answer is obvious, but don't expect it to be implemented outside a major crisis. In the meantime, there is too much talk about fairness and too little talk of individual responsibility and self-help, and of the sheer social unacceptability of people shirking work and ripping off the taxpayer.

The second problem is an endemic lack of initiative, taught in the schools, and reinforced in the business organizations, where there is a nasty little story that circulates about a major German corporation that went shopping for high-tech boutiques in California. On the home front, the research team rebelled: "We can do the same things," they said. "So why haven't you?" management asked. "Because nobody told us to," was the answer. Germany excels at, and is stuck in, mid-level technologies—great cars. But it has little of the upper-level technologies that matter today to be a frontrunner, nor the mindset and the structures to quickly become a player. True, education levels are far superior to those in the United States; but formal education does relatively little if the mindset is passive and the reward structure set by business discourages innovation adventures. The government's attempt to foster a learning society, reminiscent of Al Gore at his worst, completes the picture of a country that can see where it should be, but cannot get itself to make the big leap. That is not surprising; things are basically okay, so why rock the boat?

What then is a plausible assessment of Germany's economic future? The central scenario is thoroughly average behavior: 2 percent growth, stable unemployment, increasing fiscal problems, and substantial vulnerability if the world economy goes wrong. Not a winner by any stretch of the imagination, nor a problem case for sure. Being part of Europe, and Europe becoming a key player in the world economy, will detract increasingly from comparisons of economic performance between one country and another. The American Century is over and the European one is not about to start. More likely than not, Japan's formidable economic problems and the emerging security issues of Russia and China will be on the agenda soon, and the economic race of post-communism will look like a golden age even for the losers.

III

Global Financial Markets: Ideas Whose Time Has Come

9

Capital Controls: An Idea Whose Time Is Gone

When capital development of a country becomes a by-product of the activities of a casino, the job is likely to be ill-done.
—J. M. Keynes, *General Theory*

In the aftermath of the Mexican crisis, and even more so after the unexpected Asian collapse, capital market opening has come sharply into question. Chile, which was always rated high by the interventionists, moved up yet another notch with what is considered an effective way of sheltering the economy from the instability of international capital flows. As in the aftermath of every crisis, everybody wants to draw some lessons and preferably systemic ones.

Japanese officials are out in front declaring that Asia's collapse is the first of a new kind of crises, crises of global capitalism. Their deep ignorance of Latin America—"Asia is different ..."—overlooks the fact that Mexico had been doing fine on fundamentals, including a balanced budget, but still experienced a collapse just as Korea. Malaysia's Mahtir calls for a new system in which speculators are ostracized, and even the IMF, while flirting with mandatory capital account convertibility, cannot deny some role for short-run, ad hoc capital controls. The issue of opening the capital account has been coming on for twenty years; now it is as urgently calling for an answer as the question of the right exchange-rate system in a world of intense capital mobility.

The right answer is that there ought to be unrestricted capital mobility. Countries must urgently recognize two corollaries. First, that the scope for discretionary policies has become extremely limited and that they stand to gain from enlisting the capital markets in support of good policies.

Second, that intense capital mobility puts greater burdens on a country to assure that the financial system is well supervised and regulated. Any question of sequencing is not one of trade versus capital, but rather cleanup followed by opening. Postponing both, as Korea did, is just an invitation to a mega-crisis.

Old Answers

The old discussion revolves around two themes. One theme, most articulately proposed by James Tobin (1984), argues that the goods markets should be sheltered from the vagaries and fancies of international capital markets. The more scope there is for short-term roundtripping, the more the goods market will reflect the volatility of capital markets. Since capital market disturbances are not necessarily connected to changes in fundamentals, "throwing sand in the wheels" in the form of a foreign exchange tax is the remedy. The other strand of the discussion, best represented by McKinnon and Pill (1995), focuses on sequencing: which should come first, the capital account or the current account? In McKinnon's rendition, there is no question; the capital account must come first. Various accidents in Latin America are adduced as evidence for misguided sequencing.

Consider first the Tobin tax, advocated in the context of rich countries, but now just as relevant, if not more so, for emerging economies acing their first encounters on free market terms with the international capital market. Tobin argued that a transactions tax would lengthen horizons, just as Keynes had done, shifting attention from *speculation* to *enterprise*.

In Dornbusch (1986, 1996, 1997), I have joined the argument for a cross-border payments tax by emphasizing just the same point Tobin had made: a small fee lengthens the horizon, no more. I added that if sand is not enough, try rocks. But the later paper also recognized that however desirable a Tobin tax is in the control of noise, it cannot accomplish much. It just screens out some noise: it does not afford governments any room to pursue policies that deteriorate the long-run prospects for capital without any impact on current exchange market conditions. Asia was not brought down by short-sighted roundtripping. A Tobin tax would not have avoided the Asian bankruptcy. Anyone who contemplates 30 percent depreciation will happily pay a 0.1 percent Tobin tax!

A Tobin tax is not an answer to capital flight arising from the prospective collapse of asset prices, financial institutions, and even political continuity. The answer here, dull as it is, has to be foresight, not safety belts.

If Tobin's point was that a foreign exchange tax limits short-term roundtripping, the reality is that in emerging markets such a tax already exists. As a matter of fact, segmentation is still such that transactions costs are very substantial. The fees and bid-ask spreads are such that they effectively amount to a Tobin tax. Moreover, at the outset of a crisis, they sharply widen. Thus a Tobin tax is in place. Even so, facing a major prospect of meltdown, money will want to leave. Something more basic is required.

The McKinnon debate as to which should come first, free trade or the free flow of capital, likewise misses the practical point. Both trade opening and financial opening involve industrial restructuring—in one case goods and services industries and in the other the financial sector. There is no presumption as to which should wait or which must come first. Since a protective situation wastes resources, the sooner the better is the answer on both counts. Since gradualism and sequencing are more likely to be hijacked by political pressures adverse to the best utilization of resources and a persuasive case for gradualism has never been made, full steam ahead is the right answer.

But the McKinnon analysis focuses rightly on a basic issue that must be highlighted, namely, the balance sheet question. For import-competing textile producers, the balance sheet question is not of interest—they may or may not go bankrupt, but the welfare economist should not care. For banks and other financial institutions, however, that question is paramount because banks are special: implicitly or explicitly their liabilities are guaranteed. Coming out of a period of financial repression and political control, banks will tend to be bad or very bad.

Even before the crisis, the IMF (1996, p. 114) reported on the financial strength of banks in emerging markets. Of a total of 151 major banks, only 11 percent were rated C+ or better. In fact there were no A banks at all, and only Singapore had B+ banks and Hong Kong B banks. No surprise, the remaining 90 percent fall in the slightest tempest.

Opening the capital account therefore drives a process of almost inevitable bankruptcy: with bad loans on the books, bad banks will borrow abroad to carry bad loans at home. Their borrowing creates a national hazard because, by definition, they cannot repay. But the dynamics go further: good customers will leave bad banks because they can get better terms from new entrants. Thus bad banks have reduced earnings on their loan portfolio and will pay more in funding costs. They will make more speculative loans and thus get worse, and they will borrow at shorter maturities because that is the only money they can get. They will borrow unhedged in foreign exchange because you can go bankrupt only once, and this seems the best way to avoid slow death. It does avoid it, indeed, but can result in an unexpected quick death, as we have seen throughout Asia.

The message is that financial opening must not happen in an environment where the banking and financial system are badly regulated and badly supervised. This is not so much an argument to wait on opening, but the case for hastening the cleanup of financial repression, bad regulation, and lousy financial supervision.

New Thinking on Capital Controls

The current debate on lessons from the crisis carry two kinds of advocacy. Some quarters favor ad hoc, ex post capital controls. Staring a crisis in the face, in this school, the authorities would simply suspend capital account convertibility. Those who are in are trapped, cannot leave, cannot push down the currency, and thus amplify the crisis. They would become part of the solution rather than causing a magnification of the crisis.

This is a simplistic and deeply flawed answer. It is true that in a particular situation, ad hoc capital controls would limit the immediate damage. But that is superficial. Two consequences would ensue. First, in a global setting, ad hoc capital controls in one country would immediately cause contagion not only to the usual suspects but even beyond. Fearful that the crisis might or will spread, investors would act preemptively everywhere. They would pull out their money without waiting for more bad news. Inevitably, capital controls would be slammed on everywhere. And with that, the scope for stabilizing speculation would be severely limited. Nobody wisely lends into a situation where in bad states they become illiquid. Premia for those states would emerge, maturities would shrink, and preemptive capital flight would become the rule. Ad hoc capital controls are thus just about the worst kind of system.

Far preferred is a system of preventive capital control that limits the extent of capital inflows in the first place, or at least structures the maturity. In this perspective, equity investment is best, followed by long-term bonds and a great disdain for short maturity borrowing. If that can be done, the problem of an avalanche of outflows does not happen in the first place or, if it does happen, a flexible rate becomes an important stabilizing mechanism. If a country owes mountains of short-term debt, exchange-rate movements add to the bankruptcy risks. Not so for long-term bonds or equity, where rate movements widen the yields and bring in stabilizing speculation. Throughout Asia, the predominance of short-term debt far in excess of reserves shut out this mechanism of stabilizing speculation.

Of course, implementing capital inflow control is the hardest part. Chile has been effective, but it is hard to believe that countries with poor governance can effectively manage the situation in the way honest Chile has. Korea is a case in point. External capital was limited to short-term borrowing; equity and long-term bonds were a no-no. Much of the short-term borrowing went into Russian bonds and Brazilian Brady bonds and never even entered the country. Is the answer capital controls, or isn't it really a better structure for handling risk?

As some have argued, limiting capital *in*flows is the better strategy. Forcing long maturities and taxing short-term borrowing mean better answers.

Better Answers

A modern answer to the question of integration with the world capital market is enthusiastically positive. The capital market offers an important supervisory function over the temptations of poor economic policy. Governments may be disinclined to have the bond market look over their shoulder; savers and investors should be enthusiastic. That message is clear from a decade of adjustment policy reorientation in the United States and Europe. Now government's first thought is the bond market, and as a result their policymaking has become more disciplined.

Emerging economies can even less afford to be at odds with the world capital market—most of them need capital—and hence should not switch off the monitor that helps provide it on better and more lasting terms.

A look at the financial crisis of Asia, or that of Mexico before, reveals a shocking lack of appropriate supervision from all concerned. The IMF is obviously guilty. After Mexico they touted a new system of data dissemination including maturity structures of debt. Nobody ever saw any of this, and surely no system that would have drawn attention to the great vulnerability in place.

The rating agencies are next in line for criticism. Their analysis of risk is absurdly outdated, and their competition to provide upbeat ratings to drum up demand for business is very questionable. Surely they must have learned something from the crisis, but it is doubtful that their existing staff and technical resources have anywhere near an ability to assess country risk. The focus on debt export ratios, for example, highlights how little they perceive balance sheet crises as the issue rather than old-fashioned current account problems.

Lenders come in for criticism, as after every crisis. Long ago, Frank Taussig (1928, p. 130) had this to say about excessive capital flows and their abrupt reversal:

The loans from the creditor country begin with a modest amount, then increase and proceed crescendo. They are likely to be made in exceptionally large amounts toward the culminating stage of a period of activity and speculative upswing, and during that stage become larger from month to month so long as the upswing continues. With the advent of crisis they are at once cut down sharply, even cease entirely.

It is obvious that the pattern remains the same, all experience notwithstanding. Crisis country governments, of course, bear a large part of the responsibility. Cronyism and generalized sleaze are key factors in the crisis, from Thailand to Indonesia and Korea. Bad exchange-rate policy adds to the setting that have risen to the crisis. (See Dornbusch and Park 1995.) And so is the extraordinary incompetence of bureaucrats who gamble away the last nickel of reserves only to invite an even more acute crisis.

An effective supervisory system would, at the least, put in place a mandatory *value at risk* (VAR) analysis not only for the individual financial institutions (as is in place in the United States, for example) but in fact for the entire country. The great question of how the IMF could become more effective in preventing rather than resolving crises has an easy answer. Allowing for a transition period of say a year or two, any member of the IMF would be required to have in place both a supervisory and regulatory system that meets international standards but also a VAR evaluation. All these would be monitored by the IMF, and any country that is found deficient would not qualify for IMF support.

Thus honest crises would be generously solved with IMF credits, and predictable crises due to sleaze and regulatory failure would fall heavily on the deficient country with no international relief. Capital markets would, of course, look out for the IMF endorsement of financial conditions and punish severely with increased spreads a shortcoming in the risk assessment. In a postmortem of the crises, a single factor stands out: large dollar-denominated short-term liabilities. It is clear that any VAR analysis would immediately seize on the resulting risks: large exchange-rate swings could devastate balance sheets unless hedged. Adverse conditions could lead to a funding crisis. A finding crisis would bring with it a generalized country-credit risk with the resulting disappearance of orderly markets. Exactly what happened? In some remote sense this could happen to anyone, but this is far more likely the larger the dollar debt relative to balance sheets and reserves—hence gigantic debt-equity ratios, as in Korea, blow up the drama potential manifold—and the shorter maturities. The moment the focus shifts from sustainability to vulnerability, the whole discussion changes. Then the focus is on the bad scenario and just how bad it might be. A systematic VAR analysis highlights just this. Accordingly, countries would pay attention to alleviate excessive exposure by lengthening maturities and calling for hedging of liabilities, increase reserve, tighten budgets, and do all the things required to push down risk levels. As a result, countries could perfectly well live with an open capital market and highly mobile capital.

Another dimension of a response to a vulnerability perspective is to set up reinsurance mechanisms. Bankrupt governments that have gambled away their foreign exchange reserves and international credit standing cannot provide lender of last resort functions either for their financial institutions or the country at large. The appropriate response to the risk of an international credit crisis is to set up backup facilities. It is totally appropriate for a country's commercial banking system to be required to have international recourse facilities. Argentina has, in fact, put such a system into place. The charm of the mechanism is not only that, in need, resources become available and hence mitigate the meltdown. More important, the resource lenders have a strong interest of not lending into a bad situation. Accordingly, they will themselves supervise the solvency and liquidity of their potential clients. That mechanism works to prevent cumulative bad lending and, as a result, prevents crises or limits their severity. The world capital market is there to provide not only money but also monitoring, if only we empower it.

References

Dornbusch, R. 1986. "Flexible Exchange Rates and Excess Capital Mobility," *Brookings Papers on Economic Activity*, 1.

——— 1996. "It's Time for a Financial Transactions Tax." *The International Economy*, August/September 1970.

——— 1997. "Cross-Border Payments Taxes and Alternative Capital-Account Regimes," in *International Monetary and Financial Issues for the 1990s*, Research papers for the group of twenty-four, volume 8, United National Conference on Trade and Development, United Nations, New York and Geneva, pp. 27–35.

Dornbusch, R., and Y.C. Park (eds.) (1995) "Financial Integration in a Second Best World," in *Financial Opening*. International Center for Economic Growth.

International Monetary Fund (1996) *International Capital Markets*. Washington, D.C.: International Monetary Fund.

McKinnon, R., and H. Pill (1995) "Credit Liberalization and International Capital Flows." Mimeo, Stanford University.

Taussig, F. (1928) *International Trade*. New York: Macmillan.

Tobin, J. (1984) "On the Efficiency of the Financial System." *Lloyds Bank Review*, July.

10

Why Bailouts Are Bad Medicine

Financial authorities around the world are edgy. Hardly a month passes without the discovery of a major fraud—Metall Gesellschaft, Barings, Daiwa Securities, Sumitomo Bank, and countless others. From time to time, an entire country goes over the financial cliff. Policymakers hope that new controls, regulations, and surveillance will soon be in place before some new disaster undermines the whole global financial system.

Until then, it's up to the market to punish transgressors. The disintegration of Barings and the vigorous prosecution of Daiwa in New York are cases in point. But punishment is much harder when entire economies are financially mismanaged.

Take the postmortem on Mexico's crash and rescue. The consensus view is that the crisis showed the need for two things: better surveillance and greater financial resources. But a third—no automatic bailout for investors—could be even more important.

Individual countries have the capability of regulating and supervising their own markets. If these jobs are performed conscientiously, large-scale accidents are less likely to happen.

But in the international community, it doesn't work that way. There is no internationally recognized body to establish rules for conduct on exchange rates or other macroeconomic management. If a country decides, for example, to secretly boost its money supply, no one is likely to challenge the policy. As long as foreign money continues to pour in, the Finance Minister rides high. By the time foreign investors discover the

Originally published in *Business Week* (8 July 1995): 20. Reprinted with permission.

problem and money starts to dry up, it's too late to prevent a crisis. Then, when the International Monetary Fund and central banks try to help, the country is already deeply in trouble.

No Lack of Data

We should not kid ourselves into believing that better availability of data would prevent this kind of crisis. There is plenty of information on growth, banking problems, interest rates, and trade. More data won't help investors who refuse to look at the facts.

In the Mexico rescue, the U.S. Treasury and the International Monetary Fund got together to arrange a colossal loan. Europeans in the IMF were railroaded into participating. The German position was that bailing out investors is a mistake. The Bundesbank in particular believes that bailouts give investors a false sense of security and should be reserved for problems that threaten an entire financial system.

The U.S. view, by contrast, is that the global financial system is highly fragile. The Mexican crisis shows the risk of not having lots of money on hand for speedy intervention. The Clinton Administration had to battle Congress for money even as Mexico was in meltdown.

Both views of the bailout problem are, of course, correct. There is a hazard in telling investors that they will always be rescued. But there also is a risk if a country crisis gets out of hand and threatens the entire global financial system. The question is how to strike a balance. In the nineteenth century and until the early 1980s, governments stayed away from bailing out private investors. The history of foreign lending is replete with distressed countries, defaulted loans, and disappointed investors. Foreign Bond Holders Protective Councils organized the multitude of creditors and renegotiated the terms of settlements with defaulting countries. These councils worked pretty well. The U.S. council lasted till the mid-1960s.

Confusing Signals

Nothing in the history of foreign lending suggests that the private market cannot handle credit or that country defaults inevitably become systemic crises. It is important to allow markets to work again and get governments out of the bailout business. Private investors have to learn about risk again and pass on their skepticism about bad policies to would-be borrowers. In such a system, good policies get rewarded by low interest rates and plentiful credit; bad policies bring about high penalty rates and a dearth of credit. The current system of presumptive bailout—based on the assumption that countries are too big to fail—confuses market signals, leads to bad policy, and, thus, creates recurrent problems.

So the next time a country goes into distress, international financial institutions and the major powers should turn their backs. That will demand ice water in the veins of international policymakers, but the world will go on, as it has for 150 years of country defaults. Teaching a lesson on a smaller level frees up the financial system to intervene with great vigor when there is a real crisis.

11

Check the Laws Before You Invest Abroad

Cross-border investment in stocks and bonds has been the rage for most of the 1990s. One would have thought the Mexican meltdown would have tempered enthusiasm for these capital flows, but no. Capital is rushing into all kinds of emerging markets, from Mexico again to Russia, the Philippines, and Argentina. At last count, more than 1,200 emerging-market funds managed more than $100 billion in equity. Add to that the additional billions put into dollar-bond and local currency instruments, and the amount is staggering. But do people actually know what they are buying? Do they understand the risk?

A team of scholars from Harvard University—Rafael La Porta, Florencio Lopez De Silanes, and Andrei Shleifer—and Robert W. Vishny, from the University of Chicago, have written a report, published by the National Bureau of Economic Research, that deals with just this question. *Law and Finance* asks what institutions are in place to protect stockholders against abuse and appropriation. What happens to holders of corporate bonds when countries or foreign companies default?

The questions are not academic. Investors in Russia have discovered that they can't get into stockholder meetings without getting beaten up. In Brazil, domestic stocks tend to be cheaper than those of multinationals because management often siphons off profits through fully owned sub-contractors, leaving little for shareholders. Corporate bondholders in Mexico have discovered that bankruptcy proceedings can take a decade. They wind up renegotiating the debt rather than spending years trying to

Originally published in *Business Week* (28 October 1996): 34. Reprinted with permission.

take possession of collateral. In Japan, T. Boone Pickens Jr. discovered that stockholder meetings are rigged to protect management. Having a significant investment does not translate into meaningful control.

Common-Law Protections

The report scrutinizes national legal systems to identify whether investors have effective recourse. It concludes that there are two dominant legal regimes, Anglo-Saxon common law and French civil law, that have been adopted around the world and that provide the basic setting for investing. French law protects investors least. Those countries with common law give investors plenty of ways to safeguard their interests: voting by mail, permitting transfer of shares during stockholder meetings, fewer shares required to call an extraordinary meeting, laws to protect minority holders, etc. This is true for both equity holders and creditors.

In countries operating under French civil law, it's caveat investor. Investors get a poorer deal across the board. All of Latin America is on the French system, while most of Asia uses common law. Japan has adopted German common law, which is somewhere between the two when it comes to protecting investors' rights.

Does all this make a difference to capital flows and the availability of finance around the globe? Absolutely. If investors get poor protection, they will stay away. Outside finance will dry up, and fewer resources will be available for growth. Thus, applying anything other than common law to investors is a poor growth strategy.

A Rising Tide

There are ways for investors to circumvent weak protections. One way is to simply take a majority equity stake and join the prevailing local team as a business partner, not just as an investor. The downside is that this strategy is not nearly as efficient in broad macroeconomic terms, and there is no guarantee that local partners will protect foreign investors anyhow. Another strategy would be to go into partnership with foreign governments themselves.

Right now, we are living in a world of rising equity and bond markets, and a rising tide raises all ships. The legal environment makes little difference because management and stockholders are on the same side. But when the current atmosphere subsides and markets decline, investors will have to think seriously about how they can recoup their losses when trouble comes.

Emerging countries around the world are reforming their financial systems, opening up to external capital, and reducing the size of government. The question of how to protect investors is central to their performance. Stable macroeconomics and the absence of currency crises is just a starting point.

In the rush to diversify internationally and in the haste to collect capital gains on seemingly underpriced assets, investors have bought foreign securities on an extraordinary scale. It would be surprising if, contrary to the experience of the past century, this atmosphere continued forever.

12

How the Fed Can Tame the Savage Currency Markets

In 1944, the financial leadership of the free world met in Bretton Woods, N.H., to map out a postwar financial system. In the 1930s, the world economy had disintegrated, and the postwar world needed a structure to keep trade routes open. The experts sought to create new institutions that would prevent currency instability, competitive devaluations, tariffs, and quotas. They wanted to fix exchange rates and realign them only in case of "fundamental disequilibrium."

In large part, they succeeded. After World War II, international trade expanded faster than world production. Vanquished Germany and Japan made strong economic comebacks. Despite day-to-day trade frictions, the world moved from a closed system to an open one.

Bretton Woods is given much of the credit, but in fact it had little to do with it: most of the credit goes to the United States. Starting with the Reciprocal Trade Agreements Act of 1934, the United States reversed protectionism at home and fostered free trade abroad.

The Bretton Woods world of fixed rates was never as idyllic as many would have us believe. Many currencies remained inconvertible for years after the war. Exchange-control laws prevailed, and bureaucrats decided on specific currency transactions. In Britain, that awkward state of affairs continued right up till Margaret Thatcher became Prime Minister in 1979. In Japan, it lasted into the 1980s.

Exchange rates were never completely fixed, either. Realignments constantly took place. Currency crises were routine, centering around a

Originally published in *Business Week* (22 August 1994): 18. Reprinted with permission.

strong German mark, an anemic British pound, a shaky French franc, and an overstretched U.S. dollar.

Pragmatic Policy

The system of make-believe fixed rates crashed in the early 1970s, when the United States found it inconvenient to run its economy by standards the Bundesbank set for Germany. A major devaluation of the dollar showed the greenback had been overvalued for years, hurting U.S. growth.

The floating-rate world since then has been no Camelot, either. This was especially true in the 1980s, when a misguided U.S. Treasury turned dogmatic, practicing a hands-off approach to the dollar in the currency markets. In the midst of superhigh interest rates during the Volcker recession, the dollar soared, reaching a glorious overvaluation of 30 percent to 50 percent.

Compared with the 1980s, we now have a pragmatic policy. There is plenty of "dirty floating," with governments intervening in the markets. Whatever the dreams of the Bretton Woods romanticists, governments are determined not to make the mistake again of locking their currencies in place, only to have them become targets of speculative attacks.

It's true that the volatility of the mark-dollar rate is almost three times as high under current floating rates as in the fixed-rate period. But what are the consequences? One is that flexible rates have given countries the ability to follow an independent policy geared to domestic needs rather than to the demands of the currency markets.

No Return

Yet this pro-growth policy may bring with it an inherent inflationary bias. Those who would return to a fixed-rate system feel that linking a country to more responsible central banks abroad would limit that tendency and reduce instability in the financial markets. Unfortunately, there can be no return to Bretton Woods systems: the Bundesbank will not accept monetary policy set by the United States, and the United States will not accept a Buba-managed straitjacket on its economy. So, for better or worse, fixed rates are a nonstarter.

Of course, there is the experience of the European Monetary System (EMS). As soon as European countries fixed their currencies to the German mark, they began to let the Buba run their monetary policies. Countries gained on the inflation front, but Britain, Italy, and Spain saw their currencies collapse in a speculative free-for-all. The only nations sticking with fixed rates were the true believers in Buba policy. Even so, exchange-rate margins have since been widened for EMS countries.

Yet the question remains: why not announce target zones for major-currency relationships—such as dollar-to-mark or dollar-to-yen—to generate more predictability? The answer is that, unless there is tight monetary coordination, such a system is just as prone to attack as a rigidly fixed system.

A better strategy is to let the Federal Reserve publicly announce an inflation target for the coming years—of 1 percent to 3 percent. Let Congress monitor it and have the Fed vigorously pursue policies that achieve it. In time, the target will be accepted by markets around the world. Then the chief reason for wild currency swings—worry about inflation and the Fed's ability to stop it—will disappear.

The international monetary system matters. The best combines the advantages of exchange-rate flexibility with firm inflation targeting. There are great benefits to predictably low inflation. Currency stability is one. Purists won't be satisfied because currencies will still move. But large and disruptive swings will mostly be gone. And if, on occasion, governments intervene in foreign exchange markets to help cool them off, so what?

13

The Effectiveness of Exchange-Rate Changes

1 Introduction

This chapter addresses the question of whether exchange rates are a useful policy instrument.[1] The very question will raise tempers: the suggestion that the *real* exchange rate is a policy variable is firmly rejected by any student in the "new classical" tradition, and even by a broader group who are reluctant to declare a broad policy role for the nominal quantity of money or the nominal exchange rate. Either can, of course, be manipulated. But whether there is scope to change in this manner the *real* quantity for money or the *real* exchange rate is quite another matter.

The article seeks to highlight where exchange rates fit into the policy mix. Two issues must be given consideration: first, are trade flows responsive to relative prices? Second, can nominal exchange-rate changes change relative prices? If the answer to both questions is affirmative then exchange-rate adjustment can play a useful role.

Exchange-rate adjustments are decidedly not a panacea—in case of doubt, devalue is the wrong answer. But in circumstances where there is unemployment and a deficit—that is, the need for deflation to restore competitiveness—exchange depreciation is often the right answer. Dogmatic insistence that devaluation simply means inflation, always and everywhere, is plain wrong. Just as an increase in the nominal quantity of money, in certain circumstances, may relieve a deficiency of demand, a currency depreciation may obviate the need for deflation. Purists are

Originally published in the *Oxford Review of Economic Policy* 12, no. 3 (1996): 26–38. Reprinted with permission.

right; deflation is always an alternative. But it remains an appropriate policy assumption that deflation does not come easily.

Allowing the possibility that nominal depreciation may change relative prices is a far cry from claiming that a strategy of recurrent, predictable, and large depreciations is an effective exchange-rate strategy. There is little question that expectations would come to reflect this regime, that wage setting anticipates the devaluation strategy, and that policymakers are left with inflation rather than lasting real exchange-rate changes.[2] Successful devaluation, then, is a very rare and very special event. Having limited the claims, it is also appropriate to defend vigorously this narrow ground against preposterous assertions that it never works, cannot work, and has never worked.

The stigma against advocating devaluation as a policy that in certain circumstances might work can obviously be traced to the fear of endorsing policies from the toolkit of times and mindsets long gone, a world of downward sticky wages and fixed prices—in one word, old-fashioned *Keynesianism*. But the pendulum is swinging back; limited wage–price fixity in the form of contracting is back in vogue and, as we move closer to deflation in the advanced economies, even downward stickiness of wages is becoming a respectable topic of research.[3]

In the past thirty years, hard money talk and equilibrium theory, including credibility concepts, have gained ground. That is all for the good. In the preceding decades very narrow Keynesianism had ruled unchallenged, prices were a decoration and not the corner-stone of macroeconomics, activism over and over again was the rule, and inflation was the result. It is necessary now to strike a balance. With inflation gone in many economies, with *de*flation an active prospect—and a painful one, as the examples of Argentina, Canada, Finland, or Switzerland already show—we are not giving too much away in asking under what narrow and special circumstances a nominal depreciation can be effective. In answering that question we must, of course, have a response to the central question of whether a devaluation can change relative prices on a lasting basis. It will not come as a surprise to find that devaluation works if, and only if, there is a need for a real wage cut, wages are downwardly inflexible, but there is no real wage rigidity. Do these circumstances exist? Yes, sometimes.

II The Equilibrium Model

A convenient starting point for discussion is an equilibrium model of a small open economy. The focus is on the labour market (internal balance) and the trade account (external balance). For the points to be made, there is no need to consider asset markets and international capital mobility. We thus focus only on the labour market and the external balance.

There are two determinants of output and employment: the wage in dollars, W/e, and the money stock in dollars, H/e. Here W and H denote the money wage and the money stock and e the exchange rate (measured as the number of units of home currency per dollar.) A rise of the wage in dollars hurts employment because it worsens international competitiveness.[4] To maintain employment there is a need for an off-setting increase in real balances and, as a result, in spending. This is shown by the upward-sloping schedule LL in figure 13.1. Along that schedule we have internal balance; points above and to the left correspond to unemployment, points below and to the right to an excess demand for goods and labor.

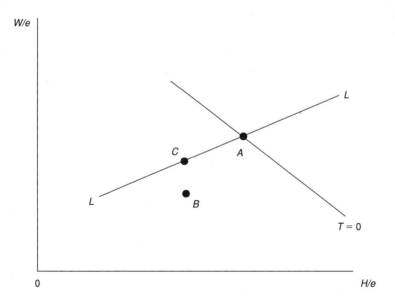

Figure 13.1
Finland-Germany Interest-Rate Differential

On the external front, a rise of wages in dollars hurts competitiveness and therefore leads to a trade deficit. An offsetting cut in real balances and spending is necessary to balance the external account. Thus the trade balance equilibrium schedule $(T = 0)$ is shown as downward sloping. Points below and to the left of $T = 0$ represent surpluses as a result of high competitiveness or low spending. Conversely, points above and to the right involve poor competitiveness or high spending and hence a deficit.

With this general framework we can now portray a number of scenarios about the adjustment process. The simplest world is one of fully flexible exchange rates and flexible prices—the equilibrium approach.[5] We would always and continually be at point A, with both internal and external balance at point A. Real disturbances could change relative prices, namely, the wage in dollars. Monetary disturbances would have no real effects—wages and the exchange rate would jump in the same proportion so that the real equilibrium is undisturbed.

A more interesting world still allows for flexible wages and prices, but holds the exchange rate fixed. This implies foreign exchange market intervention and hence an endogenous money stock. When there are surpluses (below $T = 0$), money is rising, and when there are deficits, money is falling. Thus the economy moves along LL because of wage flexibility, but it only converges over time to point A. In the short run, money matters. In the long run, the economy is always at point A. Once again, real disturbances can change equilibrium-relative prices.

Consider now an initial situation at point A and a devaluation. The instant effect is to reduce wages and for the money stock in dollars to move to a point such as B. Of course, the devaluation has made domestic labor cheap and thus there is an excess demand. Wages will rise *immediately* to point C on LL so as to restore labor-market equilibrium. Thus, with wages flexible, part of the devaluation is immediately undone. But the monetary impact lasts at least for a while. Only when a period of surpluses, as the economy moves up LL from C towards A, has restored the initial real balances will the economy be fully back to the initial equilibrium. Thus, in the equilibrium model a devaluation is a purely monetary phenomenon—it works if and because it results in a reduction of the real money stock. Because money is endogenous, it cannot last.[6]

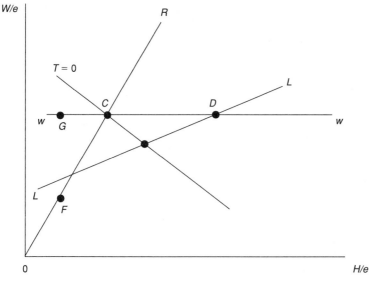

Figure 13.2
Wage-Money Stock Relationship

With fully flexible *nominal* wages, accordingly, exchange-rate changes have no interesting role to play. That is a critical insight: it forces us to ask why and how an exchange-rate change *should* work on employment or the external balance. For example, in a situation where money is passive in the sense of responding, say, by the budget deficit to wages and the exchange rate, even short-run effects cannot be expected. Exchange depreciation just means another round of inflation.

At the other extreme of fully flexible money wages are fully fixed *real* wages. This, too, is a world where exchange-rate changes cannot do anything. Suppose, in figure 13.2, the real wage is fixed at a level shown by the horizontal schedule *ww*. Labor-market equilibrium at *D* is incompatible with external balance at *C*. The monetary mechanism will make the economy converge to point *C*. A devaluation brings the economy immediately to *F*, but the sticky real wage implies a rapid adjustment to the initial level at *G*. From there, because of the reduction in real balances, there is a transitory surplus. Soon we are back to point *C*, where everything started. Thus, inflexible real wages do imply a policy problem in the sense of unemployment, but exchange-rate changes are not an answer.

The final case is the one and only one where devaluation is genuinely helpful: if money wages are sticky downwards but there is no real wage rigidity, then devaluation can help. A devaluation cuts the wage in dollars, fosters competitiveness, and in that manner helps create employment and an improved external balance. It is the missing tool in a situation where internal balance calls for expansion, but the external constraint (and possibly the budget) stands in the way of tax cuts or other fiscal measures. At this stage two questions come up. First, is there downward wage stickiness? Second, is devaluation a useful instrument?

III What Is the Model?

The suggestion that wages and prices are sticky downwards has been with us for the better part of the century. But it remains an assumption or an assertion about the world, rather than an implication of a model. In other words, it does not follow from any common mode of optimization and there is no theory to project this result, and hence the assertion must be suspect. Yet, it stays around.

There are, of course, suggestive models of contracting or pricing that imply protracted stickiness.[7] For example, the Taylor model of wage–price setting envisages overlapping wage contracts that are set partially in a forward-looking fashion. In such a world a permanent reduction in the demand for a country's goods—with unchanged monetary and exchange-rate rules—will lead to gradually falling wages and prices. Only over time—years, not days or months—will the price level fall enough to generate the level of real balances and the real exchange rate to restore full employment.

Similarly, in the Calvo-pricing model firms set prices in a forward-looking fashion and for a random duration. At any point in time the price *level* and, for a given exchange rate, the real exchange rate are given. A permanent reduction in demand will only over time lead to a set of new prices and gradually a new price level that restores full employment. Just as in the Taylor model, devaluation—while inconsistent with the assumed exchange-rate regime—will solve the problem from one moment to another.

Of course, that is not quite the end of the story. Breaking the established exchange-rate regime in itself has consequences since it raises the question of what comes next. It inevitably restricts the use of devaluation to circumstances that involve a disequilibrium sufficiently dramatic and exceptional to warrant the investment of a breach of regime.

It is also helpful to put the question in another fashion: what is the basis on which we assume that, left to itself, the market would rapidly and effectively respond to a severe reduction in demand by a fall in wages and prices? That evidence is definitely not there, perhaps because markets never get a chance really to show what they could do when there are no safety nets nor confusions about policy regimes.

In sum, there is no special model here to explain how devaluation can work; the story is still the old one: when there is unemployment caused by a fall in demand (not a hike in real wages), and when markets fail to coordinate a drop in wages and prices easily and rapidly, devaluation can provide a short cut, as is, indeed, suggested by some recent episodes of depreciation.

IV Some Examples

In this section we review a few episodes of major real exchange-rate changes. Few governments actively seek a major real depreciation. More likely, it is accepted as an inevitable measure in an attempt to reconcile internal and external balance objectives, or it is forced on the authorities in the market. One way or another, real depreciation does happen and it does last. When it does occur, it improves the external balance and it contributes to growth. It is no panacea and it is not painless, but it does work.

In the early 1990s, Finland went into a deep crisis: pulp and paper prices fell sharply, Russia vanished as a major market, world recession hurt exports, and the banking system went bust as a result of a "credibility-oriented" exchange-rate policy. Unemployment skyrocketed and the cyclical impact on the budget created gigantic deficits. The government finally gave up the misdirected support of the currency (figure 13.3), and the exchange rate took a deep dive.

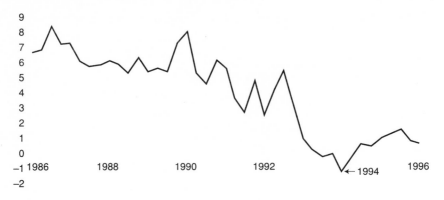

Figure 13.3
Finland-Germany Interest-Rate Differential
Source: IMF, *International Financial Statistics.*

Table 13.1
Finland: Response to Depreciation (% changes from previous year)

	1991	1992	1993	1994	1995
REER (1990 = 100)[a]	92	75	63	65	71
Imports[b]	−11.7	1.1	0.8	12.6	9.6
Exports[b]	−6.6	10.0	16.7	13.3	7.6
Foreign balance[c]	1.4	2.1	4.2	1.4	1.1
GDP	−7.1	−3.6	−1.2	4.4	4.2
Consumer prices	4.1	2.6	2.1	1.1	1.0

Notes: [a]Real effective exchange rate (relative normalized unit labour costs) as reported by the IMF. A decline of the index is a gain in competitiveness. [b]Goods and services, volumes [c]Change in net exports as a percentage of GDP.
Sources: IMF, *International Financial Statistics*, and OECD, *Economic Outlook.*

An obvious problem in analyzing the data is that the exchange rate is only one of the many factors impinging on the external balance. In addition, domestic demand plays a key role, as do foreign cyclical conditions. There is no way around that problem. The point to be noted, nevertheless, is the strong external balance support to domestic growth (table 13.1). Even though output is falling, the foreign sector acts as a shock absorber and mitigates the extent of decline. The current account (as a ratio of GDP) shifted from a deficit of 5 in 1991 to a surplus of 3.5 percent in 1995.

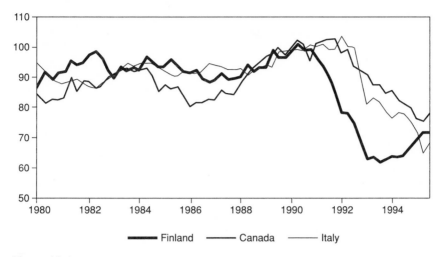

Figure 13.4
Real Effective Exchange Rates (1990 = 100)[a]
Note: [a]Relative normalized unit labor costs.
Source: IMF, *International Financial Statistics.*

Figure 13.4 shows the real effective exchange rate for three countries, Finland, Italy, and Canada, for the years 1980–95. It is obvious that, in the Finnish case, real depreciation lasted quite a few years. The reason, most plausibly, is the very high level of unemployment and the ongoing severe domestic recession. Here is a case where we do not seem to have full wage–price flexibility and, as a result, nominal exchange depreciation can play a useful role in bringing about stimulus of demand together with correction of a large external deficit. Strict adherents of the flexible wage model might argue that in the presence of unfavorable external shocks, of course, real depreciation is the equilibrium response. They might also argue that high unemployment is a reflection of overly generous unemployment benefits. Hence, in their view, there is no evidence here—in the absence of depreciation we would have observed vigorous deflation.[8] Given the unemployment benefit structure, depreciation at least reduces the cost of adjustment.

Another case of effective exchange-rate adjustment is Italy in the early 1990s. An essential part of the story was the abandonment of the *scala mobile*, a system of automatic wage indexation including price effects of exchange-rate depreciation. Table 13.2 shows the large real depreciation

Table 13.2
Italy: Response to Depreciation (% changes from previous year)

	1992	1993	1994	1995
Nominal effective exchange rate (1990 = 100)	96	80	77	69
REER (1990 = 100)[a]	99	82	77	67
Import prices	−0.7	10.6	4.9	16.2
Export prices	0.8	8.8	3.9	13.6
Import volume[b]	3.3	−9.3	10.5	7.7
Export volume[b]	3.6	11.1	10.5	10.4
Foreign balance[c]	−0.1	4.6	0.3	0.4
GDP	0.7	−1.2	2.2	3.0
Consumer prices	5.1	4.5	4.0	5.2

Notes: [a]Real effective exchange rate (relative normalized unit labour costs) as reported by the IMF. A decline of the index is a gain in competitiveness. [b]Goods only, volumes. [c]Change in net exports as a percentage of GDP.
Sources: As for table 13.1.

of 1992. The price effects of depreciation are of special interest. Import prices reflect very substantially the cumulative depreciation, but export prices or the inflation rate do not. As a result, a significant gain in export-competitiveness is sustained. Predictably, imports declined, export growth picked up, and the net external balance contributed substantially to growth.

In the case of Italy, real depreciation was an effective offset to fiscal tightening. This is a textbook case, where expenditure-switching effects of depreciation and expenditure-reducing fiscal policies combined to sustain growth.

In Canada's case (table 13.3), real depreciation made up for a terms-of-trade deterioration and a significant fiscal consolidation. The structural budget deficit declined by 2 percent of GDP between 1992 and 1995. That this was possible while sustaining some growth was because real depreciation kept up the external contribution to growth. Note, too, that just as in Italy, inflation declined in the face of a major depreciation.

Mexico (table 13.4) is another example of successful real depreciation. In 1990–94 a policy of exchange-rate-based disinflation had led to a significant overvaluation. Growth slowed down, the banking system deterio-

Table 13.3
Canada: Response to Depreciation (% changes from previous year)

	1992	1993	1994	1995
REER (1990 = 100)[a]	96	88	83	77
Foreign balance[b]	0.4	0.3	1.1	1.0
GDP	0.8	2.2	4.6	2.2
Consumer prices	1.5	1.8	0.2	2.2

Notes: [a]Real effective exchange rate (relative normalized unit labour costs) as reported by the IMF. A decline of the index is a gain in competitiveness. [b]Change in net exports as a percentage of GDP.
Source: As for table 13.1.

Table 13.4
Mexico: Response to Depreciation (% changes from previous year)

	1993	1994	1995
REER (1990 = 100)[a]	117	112	79
Foreign balance[b]	0.9	−0.9	10.8
GDP	0.6	3.5	−6.8
Consumer prices	9.8	7.0	35.0

Notes: [a]Real effective exchange rate (relative wholesale prices), as reported by J. P. Morgan. [b]Change in net exports as a percentage of GDP.
Sources: J. P. Morgan and OECD.

rated, and the external balance showed a massive deficit. The collapse of the peso in late 1994 and early 1995 has since set the stage for a more balanced macroeconomic situation. The external balance has sharply turned, in part as a result of real depreciation and in part because of the deep recession. In the midst of the adjustments in the budget, and as a result of a bankrupt banking system, external stimulus was the only source of growth.

The Mexican story is, of course, far from complete. The massive nominal depreciation of the peso—150 percent between mid-1994 and 1996—produces a large inflation shock. That is now wearing off. But, as in the past, the government continues to use the exchange rate for disinflation purposes and as a result the real exchange rate is appreciating. By mid-1996 it was only 20 percent below the pre-crash 1994 level.

Table 13.5
Consensus Estimates of Price Elasticities

	United States	Japan	Germany
Exports	−1.31	−1.68	−1.06
	(0.92)	(3.70)	(1.87)
Imports	−1.35	−0.97	−0.50
	(0.93)	(0.78)	(0.44)

Note: Numbers in parentheses are the standard deviations of estimates reported in various studies.
Source: Hooper and Marquez (1995, Table 4.2).

V   Reviewing Estimates for Industrialized Countries

The next step is to ask what is known more systematically about the effect of exchange-rate changes on prices, trade flows, and the external balance. These topics have been studied for the past fifty years. The early view was that trade flows are relatively unresponsive—elasticity pessimism—and that, accordingly, devaluation was a relatively unattractive if not outright ineffective instrument. That view was further reinforced by a misleading debate about elasticity versus absorption approaches, which is best forgotten.

A comprehensive survey by Hooper and Marquez (1995) brings together a massive amount of evidence on just how responsive trade flows in fact are to changes in relative prices. The large sample of various estimates is reported in table 13.5.

The most important point of these numbers is that they are large: the elasticity of trade flows with respect to relative prices is far into the region where devaluation works! This is the case for the major industrialized countries, and it is presumably the case for all countries. Trade flows that are unrelated to prices would be an extraordinary finding; small responsiveness—elasticities of, say, 0.1—would be very unusual. Note, too, that these estimates easily satisfy the famous Marshall–Lerner condition, which stipulates that a devaluation will improve the trade balance if the sum of the elasticities of imports and exports exceeds unity. Thus, after fifty years of research on this topic, the finding is sturdily in support of the effectiveness of the price mechanism.

Table 13.6
Hooper-Marquez Estimates of Trade Elasticities

	United States		Japan	
	Exports	Imports	Exports	Imports
Trade volume				
Income	1.00	2.50	1.06	1.03
Relative prices	−1.01	−1.03	−0.80	−0.73
Trade prices				
Home costs	0.77		0.61	
Foreign costs		0.55		0.78
Home prices		0.51		
Foreign prices	0.16		0.15	
Commodity prices			0.34	0.33

Source: Hooper and Marquez (1995, Tables 4.4 and 4.5).

To get some further detail, beyond the consensus estimates, we report in table 13.6 that Hooper-Marquez preferred estimates of their own trade model. As before, the volume of trade flows is significantly responsive to relative prices.

The other question concerns the determinants of export and import prices. Note that, on the export side, home costs, not foreign prices, carry the most weight. Hence exchange-rate changes will affect relative prices.[9] The same is true on the import side. Hence there is no doubt that nominal exchange-rate changes translate substantially into real exchange-rate changes even though, from country to country, there will be differences in just exactly how that translation works out.

Putting the pieces together, it may be useful to look at the combined effects of a currency realignment. A set of estimates is available, for example, for the U.S. economy.[10] Here a 10 percent depreciation relative to the G10 countries has the effects shown in table 13.7.

Note first that the impact of depreciation on the price level is minor— the trade-off 10:1 is highly favorable in translating nominal depreciation into (relatively lasting) real depreciation. Does a large depreciation—that is, 10 percent—have major effects on the economy? In the U.S. case the answer is not overwhelming but, yes, substantial. An extra half percentage point growth, when trend growth is about 2 percent, is a sizeable

Table 13.7
Simulated Impact on the United States of a 10 Percent Dollar Depreciation (differences from baseline)

	Year 1	Year 2
Consumer prices (%)	0.4	1.3
Current account ($ billion)	15	38
Real GDP (%)	0.5	0.6

Source: Federal Reserve, unpublished model-based simulation.

Table 13.8
Simulated Impact on Japan of a 30 Percent Yen Appreciation (differences from baseline)

	1993	1994	1995
GDP deflator (%)	−0.7	−2.1	−2.0
Foreign balance (%)[a]	−1.2	−1.3	−0.1
Real GDP (%)	−0.5	−1.1	−0.4

Note: [a]Change in export as a percentage of GDP.
Source: OECD, *Economic Outlook*, December 1993, p. 10.

impact. So is the exchange-rate effect on the current account. In the second year, the current balance improvement is of the order of a half percent of GDP. Clearly, that is sizeable when the actual deficit is about $160 billion.[11]

Another set of simulation results is available from the OECD (table 13.8). Here the experiment was a 30 percent yen appreciation, as occurred in the early 1990s.[12] As expected, nominal appreciation means real appreciation, almost one-for-one since the impact on prices is negligible. Second, there is a substantial decline in Japan's real GDP, but not a lasting one. To some extent this is a reflection of the accompanying monetary and fiscal policies. But, clearly, the improvement in the terms of trade in the form of lower real commodity prices works at least in part to offset the loss in competitiveness. Finally, net exports continue declining, and substantially so.

Both simulation results reported here apply to relatively closed economies. In far more open economies the impact of devaluation on the price level, and the potential feed through to wages, is of course more significant. Even so, as the examples in the earlier section showed, often devaluation simply is not tantamount to inflation. This is more likely to be the case when unemployment is high.

We return for a moment to the size of elasticities. From the perspective of the working of the price mechanism or the Marshall-Lerner condition, these elasticities are large, that is, large enough for devaluation to work. But from another perspective they may be disappointingly small. Suppose a current account deficit of, say, 3 percent of GDP had to be eliminated, just how much of a depreciation would that require? The right answer here is that an exchange-rate change by itself is not the right policy setting. Correcting an external imbalance requires both an expenditure-switching and an expenditure-adjusting strategy. For example, one might look at the combined impact of balancing the U.S. budget and a real depreciation of the dollar. Looking at the right experiment brings into play expenditure effects along with price adjustment and hence requires less work to be done by relative prices.[13]

In summary then, both the structural estimates as well as simulation results show that, in the case of industrial countries, exchange-rate changes can work. There is substantial responsiveness of trade flows to relative price changes. Moreover, changes in nominal exchange rates are not routinely offset by inflationary adjustments that leave real exchange rates unchanged. This is not to say that they work always and in any place. In a fully employed, booming, and inflationary economy they evidently could not do much.

VI Developing Countries

Increasingly, the group of developing countries is becoming an important part of the world macro economy and of adjustment scenarios. This is especially so since they are now increasingly producers of manufactures rather than only of commodities. As they move out of a repressed and controlled economic mode, their exchange rates will start playing a role in policy analysis. Not surprisingly, much of what is true for industrialized countries is also true in emerging economies: relative prices influence

Table 13.9
Regional and Aggregate Import Demand Elasticities

	Developing countries		Industrial countries	
	Relative price	Income	Relative price	Income
Latin America	−0.36	0.964	−0.19	2.07
	(0.07)	(0.08)	(0.08)	(0.12)
Asia	−0.40	1.34	−0.40	2.49
	(0.07)	(0.05)	(0.09)	(0.14)
Africa	−1.36	1.14	−0.27	1.25
	(0.54)	(0.12)	(0.1)	(0.17)
All developing countries	−0.53	1.22	−0.32	2.05
	(0.05)	(0.04)	(0.05)	(0.98)

Note: The industrial countries' demand refers to their import demand from developing countries.
Source: Reinhardt (1995, Table 6).

their trade flows. Thus, at least in part, the conditions for an effective use of the exchange rate are given.

The evidence on the adjustment of trade flows has been brought together in an important paper by Reinhardt (1995) from which table 13.9 is derived. Reinhardt shows that for developing countries, in the aggregate and by region, trade flows are significantly responsive to relative prices. The same is true for the import elasticities of industrial countries in their trade with emerging economies, which is reported on the right-hand side of the table. Note, however, that the elasticities shown here are far smaller than is the case for the industrial countries reported above. The reason for this finding needs still to be investigated and elasticity pessimism should be held in suspension until further notice.[14]

Of course, showing that trade flows respond to prices is not enough in making the case for the effectiveness of exchange-rate changes. It must also be the case that nominal exchange-rate changes translate substantially into real exchange-rate movements. That is very often not the case! The more inflationary the economy, the more it is indexed, the less likely that a devaluation has lasting real effects.[15] The fact that most developing economies are very open increases the difficulty of making a major real depreciation stick, since it is so obviously a cut in real wages.

Table 13.10
Simulated Impact of a 10 Percent Appreciation by the NIEs (differences from baseline in year 2)

	Real GDP (%)	Current account (% of GDP)
NIEs	n.a.	−2.7
OECD	0.3	0.2

Note: NIEs refers to Hong Kong, Singapore, South Korea, and Taiwan.
Source: OECD, *Economic Outlook*, June 1996, p. 138.

Two applications help round off the discussion of developing countries' real exchange rates. The first concerns trade liberalization and the appropriate response of relative prices. When a country—the typical emerging economy with three layers of protection: tariffs, quotas, and permits—opens up, imports become relatively cheap, but exports are not more competitive just because trade has been liberalized. True, some imported intermediate goods may now help improve export competitiveness, but that will not be enough. Real depreciation is the required equilibrium move for the real exchange rate. Because of inflation fears, particularly when trade liberalization is used to fight inflation, governments resist this real depreciation and, as a result, find liberalization very painful. If they allow, under the pressure of capital inflows, the real exchange rate to appreciate, they will almost certainly face a payments crisis in short order. That was the case in Mexico recently and in Chile in the late 1970s.

Our second application concerns Asian exchange rates. Asia, as a block, has enjoyed a model of development centred on export-led growth, much as Europe in the postwar period. At some point, catching-up gives way to a significant real appreciation that takes away the undervaluation support for the export model. It is interesting then to ask, what would be the impact of a simultaneous appreciation of the developing Asian economies relative to the OECD economies (table 13.10).

The impact of Asian appreciation on the OECD economies is an external balance improvement and some extra growth. The impact cannot possibly be vast simply because OECD trade with the Asian emerging economies (including China) amounts to barely 1.6 percent of OECD GDP. Even so, the impact of Asian appreciation is more than a rounding error. And in the Asian economies themselves the impact is very substantial: a shift in the current account equivalent to 2.7 percent of GDP is a massive adjustment. Note further that if China, India, the Philippines, and Thailand are included in the exercise, the impact is increased by about 60 percent.

VII   Conclusion: Depreciation and Credibility

More often than not, depreciation is resisted fiercely. The arguments against a realignment are many. But high on the list are two: one, it does not work—exchange-rate movements will not translate into real depreciation; they will just be inflated way. The other, depreciation means throwing away credibility, giving up all that has been gained by holding on to a nominal anchor. In combination, the arguments lead to a fearful case against currency depreciation. The case is even stronger when the political economy is taken into account. Cooper (1978) reports that depreciation is routinely followed by the fall of the finance minister; Lamont in Britain and Serra in Mexico are mere additions to a long list.

Depreciation, then, has a bad press. Is there an alternative? The obvious answer is to try and hold out, restrain demand, limit external deficits, and work on the financing of deficits. All that comes at the expense of growth. The evidence in Europe in 1992, surely, is that any loss in credibility—if, indeed, there is one—is relatively small. Moreover, just hanging in is surely not free: it hurts growth and the budget, as the case of France makes clear. Returning to our earlier examples, Finland today has lower interest differentials from France or Germany than it had before its 1992 depreciation. The explanation presumably is that depreciation was not tantamount to throwing all discipline overboard, but rather a gathering of forces for a more sensible macroeconomic strategy.

In sum, exchange rates are useful, and they should be used, early and wisely. They are no panacea, they can be overused, and they cannot do their work alone, out of the macroeconomic context and without supporting macroeconomic policies. The more exchange rates are misused, the less they can be expected to deliver and their use may even become outright counterproductive. But when the setting is right, exceptionally, they form an essential part of the policy toolkit.

Keynes remains the accepted wisdom—it is better to fail by conventional means than to succeed by unconventional ones. A successful devaluation in preference to protracted unemployment would be the unconventional way. Nothing creates more envy and acrimony on the part of traditionalists of hard money than a highly successful devaluation. Much of the 1992 assessment is just of that kind. So far, four years later, countries like Italy are still ahead.

Notes

1. I am indebted to two anonymous referees for very helpful suggestions. They have persuaded me to tone down the claims and show more of the cards.

2. See Taylor (1979) and Dornbusch (1980) where the policy regime, including exchange-rate rules, is embedded in expectations and as a result in the inflation process.

3. See the important paper by Akerlof, Dickens, and Perry (1996) where evidence is offered that, in the U.S. economy, the alleged downward flexibility of wages is actually not present. The paper draws the conclusion that a strategy of zero inflation, because it goes to the cliff of deflation, may be hazardous.

4. There is already a hidden assumption here, namely that the income effect of a rise in wages on spending is more than offset by the substitution effect arising from an increase in relative prices. Conservatives favour the view that substitution effects dominate. This point is important in the discussion of "contractionary devaluation." See Lizondo and Montiel (1989) and Agenor and Montiel (1996).

5. See Stockman (1987) and Obstfeld and Rogoff (1995, 1996).

6. In the presence of capital mobility, the effectiveness of devaluation is further reduced by the fact that money is endogenous even in the short run. The reduction in real balances relative to the demand for real money leads to capital inflows and their monetization. Devaluation only affects the portfolio composition of the central bank; it does not even last for any length of time in its real effects.

7. Among the extensive literature, see Taylor (1979), Calvo (1996), Obstfeld and Rogoff (1995, 1996), and Dornbusch (1980) for possible approaches.

8. Argentina in 1995–6 is a case in point: the nominal exchange rate is fixed on the dollar, unemployment exceeds 17 percent, unemployment benefits are insignificant, wages are barely falling.

9. For more detail on the price issue in the case of Japan, see Gagnon and Knetter (1995) and Klitgaard (1996).

10. Simulations of exchange-rate shocks are hard to come by since, under flexible rates, they are typically the byproduct of policy shocks such as monetary or fiscal disturbances.

11. Of course, there is a large number of issues not even addressed in this simulation, as, for example, impacts on direct investment or hysteresis effects, as in Baldwin and Krugman (1989).

12. For details refer to the table's source. Note, too, further discussion in the OECD December 1995 *Economic Outlook*.

13. For further discussion see, too, Vines and Currie (1995).

14. Studies that focus on the substitutability among competing emerging market suppliers in manufacturing find, in fact, very high elasticities.

15. See Cooper (1978), Rodriguez (1978), Dornbusch (1980), and Agenor and Montiel (1996).

References

Agenor, P.-R., and Montiel, P. (1996), *Development Macroeconomics*, Princeton, NJ, Princeton University Press.

Akerlof, G. A., Dickens, W. T., and Perry, G. L. (1996), "The Macroeconomics of Low Inflation," *Brookings Papers on Economic Activity*, 1, 1–76.

Baldwin, R., and Krugman, P. (1989), "Persistent Effects of Large Exchange Rate Shocks," *Quarterly Journal of Economics*, 104(1), 16–32.

Calvo, G. (1996), *Money, Exchange Rates and Output*, Cambridge, MA, MIT Press.

Cooper, R. N. (1978), "An Assessment of Currency Depreciation in Developing Countries," in G. Ranis (ed.), *Government and the Economy*, New Haven, CT, Yale University Press.

Dornbusch, R. (1980), *Open Economy Macroeconomics*, New York, NY, Basic Books.

Gagnon, J., and Knetter, M. (1995), "Markup Adjustment and Exchange Rate Fluctuations: Evidence from Panel Data on Automobile Exports," *Journal of International Money and Finance*, 14(2), 289–310.

Hooper, P., and Marquez, J. (1995), "Exchange Rates, Prices and External Adjustment in the United States and Japan," in P. Kenen (ed.), *Understanding Interdependence. The Macroeconomics of the Open Economy*, Princeton, NJ, Princeton University Press.

Klitgaard, T. (1996), "Coping With the Rising Yen: Japan's Recent Export Experience," *Federal Reserve Bank of New York Current Issues*, 2(1), 1–5.

Lizondo, J. S., and Montiel, P. (1989), "Contractionary Devaluation in Developing Countries: An Analytical Overview," *IMF Staff Papers*, 36(1), 182–227.

Obstfeld, M., and Rogoff, K. (1995), "The Intertemporal Approach to the Current Account," in G. Grossmann and K. Rogoff (eds), *Handbook of International Economics*, Vol. III, Amsterdam, Elsevier.

—— (1996), *Foundations of International Macroeconomics*, Cambridge, MA, MIT Press.

Reinhardt, C. (1995), "Devaluation, Relative Prices and International Trade," *IMF Staff Papers*, 42(2), 290–312.

Rodriguez, C. A. (1978), "A Stylized Model of the Devaluation–Inflation Spiral," *IMF Staff Papers*, 25(1), 76–89.

Stockman, A. (1987), "The Equilibrium Approach to Exchange Rates," Federal Reserve Bank of Richmond, *Economic Review*, 73(1), 12–30.

Taylor, J. (1979), "Staggered Wage Setting in a Macro Model," *American Economic Review* (Papers and Proceedings), 69(2), 108–13.

Vines, D., and Currie, D. (eds) (1995), *North–South Linkages and International Macroeconomic Policy*, Cambridge, Cambridge University Press.

14

No Way to Rescue the Greenback—And No Need To

The dollar has reached all-time lows against the Japanese yen and the German mark. But don't worry: reports of the greenback's demise have been vastly exaggerated. There is nothing that can be done—or needs to be done.

Despite large swings, the dollar has been declining against the yen and the mark for more than twenty-five years. Japan and Germany have performed better than the United States on productivity and inflation during that time, and they have taken a more conservative fiscal stance. Hence the steady appreciation of their currencies against the buck. Added to this have been the growing indebtedness of the United States and the rising net-creditor status of Japan and Germany.

This is not the first time the dollar has seemed to slip into a bottomless hole. Of course, the dollar won't plunge an extra 20 percent or 30 percent, as though it were the lira or the peso. The extent of the dollar's decline so far, however, is not surprising.

Aspirin Power

Why is a falling dollar no big deal? The dollar has not really dropped so far—in trade-weighted terms, the depreciation has been barely 3.5 percent since December 1994—and there have been large offsets to the weakness against the yen and mark. The Canadian and Mexican currencies have both depreciated against the dollar. The trade effects are

Originally published in *Business Week* (10 April 1995): 26. Reprinted with permission.

muted on Germany because most of its trade is with Europe or in competition with Japan in developing markets. And as for Japan, the yen's appreciation has kept a rival producer at bay. The upshot is that not much has happened—for growth or inflation—and certainly not enough to divert interest-rate policy from its primary responsibility, which is price stability with steady growth.

Whenever key currencies move sharply, hard-money gurus demand a return to the gold standard, and more moderate reformers call for a "new Bretton Woods." We don't need gold, thank you. The past decade bears witness that central banks around the world are taking inflation seriously. In the United States particularly, fighting inflation before it strikes—like taking an aspirin before you get a headache—does wonders for monetary-policy performance. Likewise, a new Bretton Woods agreement—on fixed rates and common monetary policy—just isn't an option, even if it were a good idea. Since the Europeans can't keep their currencies fixed, there's no reason to think a North Atlantic fix is workable.

A more moderate option for stabilizing currencies is coordinated intervention: get into the currency market with strength and inflict deep wounds on speculators by throwing billions at them. The notion of a new coordinated-intervention agreement, like the 1985 Plaza and Louvre accords, is just a pipe dream. Unless central banks enlist interest-rate policy to support their intervention, drawing lines in the sand won't work.

True, there is evidence that intervention alone may have at least short-lived effects, particularly if it hits an uncertain market late in the afternoon with all central banks standing firm when exchange rates have gone wild. But none of these conditions are met today. More likely, we will see Brussels eager to get its hands once again on European monetary issues, now that its initiative on a common currency is on the rocks. No surprise it seizes on the dollar. To a man with a hammer, everything looks like a nail.

Is all this too complacent? Won't U.S. inflation rise? Won't Japan and Germany collapse under the weight of appreciation? Won't central banks dump the trillions of dollar-denominated assets they have traditionally held? Germany can cope well, but the same is not true of Japan, where such concerns are amply justified. Its anemic economy stumbles from one recession to another, with reprieves only from projects such as public works following an earthquake.

Big Buba?

Japan's strong yen may be driven by its trade surpluses, but that is hardly a cure, since the weakening of the economy reduces the level of imports even faster than the loss of competitiveness raises them. Japan needs a cut in interest rates—down to zero—to cope with pervasive bankruptcy and slack. Fed Chairman Alan Greenspan's driving short-term rates down to 3 percent cured the U.S. economy. Japan's dead-in-the-water economy with falling prices needs some of the same medicine.

Don't worry about the dollar losing its status. That alarm rings every time the currency slides. Soon, the dollar will take an upturn, and people will be happy they did not jump ship. Over time, the greenback has had rivals as a reserve currency, but we are nowhere near a time when the world wants to entrust all its assets to Japan's Finance Ministry or even to the Bundesbank.

15

Lessons from the Mexican Crisis

While the memory is fresh, two lessons are to be drawn from Mexico's collapse. First, sharp practices in currency and debt management can go badly wrong. People who buy junk bonds should only blame themselves. Second, surely we should not institute a world rescue fund for the debts and currencies of mismanaged economies. A lender of last resort makes sense when there is substantial preventive supervision, not in a situation of fait accompli around the globe wherever opportunity beckons.

Just a while back, Mexico was everybody's darling and now it is anyone's goat. All fine reforms notwithstanding, Mexico made the critical mistake of overvaluing its currency and hanging on and on. To offer apprehensive lenders the impression of reduced currency risk and increased liquidity, public debt was indexed in dollars and maturities were shortened. Major Mexican companies and banks were encouraged to speculate by borrowing dollars to bypass high Mexican interest rates on peso loans. Incomes policy perpetuated inflation and stood in the way of competition and employment. The newly "independent" Central Bank expanded credit at a vigorous rate, financing rather than stemming the capital flight.

When Mexico ran out of money it had two crises in one: a currency crisis that could only be remedied by a deep depreciation of the peso and a debt crisis that arose from the totally liquid dollar debt. The disillusionment of investors was such that nobody knew whether Mexico was illiquid or insolvent, and that meant even 30 or 40 percent in dollars was too little to buy in. Moreover, history teaches that anyone who promises to pay 30 or 40 percent is very unlikely to ever pay.

For hundreds of years, Latin America and other parts of the world have disappointed foreign investors. As far back as the South Sea Bubble and as recently as the Latin default of the early 1980s, investors have been had in stocks and bonds across the border. Shouldn't they have been surprised at 52 percent stock returns *on average* in 1989–93? A realistic assessment of Mexico would have looked at the downside. Among the indications foreshadowing trouble were these: no growth to speak of (compared to, say, Chile or Asia), a huge external deficit, a conspicuous overvaluation, a rising incidence of nonperforming loans in the banking system, and capital flight by wealthy Mexicans. Investors were blinded by past returns and they wanted their own ride on the bubble. Don't feel sorry for investors in Cetes, Tesobonos, or Telmex. From tulip booms to Mexican losses, junk bonds, Orange County, and commercial real estate collapses, the lesson is caveat emptor. The next round of investors in Mexico should move in no sooner than when they see a genuinely independent central bank, a competitive exchange rate, a moderate external deficit, the end of incomes policy, and a prospect of growth. Anything else means instability, both financial and political.

Another lesson concerns the lender of last resort. Should we institutionalize rescue operations to have them on hand in a more timely fashion? There are two ways the international community authorities can face a financial crisis in any country. One is to look the other way. In that case, holders of stock suffer capital losses and bond holders are exposed to default and a restructuring, unilateral or with creditors. There is ample precedent in history, as witnessed by the Bond Holders' Protective Associations that flourished over the past century and functioned into the 1960s. The other way is for G7 and the IMF to intervene in a crisis and ward off capital flight and the speculative attack with an overwhelmingly large financial package. If only the war chest is large enough, even George Soros would have to back off. Whatever the merit of the United States trying to shore up Mexico, it must be clear that a world anti-speculation fund is a terrible idea. There are serious questions about the appropriateness of bailing out large banks or firms within a country. It is preposterous to imagine bailing out countries who over the past twenty years have built up a record of refusing to privatize, perpetuating fiscal laxity and poor currency management. Their bad debts are in place, waiting for a showdown with disillusioned investors. A fund to support these economies—say, Greece or Italy to be concrete—would cost a fortune, reward poor policies, and more likely than not give mismanagement an extra half year. The international community is unwilling and unable to effectively regulate and supervise what happens in a sovereign country's public finance and monetary management. The implication is clearly that the community must give a firm "no" to any bailout scheme.

The best assurance for sound monetary and fiscal policies are weary investors who kick the tires and policymakers who rise or fall by their policies. Nobody wants a crisis, and even less one that spreads to innocent bystanders. Yet, in a world of sovereign investors and sovereign policymakers, socializing the losses will maximize the losses. Europe's reluctance to follow the U.S. leadership in the Mexico program reflects, in part, a perception that there was really no system crisis but rather a U.S. overreaction. In part and rightly, it reflects the concern of being drawn into a much more expensive situation that is already on the horizon in Southern Europe.

16

After Asia: New Directions for the International Financial System

In Mexico's massive earthquake, some years back, many of the splendid new buildings collapsed, burying and killing a large number of people in the debris. Without the earthquake, they surely would not have crashed; in fact, they had graced the skyline for years, monuments to their proud owners and builders. But examination revealed that the concrete had far too much sand and too little of the real stuff. Not surprisingly, under stress they went. That surely was not an accident—the building codes were there, and the inspectors stood by collecting the payoffs for overlooking unsound construction. Just the same has been happening in cross-border finance. Emerging market balance sheets stand up in fair weather, but under stress they collapse. *Vulnerability* is the key word; *risk* is another way of looking at it. No two crises are quite alike, but they all have in common that without significant vulnerability, currency and financial collapse is very unlikely. In the aftermath of every crisis, whether war or currency collapses, there is a soul-searching effort to build a better world. Just such an effort, short-lived and without leaving a trace, got under way after the Mexican debacle. Another one is being conducted just now. Asia's collapse and Japan's implosion are the obvious triggers. This is a great occasion for bad ideas, or just impractical ones, to draw attention and gain respectability. Let us set out here where the crises come from and what the most effective way of dealing with them is before we rush headlong down the wrong path.

In the past, balance-of-payments crises were predominantly current account crises, and the story would go somewhat like this. A country had a large trade deficit from overvaluation or overexpansion or from both. There was some debt service, and there was not enough money around.

Reserves would already have run off, new loans were not to be gotten. Sooner or later a devaluation and/or recession would rectify the situation and, for habitual offenders, they would soon be back in the same situation. More often than not, the external deficit was just the counterpart of a budget deficit, happy twins of overspending. Invariably, they would be supplemented with fixed rates to contain inflation and thus give the public a boon, too, by raising real wages in dollars. Social peace means high wages in dollars, big government, and full employment, while external balance means just that: you can pay your way. Obviously, the two goals can come in conflict; reality, meaning the external constraint, always wins out, sooner or later. When it comes to the showdown, spending needs to be cut and wages in dollars have to fall, with austerity the answer.

More recent crises, starting with the early 1980s in Latin America, Mexico in 1994–95, and now Asia and Russia are fundamentally different in that balance sheet issues are entirely central to the fact and surely the propagation of the crisis. Moreover, they increasingly involve the private-sector, and not just public-sector external debt as in the 1980s debt crisis or in the case of Mexico. These crises have to do with an inability to roll over an existing debt, a liquidation scramble, and a resulting currency collapse.[1] Balance sheet crises by their nature have far more leverage both in collapsing a country's financial structure and hence its economy, but also in spreading contamination. They are capital market crises. Capital market crises have more oomph once they happen; meltdown is the best description. Their resolution is also more complicated and certainly more costly.

Designing an international system that is less crisis-prone must address the central issue of capital market crises—unsound finance, which translates into national balance sheet vulnerability. It is naive to believe that we can abolish crises altogether, but surely we must be able to do far better in limiting the fallout once crises happen.

Interpreting the Asian Crisis

The Asian crisis is easily interpreted as a capital market crisis—not a crisis of capitalism as the Japanese officials like to argue. Central to that interpretation are several ingredients:

• In the balance sheets of the financial system and large corporations, there was systematic mismatching of *maturities*. Emerging market banks and firms borrow short either because it is cheaper or because nobody is willing to lend to them at long maturities. On the asset side, they are funding with these loans long-term investments such as real estate development, corporate capital formation, or even infrastructure. (Not a good idea to fund highways with overnight money.) In referring to loans, we already make implicit the point that equity might have been a much better vehicle. The resulting vulnerability takes the form of liquidity risk—the sudden inability to roll over debts that moves companies and countries from sunny skies into the midst of a funding crisis.

• The second source of vulnerability was mismatching of *denominations*. Asia borrowed in dollars or yen to fund investments with payoffs in local currency. As a result, balance sheets were exposed to the risk of currency movements. A major currency depreciation would carry the risk of bankrupting a large part of the financial system or their loan customers. Mismatched denominations are like driving without car insurance: every day there is no accident, it is money saved. But when there is an accident, the absence of a currency hedge comes in disastrously expensive.

• The third source of vulnerability was *market risk*—borrowing to carry assets that are exposed to large fluctuations in their capital value: stocks, commodities, foreign exchange, or high-risk instruments such as Brady bonds. Korean financial institutions, for example, had taken a large position in Russian bonds and Brazilian Brady bonds. When their prices fell sharply, the balance sheets of the Koreans had instantly a huge hole.

• The next source of vulnerability is *national credit risk*. Because the various banks and companies had collectively assumed a large risk position, the national credit rating had been put at risk, with spillover effects to anyone in case of a liquidation scramble both in terms of the capital value of their assets and the access to alternative sources of credit.

In a well-supervised financial system—say the United States or the United Kingdom today—all this could not have happened. But, of course, it is routine in Japan, Russia, or anywhere in Latin America. The negligent or deliberate lack of regulation, supervision, and transparency then comes in as an explanation for the fragile financial structure. This is further complicated by a key mistake on the part of central banks: gambling away the reserves. Central banks in both Thailand and Korea went out of their way to take gambles in forward markets until their reserves were gone; they went out of their way to cheat on the numbers. Any sense of sleaze or lack of transparency was certainly reinforced by the active cooperation of bureaucrats who have worked untiringly taking bribes, overlooking flagrant risk taking, and adding to the vulnerability by misrepresenting central bank assets. All this would not be possible without active help from politicians. In this last sense, the Asian crisis is also a crisis of corrupt governments.

Of course, vulnerability alone is not enough to have an accident. Something has to happen to bring the fragility into play. Here external factors play a role. It would be wrong to place the entire blame on mismanagement in the Asian economies themselves. Two critical complications came from the outside. But that is by way of explanation—vulnerability has to do with just such possibilities! First, Japan went into the tank and the resulting deterioration in Asian economies' trade environment accounts for some of the problem. The shadow falling over Asian investment opportunities added to the problem.

Second, and perhaps more important, movements in the dollar/yen rate moved sharply, thereby leaving the dollar peggers high and dry. That, too, is only by way of explanation. The yen had been as strong as 80 yen/$ only as recently as 1995 and as weak as 200 yen/$ in the mid-1980s. The idea that the yen could depreciate was not a brand new concept that risk takers could be excused from overlooking. Those who enjoyed the stark yen overvaluation with its resulting export competitiveness for dollar peggers surely must have understood that the pendulum swings wide *both* ways.

The summary of factors can be customized to country experiences. How, for example, did the Philippines avoid meltdown? They came late to the game, took little of the external money, and hence had less of a balance sheet problem and less of a meltdown—more nearly the old style of crisis. Or Malaysia, banking problems, yes, but much less of an external debt problem because financing took the form of direct investment. Or Korea, where the aggravation of circumstances lies in the dysfunctional corporate structure—debt equity ratios of 500 percent plus for the chaebols, which control 50 percent of GDP. If so much is made of vulnerability now, how come nothing had gone wrong in the past? The answer is that the vulnerability was of very recent vintage—three or four years and not more. Financial opening and hence the very possibility of taking on big risks rather than just bad loans on balance sheets is a matter of the last few years.

The typical scenario, following financial liberalization, is a lending boom funded by offshore borrowing under the cover or a fixed or at least very stable exchange rate. Then, once positions are in place, a disturbance comes on the horizon: domestic investment, notably overdone, goes sour, and soon there is a conflict between keeping up the financing by high interest rates or the domestic institutions, banks, and companies by low interest rates. If the interest rates are cut the currency crashes, and if they are raised the banks and companies crash. In the end, both crash because individual foreign lenders understand that the situation is not viable: returns don't cover the risk, the herd is leaving, and they certainly don't want to be left holding an empty bag.

Vulnerability is in part an objective fact but, just as in the case of bank runs, in part it is in the eyes of the beholder. *Contamination*, therefore, is very much part of the play. If the unsustainability of banks or debts is obvious in one place, hard questions will immediately be asked of the next—why not earlier is an interesting question but not relevant at this point. "Safety first" is the motto of investors when they smell a rat. Thus one vulnerable economy after another tumbles. They did not have to in some immutable statistical sense; it was just that they came under suspicion, and the rest is history. Countries that are not vulnerable will also be tested, but they can raise rates and defend their currency, and that quickly becomes a losing game for investors so that they call off the siege, at least until further notice.[2]

Note that neither current account deficits nor budget deficits nor even misaligned exchange rates were part of the balance sheet crisis story. In fact, the budget situation in most Asian economies was quite strong and while exchange rates collapsed, they certainly had not been crassly overvalued as measured by PPP comparisons. (At least that was the case in Asia, though not, of course, in Mexico.) If there was a sign of something amiss, it was in the boom atmosphere that had gotten to construction, consumption, and luxury imports. It had all the experience of what in the later 1970s Argentines called *plata dulce*.

Good Answers

The right answer for crisis avoidance is controlling risk. That is done routinely in the domestic financial system of the United Kingdom or the United States, where the supervisory authorities set and enforce capital standards as well as sophisticated risk measurement. The London authorities go further in imposing differentiated capital requirements for cross-border loans to regions where regulatory or supervisory standards are classified as lax. That is being serious about risk.

How could this be done at the international level? A modest ambition is to create a new culture that focuses on dissemination of the right thinking, learning from the present crisis to put in place more responsible balance sheets. A more ambitious scheme makes support in case of "honest" accidents conditional on compliance with a tightly written and audited scheme.

The starting point of any discussion is that regulators and supervisors in most countries even today have no clue, nor for that purpose do rating agencies. The appropriate conceptual framework is *value at risk*—a model-driven estimate of the maximum risk for a particular balance sheet situation over a specified horizon. There are genuine issues of modeling, but there is no issue whatsoever in recognizing that this approach is the right one. Measures such as debt-to-exports never appear in it, but the ratio of foreign liabilities as a share of total liabilities or the share that is short-dated would be as important as the variability of asset prices or the likelihood of an external shock that triggers contamination.

If authorities everywhere enforced a culture of risk-oriented evaluation of balance sheets, extreme situations such as those of Asia would just disappear or, at the worst, become a rare species. Perhaps it took a bad experience to understand that the issue is risk. And it is latent in a balance sheet rather than falling from heaven.

The more ambitious step, with an appropriate transition period, is to actually use the regular IMF consultations as the inspection opportunity for the national balance sheet. Countries who would want to have IMF support when in trouble would only qualify if they have, in fact, in the recent past been in compliance with an agreed risk control strategy. This procedure has three advantages. First and foremost, it institutionalizes risk analysis as part of the local supervisory process and as such creates the right culture. Second, it directly lowers risk levels worldwide because countries will be eager to qualify for IMF support in cases of honest accidents, which are still possible though less likely. Third, anyone who opts out and wants to run a national gambling house can do so. But it is clear to financial markets that value at risk exceeds internationally acceptable thresholds and, as a result, financing will be hard to get and will be expensive. Hence the incentive for rogue countries to join the club.

There is nothing wild-eyed about this proposal, particularly if there is a transition period in which countries can implement what each and every one of them should want to do with the greatest urgency. But that does not mean it will happen at the IMF. The IMF is owned and operated by its board, that is, representatives of countries like Japan who have no concept of sound finance and no willingness to get there soon. The IMF and its board actively enjoy crisis situations, since they give bureaucrats the opportunity to wield power, and expand the scope and mandate of their institution. The notion that anything preemptive is impractical is just far too easily accepted. Accordingly, the immediate interest of what to do with a Russia commands the only attention, and how to get a less risky system some four or five years from now gets none.

IMF Programs

Another area of contention is what exactly the IMF should ask of countries on the operating table. In the course of the Asian crisis the IMF got a bad name, just as they already had in Latin America in the 1970s. In the past, the IMF had been demonized, and it is a bit surprising how it recovered its reputation or at least lost the stigma. Perhaps it was the success of Mexico with ultra-IMF policies.

Many, but most surprisingly World Bank chief economist Joe Stiglitz, have been preaching liberation theology. Their message is simply this: the IMF is wrong, high interest rates in the process of stabilization are destructive of sound credit, and fiscal restraint is inappropriate since it adds to the recessionary forces. It is not quite clear what the stabilization is all about if it is not tighter money and sounder public finances.

A key point is to separate debt restructuring, which is unpopular but may be inevitable, from high interest rates. To restore financial stability, the first point is to put a floor under the currency. If everybody wants to get out because the risk-reward trade-off is too unfavorable, high interest rates are the way to change the equation. A successful stabilization without a hike in rates is like Hamlet without the Prince of Denmark. But that may well leave the issue of bad debts in banks and companies and, as a result, bankruptcy risks. The answer is twofold. First, you can't make omelets without breaking some eggs. Second, debt write-offs may be inevitable; not raising rates is just a bad idea, not a solution.

Mexico, for example, fully implemented a stark U.S.-IMF program of tight money to stabilize the currency and restore confidence. It implemented a tight fiscal policy to restore public credit. Starting off in a near-meltdown situation, confidence returned and within a year the country was on the second leg of a V-shaped recovery. The high interest rate policy was far from easy, economically and politically, and partial debt relief was provided, at public expense, to various sectors. That pragmatic way of dealing with the high interest rate issue ought to be the example of separating debt issue (dead money) from the problem of reversing capital flight and stabilizing exchange rates. The IMF is unqualifiedly right in its insistence on high rates as the front end of stabilization.

The fiscal issue is, in principle, more complicated. If a country runs into a currency crisis but actually has no fiscal or debt problem to speak of, why should the budget be tightened? The answer is surely that no, there is no reason to take extra pain. Of course, in practice that is not the case. In Asia, financial distress of banks and companies moved into the budget a very substantial liability. As a result, there was a major prospective fiscal deterioration and a resulting need to make provision. Taking a 30 percent of GDP hit in public credit requires an offset in the budget to restore confidence of investors. In fact, the less is done on the budget, the more will have to be done with interest rates. Thus while in some cases the IMF may have been overzealous, it is doubtful that much of a mistake was made. Public finance has deteriorated massively; calling back megaprojects at such a time is totally correct.

It must be confusing to finance ministers and central bankers around the world to see the World Bank shoot them in the back just as they try to stabilize their currencies. The World Bank's liberation theology is a very bad idea, which makes everybody's task of stabilization even harder than it already is. If somewhere in the Washington institutions there is malpractice, it surely is at the World Bank.

BUT there is a more critical issue of prevention versus remedy. Part of crisis management is to change the way the game is played. Intelligent leadership uses the crisis situation for more than just making the country function better. Surely, the IMF should go a step further than just shifting hundreds of billion dollars to the bailout front. More so, in a systemic crisis, as is claimed for the Asian situation, there ought to be improvements in the way the system is run. Its bailout function is going to say, let it be supplemented by rigorous reporting and auditing of national balance sheets so that bailouts are more in line with acceptable moral hazard rather than, as in the Russia case today, a flagrant in-your-face assertion of "too large to fail" by the client.

If IMF stabilization programs are right in basic design—there is always an issue of calibration, and so far the IMF has felt safe to err on the side of amputation without sedation—there is no excuse for the IMF's long-standing disregard for risk management. The IMF, unlike the Bank for International Settlements in Basel, has paid no attention to balance sheets and their risks, it has been plain asleep at the wheel. It has indulged lecturing about budget deficits and lack of commitment to low inflation, disregarding the far more explosive issue of mismanaged balance sheets. The Mexican crisis was not one of inflation or budget deficits, nor was the Asian crisis. There is no excuse for the disregard of risk management, more so if the IMF is eagerly calling for more resources to enhance its role as a lender of last resort. To have a fiscal affairs department that explores the nooks and crannies of budgets but not to have a balance sheet department is stark mad. The U.S. Congress should refuse further IMF monies until an entire floor of the IMF building is devoted to balance sheet and risk management supervision, even if that means closing the cafeteria.

Exchange Rate Regimes[3]

Exchange rates played a crucial role in leveraging the Asian crisis. Accordingly, it stands to reason that we should reevaluate the lessons for exchange-rate policy that come out of the experience of Mexico and Asia. For many countries, in Eastern Europe and in Latin America, there is an obvious answer: forget about nationally managed monies, and adopt the Euro in Europe or the dollar in Latin America as the national money. The notion that central banks can successfully maintain fixed exchange rates, until further notice, is not supported by any evidence. The scheme just leads to megabets on the currency and, in the end, the country sides with the loser and picks up the losses. Having no money (just giving up the "national" airline) becomes totally plausible once we recognize that capital markets rather than current accounts dominate exchange-rate issues.

If giving up the national money outright is not an acceptable answer, a currency board goes far in the same direction. It abolishes, largely though not fully, the question of credibility of the exchange rate. Such a system has functioned well in Argentina and Hong Kong. It cannot, of course, avoid the spillover of regional economic crises, but it can perfectly well avoid a collapse of the currency that makes everything much worse. The counterargument that currency boards or full dollarization sacrifice the lender of last resort function are deeply misguided. National central banks can print money, and that is rarely the right answer to a banking crisis provoked by a loss of confidence in the country. Lender of last resort support can readily be rented, along with bank supervision, by requiring financial institutions to carry off-shore guarantees. That is a system in line with modern capital markets; nationally managed currencies that are highly politicized is the stark opposite.

Denouncing Some Bad Answers

We should single out some of the bad ideas as particularly inadequate. If Goldman goes to the capital market to get more firepower, should not the IMF and the World Bank also get more ammunition? The first bad answer is, of course, to provide more money. True, the world financial system today has far more firepower than ever before. Investors have deep pockets, and countries cannot be expected to have the resources that can conceivably match what one hundred short sellers (including central banks who join the attack, as indeed happens) can put on the table. Making available more rescue money, without anything else, is much the same as the plea for bigger and better arms for the police—it raises the quality of the shootouts.[4]

It is already the case that the resources used since Mexico exceed anything one might have imagined at the beginning of the 1990s, when the last debt default was still being worked off. As we come to the hard core "too large to fail countries" Russia and Brazil—flagrant offenders both in fiscal probity and risk management—the numbers become staggering, and the violence done in terms of moral hazard unbounded. Would it not be a good idea to have a country like Russia do a forced restructuring of maturities to make the point that what seems totally liquid to the lender in fact never is in a crunch? That ought to help mismatching of maturities.

Another terrible idea is capital controls as an alternative to risk management. One might have sympathy with Chilean-style management of inflows, but one has to doubt that countries where inefficient or dishonest administration is the rule (unlike in sweet Chile!) can run a sensible system. More likely, it will be a festival of corruption.

An even worse idea, or a non-idea, is an Asian IMF. In the heat of the Thailand crisis, possibly as a very cynical move to push the U.S. Treasury and the IMF into lending and avoid a key contributing role for itself, Japan offered the idea of an Asian IMF and has kept that idea alive to this day. The Asian IMF would pool resources and do mutual surveillance in the region. Who can take this seriously? The lead country, Japan, is the most in need of a serious financial cleanup and the least able to exercise leadership since it is totally stymied by its own problems. Who can see a Korean official telling an Indonesian that they need to pull their socks up and can't be quite so corrupt? If it had gone anywhere, it would have been a festival of restrictions and circumvention and priorities for Japanese banks to get paid off ahead of the rest. Fortunately and rightly, China stayed away from the whole exercise, and it flopped.[5]

Notes

1. The term liquidation scramble comes from the 1930s, when it was used in the context of the liquidity of the national balance sheet at a time of financial crisis.

2. What is said here of Asia is not the case, however, of Russia or Brazil, where budgets are unabashedly large.

3. For a further discussion, see R. Dornbusch and F. Giavazzi, "Hard Money and Sound Credit," on the author's website at http://web.mit.edu/~rudi.

4. See "Capital Controls: An Idea Whose Time Is Gone," on the author's website at http://web.mit.edu/~rudi.

5. Flop it did, but it is not quite dead. The Japanese Ministry of Finance just released a report that, among many bad ideas, proposes once again regional IMFs and, of course, massive injection of financial support. See Ministry of Finance "Lessons from the Asian Currency Crises—Risks Related to Short-Term Capital Movement and the "21st Century-Type" Currency Crisis." Tokyo, May 1998.

17

The Target Zone Controversy

Why on earth should we believe that target zones among governments are a good and practical idea? "Target zone" is the new hot word in international policy debate. The French government has called for a new international monetary arrangement (no more benign neglect of currency fluctuations), the new German government has joined the bandwagon with great enthusiasm, and the Japanese, whether they mean it or not, have expressed great interest. Should we believe that target zones are it, that the upcoming Cologne Summit will bring a blueprint for the Euro-dollar rate to move in a narrow range, that the yen won't do its wild dance any longer? Forget it: there is no chance on earth that the United States will join a scheme that limits its policy flexibility and puts responsibility for U.S. economic performance in the hands of financially inexperienced and statist-minded socialist governments. And just as remote is the chance that the United States will agree with Japan on narrow exchange-rate margins; they can't manage their own economy, why should we tie ourselves to their ill fortune?

The superficial reason for target zones is that without large fluctuations in exchange rates between the dollar and the yen, the Asian currency crisis just would not have happened. True, the dollar-yen rate moved a lot in the last five years; it visited the high 80s yen/$ and it went all the way to the 140s. Currencies like Thailand's bhat that were fixed to the dollar went on a joyride when the dollar weakened and then they crashed when the yen tumbled. And much the same, of course, is true for the rest. The currency movements were just the straw that broke the camel's back. The fact of the crisis, and the extreme dimension of it, have above all to do with an extraordinary mountain of irresponsibly short debt and an awful banking system. That is where the dynamite was; the dollar-yen rate was at best the spark that started the explosion. Avoiding financial crises, from Mexico and Brazil to Asia, has to do with a sound financial structure and good exchange-rate policy. The message is not to fix the dollar-yen rate but to find better exchange rate policies for emerging markets. In Eastern Europe that means currency boards on the Euro, in Latin America it means full dollarization and to forget amateur-manage an exchange rate and central bank. In Asia it means flexible exchange rates. It just has nothing to do with a case for target zones among G3.

If emerging market problems are not a good or real reason for target zones, how about the risk of extraordinary instability in the world economy provoked by vast international currency swings? Again a non-reason. In the past, on an ad hoc basis, governments have gotten together on a few occasions when rates had gone extremely far. That was the case of the dollar in 1985, it was the case of the yen in 1995. Ad hoc joint intervention worked impressively on both occasions in large part because rates had gone too far in the first place. As a result, speculators were willing to be scared by governments saying "no further." There is every reason to believe that we could get the same ad hoc joint intervention should circumstances warrant it. No government has an interest in fomenting an obviously bad situation. But if intervention done right works, if there is conviction that governments in the right circumstances collaborate, why not go the extra step of formalizing it? Why not draw lines in the sand just now so the problem never emerges in the first place? This is here the judgments part. The French and the new German government always like the idea of fixing anything that moves; the British or the Americans, by contrast, are deeply suspicious of market intervention. They will point out that intervening at relatively extreme points needs nothing more than a show of force, but intervening in the small needs much more to convince markets: coordination. They rightly argue that there is no such thing as coordination. The U.S. Congress will not accept European interference, the ECB will not take instructions from the U.S. Treasury, Greenspan wants his hands free to run the U.S. economy, and all of that is an immutable fact. Target zones will just create confusion.

Of course, the European love of target zones is not quite so innocent. European policymakers have two important reasons for promoting bands for exchange rates. The first is the belief, or at least the recognition of the possibility, that the dollar and the yen will weaken on the Euro in the coming year—Japan is dying and about to monetize its debt; the U.S. stock market is running out of luck, and with it the U.S. economy; and, on the other side, the Euro has its attraction in portfolios. The obvious risk then is that Europe's unemployment problems will get even worse. And here comes the second reason and the hidden agenda: Europe's finance ministers cannot make the central bank march to their tune, but they can make currency arrangements. Thus, if there were a target zone and the Euro were to appreciate strongly, the ECB would be forced—*like it or not*—to cut interest rates and limit the appreciation. Target zones are the hidden way to recover some of the control over monetary policy, and the rest is just dressing it up as internationalism that should not fool anyone. If that were all, the United States might even agree. But imagine the target zone arrangements work on both sides, so that the United States is called upon to raise interest rates at a time when its economy and currency weaken. No way: that is where the Congress, the Treasury, and just anyone and everyone will say no thank you. No way will we have exchange-rate arrangements put in jeopardy U.S. prosperity. And that is the very last word on the topic.

Of course, to bring Japan into the discussion is plain absurd. In what is a pathetic spectacle of incompetence, the Japanese economy is sinking and public finances are moving to junk bond status. Japan cannot get a recovery, it cannot limit its deficits or at least make them produce growth, it cannot decide whether its central bank should monetize debt or support interest rates, and it can't decide whether it wants a strong or weak yen. It is inconceivable that Japan could be part of a well-functioning target zone arrangement.

European governments have used the fear caused by trembling capital markets last fall and the crashing currencies of mismanaged third world countries to shape what looks like an internationalist, responsible agenda. They are trying to drag the United States into a domestic debate about the ECB. They will fail and have to be satisfied with castigating the

United States as a dogmatic free marketeer which it is indeed, fortunately. They would do better to look for a more competitive and dynamic economy so that the exchange rate becomes a less desperate battle line. Forget target zones; markets on occasion may be irrational, but more often than not socialist policy makers are worse.

In the aftermath of the EMU and at the turn of a century of currency turmoil, it is useful to ask what the monetary arrangements of the next century might look like. There is no prospect of very coordinated arrangements among the G3—the Euro/$ and the $/yen rates are bound to fluctuate and, at best, coordinated intervention at extreme points can be expected. But there is another direction in which we should look to a far more structured currency system. Specifically, the periphery will integrate with the lead currencies in a very tight structure. It is already apparent that Latin America will move to a dollar standard. Argentina did so at the beginning of the decade and the benefits are obvious: even in the midst of a regional crisis, credible exchange rates translate into more moderate interest rates, more confidence, and more growth. Now Brazil faces that same situation that made Argentina choose the right medicine: Brazil's currency is melting, its government is hopeless and helpless, and its interest rates are near 50 percent. The answer is to close the central bank, be done with bad money, and adopt the dollar as the national money. And in Mexico, on the U.S. border, that same choice is being made. Nobody seriously doubts that Mexico in just a few years will move to the dollar, perhaps even next year in an effort to increase growth and face a much better chance in the year 2000 elections. Old-fashioned nationalism with its insistence on national money is outdated in a world of free and fickle capital movements. Governments must choose hard monies to stay clear of speculative attacks that undermine financial stability and prosperity. That point is being understood mostly as a result of Argentina's extraordinary performance both in the Mexican crisis of 1994–95 and once again today as its neighbor Brazil is on the ropes.

The same logic will surely drive countries in Eastern Europe—Poland, Hungary, the Czech Republic, and more—into the arms of the Euro. These countries will and want to be part of the European Union; they can't wait to get in. They would do well to start with a currency board arrangement that helps financial integration and demonstrates willingness and ability to practice serious money; that will speed their admission. Flexibility of monetary policy in emerging markets is long gone: flexibility is charged for by extra high and unaffordable interest rates.

It is much harder to predict whether Asia will become a monetary area. Japan might play that role, but its devastating financial weakness makes it a poor candidate, and so does Japan's inability to lead politically. China is another candidate, but it is of course very far away from having the capital market and monetary tradition that would inspire dominance and leadership. In Asia, therefore, ad hoc arrangements will predominate.

18
New Challenges for World Financial Markets

Asian emerging markets are on the move, China is definitely not devaluing, and Brazil has become the capital market's new best friend. What is there to fear; the world is hunky-dory. No more crises, no inflation, nothing to stop new records in asset valuation and prosperity. Three cheers for the New Economy, Alan Greenspan, and the U.S. Treasury. And some cheers, too, for the ECB that cut rates, the Japanese who cleaned up their banks, and reluctantly the IMF that orchestrated the Brazil express recovery. Nothing stands in the way of the longest U.S. expansion getting much longer, the rest of the world finally coming on board, and stocks seeing dazzling new heights.

Too good to be true? Of course, there might be another emerging market going belly-up. But by now we know that they mend almost faster than they falter. So that cannot be the source of much headache. Nor is the war in the former Yugoslavia; Russia may rattle sabers, but it knows better than getting close to the fire. Nor is the next crisis over deadbeat socialist governments in Europe or the Euro. The two trouble spots that may erupt and disturb the harmony around the world are the United States and Japan. Both involve overpriced assets: U.S. stocks and Japanese bonds. A major realignment of these prices would shake world capital markets really hard.

U.S. stocks are overpriced for a world in which inflation is not totally dead. In the most likely scenario, an adjustment will just be turbulent but ultimately soft. Deep confidence in the pilots and a sound economy justify a good outcome and a controlled shock to the rest of the world. Not so in the case of Japan, where bonds are vastly overpriced. The debt already in place, the state of the economy, and the irreversible aging problem come together in bad public finance. Debt escalation simply cannot be avoided; Japan deserves junk bond rating. That recognition can become the biggest financial crisis of the postwar period because the problem is out of control and the management is both distracted by politics and deeply confused as to the depth of the deterioration already in place.

Stocks and 100 Months into U.S. Recovery

Every bubble has some grain of truth plus lots of rationalization. U.S. stocks are better than that; there are a few reasons they should be very high indeed. There is business-friendly government, and stockholders have taken over to force CEOs to become efficient managers rather than corporate bureaucrats. There is the integration into the world economy, which has allowed deep cost cuts in restructured businesses, and there is formidable technology and the willingness to use it. In sum, impossible is no longer part of the corporate language, and the stockholders collect on it. And they do gain from the fact that a well-functioning labor market has replaced unions. There is also, importantly, the proposition that recessions are no longer part of the landscape. Inflation is low and hence the Fed need not stage the regular bloodletting of the past. But there is also, just in case, very strong fiscal position which means that if something goes wrong, tax cuts will be on the table in no time, and households will spend them even as the mail arrives. Recession is just not an issue: we don't need one, we don't want one, and so we won't have one.

But that is not to say that the Fed will stand by and allow inflation to build up again once the world economy gets going. Our disinflation has been helped by distress in the rest of the world. Just now we are in a virtuous circle of low price inflation and good productivity performance to translate into low wage settlements with rising real wages. On the domestic front, inflation has virtually ceased to be a cyclical issue. Not so in the world economy. With Japan and all of Asia, and Latin America tanking, commodity prices have been falling sharply and have assisted the good U.S. performance, which in turn has kept the Fed at bay. That is now over; world recovery is coming on and will gather strength. And as it does, so will commodity prices from chips to steel to a broad range of manufactures. U.S. inflation will jump.

The good news is that the impact on U.S. inflation of recovery around the globe, while certain, is also small. Hence, we are not remotely talking of inflation rates going to 4 or 5 percent and beyond. Those days are gone perhaps forever. But the bad news is that even if inflation just goes to 3 percent, that is too much for the Fed to allow. If they did not act, wage inflation would pick up, as would price inflation, and so on. Hence, if we believe in a world pickup, then we must draw the conclusion: the Fed is coming. It is a small step from there to recognize that stocks will tumble and the dollar slide. But the bad news is really not awful; the inflation issue is small and so is the cure required—slowdown and surely not recession. In fact, correction of the stock market will be most of what will happen. Piling on top sizeable interest rate hikes would be overkill. The issue is to absorb an inflation shock, not to wring inflation out of the system or go bubble-busting Japanese style. The Fed is fully capable of making this hazardous landing without crashing the plane. But the passengers will hold their breath as it happens. And so will the world economy, particularly in emerging markets. When there are tremors at the center, nobody wants to hang out on the periphery. In sum, U.S. disinflation is not complete; with one more round to go, we are okay, but the stock market will be hit.

Japan's Junk Debt

The biggest issue for the world economy is Japan. This may not be an issue this year or even next, but when it comes it will be formidable. In a narrow way, it is the Japanese recession—Japan is setting personal records for staying underwater—that pulls down world growth directly but also adds to poor performance by limiting the recoveries of its Asian trading partners. But inside every little problem there is a big one trying to get out. The one to emerge is Japan's huge public debt and its massive unfunded pension liabilities. By themselves they are awesome, but combined with a shrinking and aging economy, as they are, the debt problem is out of control. Market recognition of this proposition will mean a deep

Table 18.1
Japan's Public Finance Disaster (percent of GDP)

	Public Debt	Pension Liabilities	Deficit
Japan	130	107	−7.9
U.S.	58	26	1.4
Germany	62	111	−2.2
Italy	118	76	−2.7
France	61	114	−2.5

Source: IMF.

downgrading of the world's largest debtor and hence the potential for a spectacular credit crisis.

According to IMF data, Japan's public debt is now 130 percent of GDP. In addition, according to OECD estimates, the net present value of pension liabilities is above 107 percent of GDP. The combined debt is the largest public liability in the world, both absolutely and, of course, even more so when scaled to the size of the Japanese economy. When debt and pensions are combined, and the deficit perspective is added, Japan sticks out. Recovery is not in sight; according to the consensus forecast, growth this year is negative and next year zero. The cyclical deficits today will soon be joined by the demographic deficits of unfunded pensions. An aging population is coming on rapidly—the labor force has already peaked, while population peaks in the next few years. High debt and deficits forever are a recipe for disaster.

Yes, there are ways out. A deep deregulation of Japan to produce job opportunities, jobs, and with them taxpayers is clearly part of the prescription. But for the moment corporate restructuring is mostly defensive, resulting in fewer jobs, not more. And the central bank could play a constructive role, printing money to buy stocks and dollars to pull the economy out of the swamp. But instead, like the Fed in the 1930s, its thinking is muddled and it keeps waiting for someone else to accomplish a miracle.

Accepting that there is unlikely to be an escape from the fatal debt dynamics, one wonders how this will end. One scenario is a financial meltdown of Japan, driven by deteriorating credit ratings, increasing Japan risk spreads, worsening balance sheets and debt dynamics, loss of confidence, and deepening recession. Once the ball gets rolling, as with any distressed company or country, it goes all the way. And there is no IMF or United States for the bailout because the numbers are staggeringly large. Nor is there a preparedness to step in and engineer a preemptive restructuring because there is no consensus on who gets the haircut. There is also a firm belief that moving the furniture around can buy a lot of time, so maybe the problem will go away.

The other scenario is as drastic. Faced with an enormous financial crisis, Japan responds by reversing financial liberalization. The high savings rate is targeted at rolling over the debt; savers are taken hostage to postpone the inevitable. Much of Asia will join in an Asian financial area with repressed finance and capital controls on the way out. There is no collapse at all to speak of, except that the notion of an increasingly open world economy has ended overnight. That happened in the 1930s and is surely a very plausible result of the otherwise unmanageable Japanese debt. No surprise in this; Japan already moved two years ago for an Asian financial area where capital can't escape from problem areas, and it is seeking free trade agreements with its neighbors. A Japanese crisis, with its huge potential for asset collapses and competitive depreciation, is just the setting for where Asia readily joins Japan in turning back the clock.

In the New Economy, a shock anywhere is a shock everywhere. And with significant leverage, even small shocks become big, and big ones become nuclear financial blasts. With that in mind, complacency when it comes to Japan's debt is clearly out of line. Good luck to Chairman Greenspan and Treasury Secretary Summers.

IV

No Apologies for Free Trade

19

Is Free Trade at a Crossroads?

The failure of the Uruguay Round of trade negotiations has led to fears of world trade conflict. The inward-looking nature of Europe '92 and the pending formation of a North American Free Trade Area—possibly not including Canada are only reinforcing these fears. What are the issues, and how serious are the risks?

There is far too much gloom and doom; world trade will continue substantially free among the North Atlantic partners. There is no realistic threat of a rollback on the liberalization achieved in the postwar period. Freedom of trade with Asia, however, is a more open question; strategies for further opening may change toward regional initiatives.

World Trade Today

Following the interwar strife in trade relations, in the past four decades world trade has been prospering. World trade expanded significantly faster than output. This has been the case, in particular, for manufactures. Of course, not all the credit can go to multilateralism. A good part of the expansion is also due to arrangements that went beyond GATT and took the form of regional integration with the full elimination of internal duties. The European Community and European Free Trade Area would be the leading examples.

Under the auspices of GATT, a number of multilateral trade liberalizations proceeded rapidly in the postwar period. Important milestones were the Kennedy Round and the Tokyo Round. Current levels of tariffs in industrial countries reflect the success of multilateral trade diplomacy.

Table 19.1
Postwar Trade Growth (average annual volume growth, percent)

	1960–69	1970–79	1980–89
Exports	8.5	5.5	4.3
Manufactures	10.5	7.5	5.3
Production	6.0	4.0	2.7
Manufactures	7.5	4.5	3.7

Source: GATT.

Table 19.2
Post-Tokyo Round Tariff Rates (percent)

	Raw Materials	Semifinished Manufactures	Finished Manufactures
United States	0.2	3.0	5.7
Japan	0.5	4.6	6.0
European Community	0.2	4.2	6.9

Average tariff rates are now very moderate and do not differ much across industrial countries.

Even though world trade expanded rapidly and barriers came down for three decades, a countercurrent became increasingly visible, namely, use of non-tariff barriers and special sectoral protection. For textiles this happened early on, but it spread in the 1970s and 1980s to a large range of goods including automobiles, steel, and products in which developing countries had gained trade competitiveness. Voluntary export restraints (VERs) and quotas were the chief vehicles of this new protectionism. Moreover, vigorous enforcement of trade laws including anti-dumping provisions became itself a powerful force in impeding trade growth in special commodity groups.

It is significant that against a pattern of falling duties, non-tariff restraints have actually become a very important source of trade restraint. These new restraints are far from negligible and spread as developing countries gain competitiveness in low-wage manufactures; hence they trigger latent protectionism in industrial countries. Of course, these are

Table 19.3
Trade Restrictions

	United States	Japan	EC
VERs[a]	62	12	138
Non-Tariff Barriers[b]			
Imports from Ind. Countries	15	29	13
Imports from Dev. Countries	17	22	22

Notes: [a]Number of cases. [b]Share of trade subject to hardcore non-tariff barriers.

averages and restrictions facing the newly industrialized countries are more severe. Even so, the export success of the NICs suggests that they are not invading fortresses but rather wide open cities.

The Uruguay Round

The traditional response to rising protectionism has been a round of multilateral trade negotiations. The process has kept protectionism at bay by highlighting the benefits of multilateral reductions in trade obstacles. But as is clear from table 19.2, further negotiations to cut tariff rates would offer little because in most categories tariffs now are quite low. Attention therefore has turned to areas so far left out of the GATT. Negotiations in this newest round focused chiefly on four issues:

• Liberalization of trade in services, including especially financial services and the establishment of a Code for Intellectual Property Protection
• The reduction of agricultural subsidies in industrial countries
• A phasing out of textile protection
• A code for handling of trade conflicts, improving on such practices as U.S. Super-301 and anti-dumping mechanisms

The stumbling block in the negotiations was, not surprisingly, agriculture. For the past fifty years, agriculture has occupied a special place in industrial countries' protection structure and little has happened to erode the political influence of the lobby, at least in Japan and Europe.

The case for a phasing out of agricultural subsidies is compelling. The first column of table 19.4 shows the discrepancy between domestic and international prices for various countries. The second column reports the

Table 19.4
Agricultural Subsidies (percent)

	Nominal Protection	Effective Subsidy
Europe Community	22	38
Japan	102	72
U.S.	6	27

Source: IMF, *Staff Studies for the World Economic Outlook*, September 1990.

fraction of farm income due to subsidies or the equivalent from other support measures.

It is interesting to note that Japan managed to stay in the background in the breakdown of the Uruguay Round; clearly, Japan is most deeply into agricultural protection and even with fierce U.S. pressure has done little over the last decade to change the situation. Self-sufficiency in meats amounts to 78 percent of consumption, and in rice it reaches 108 percent.

Those who gain from agricultural liberalization would be countries including Australia, Canada, and Argentina, all of whom could expect that an end of subsidies would reduce production in industrialized countries, cut output, and therefore raise world demand and world prices for their exports. But treasuries in the industrialized countries would, of course, also benefit very substantially. Agricultural protection is very expensive. Finally, consumers would benefit in those countries where today high price supports raise the cost of food. Japan is clearly a case in point because rice prices in Japan exceed world levels by a factor of 5!

There is every expectation that ultimately agricultural protection will go. The absurd land use in Japan, budget problems in the United States, and the distribution problems among countries raised by the European Common Agricultural Policy as well as the entry of Eastern Europe and the Soviet Union as agricultural exporters force reconsideration of the issue. The timing of any resolution, however, is not close. The Uruguay Round was a good attempt to get all protecting countries off the hook by taking a joint, international plunge. There are bound to be further rounds in the next few years as the Eastern European countries come on the scene with their export potential and need for markets.

Even though lack of agreement on agriculture was responsible for the failure of the Uruguay Round, the other issues were no less important. Trade in financial services is a hot issue for countries whose financial businesses want to do banking or insurance abroad. And so is trade in services such as TV, for example.

Protection in this industry is unusually intense. In many countries, governments maintain monopolies and when they do not, they restrict entry and mostly to domestic firms. Technology runs in the opposite direction: cross-border emission of programs is all too easy and the scale economies of promoting sports events, for example, for worldwide viewing are phenomenal. Producers of world TV argue that consumers could see infinitely better sports if they were allowed access to all markets, thus creating revenues to produce extraordinary programs. National governments counter that culture suffers when TV goes international. Even though Europe has just restricted the TV market to 50 percent European, it is hard to see how in the next decade the internationalization can be resisted.

And Now?

As the GATT talks seemed to collapse, fears were created of an imminent breakdown of the multilateral trading system. There is really no indication that such a risk is on hand. Trade has always had frictions, and these will continue. But a few predictions can be offered safely.

• The services issues in the GATT round will be taken up, separately, and carried forward in the OECD. Developed countries have too much of a common interest. There may be long phase-in periods and special provisions, but ultimately trade in services will have to become as international as trade in goods. In fact, in services the scale economies that are a potent reason for merchandise trade may be even more powerful.

• Agricultural liberalization talks will be delinked, and progress will come in a piecemeal fashion. The front end will be a minor concession along the lines of the European proposal. Over the next decade, the rest will gradually follow. The entry of Eastern Europe as a producer of agricultural goods will create a major headache for the Common Agricultural Policy.

• Japan is bound to be singled out for more aggressive treatment. It is true, Japan is moving. But considering how far the country is behind other industrial nations, progress is far too slow. This applies across the board, to agricultural trade, to trade in manufactures, and to service trade.

• Plurilateral trade agreements will become more common. Everybody recognizes the great benefits Europe derived in the past forty years from regional liberalization. The United States will pursue the same strategy, first with Mexico, then with other Latin American countries. Inside Latin America, interest is already emerging in trade pacts with the United States and also in regional liberalization centered around Brazil.

• GATT is not in danger, but it may not be the chief vehicle for trade opening in the next decade.

North American Free Trade

The intense debate on fast-track (the authority for the U.S. President to negotiate a North American free trade agreement (NAFTA), which then goes to Congress for an up-or-down vote) marked an open defiance of organized labor on the part of Congress, a decisive move toward a Western Hemisphere economic area, and possibly a fresh impetus for multilateral trade diplomacy.

As for trade and employment effects, organized labor and its Congressional supporters in the United States opposed an FTA because it would ruin workers on both sides of the Rio Grande. Union Secretary-Treasurer Tom Donahue told a Senate Committee: "The enactment of a free trade agreement with Mexico would be an economic and social disaster for U.S. workers and their communities, and do little to help the vast majority of Mexican workers." None of this is plausible: an FTA will help U.S. employment and it will help Mexico. For the United States, the gains will be small relative to the size of its economy because Mexico is simply too small a market to make the United States rich.

20

2005: A Trade Odyssey

Most of Latin America has moved aggressively to stabilization and reform: Chile is the winner, Mexico has gone through a massive change with obvious benefits, and Argentina against all belief has espoused reform and harvested success. Even Venezuela seems to be on the way. Brazil is alone in indulging obsessively the view that stability and reform are "politically impossible." The fact is that the leadership is incompetent and irresponsible, and that has been so for more than a decade. But in the meantime the world goes on. While Brazil is teetering on the verge of hyperinflation and continues eroding institutions and social stability, the rest of the Americas focuses keenly on the new scene in world trade.

One of the great issues for the coming years is free trade for the Americas. NAFTA is in the making—organized labor, the Greens, and Ross Perot notwithstanding—and it thus pays to look beyond and ask what are the next steps. What comes after NAFTA? And what are the benefits of an open-trade regime for all concerned?

Today the United States faces an unusual opportunity to implement an outward-looking trade policy with Latin America. Looking for modernization as the way out of a difficult economic situation, Latin America today is open to far-reaching trade reform. That case is forcefully made by Mexico's Finance Minister Pedro Aspe, in his new book *Economic Transformation: The Mexican Way*. If we miss this opportunity, we are bound to fail building an important Western Hemisphere trade and investment block in the 1990s. Turning our back on trade opening means inviting a slowdown, if not failure, of the reform movement and a

Originally published in the *International Economy* (September/October 1993): 57–63. Reprinted with permission.

Table 20.1
Comparative Data: 1991

	Population (million)	GDP ($U.S. bn)	GDP Per Capita ($U.S.)	Compensation ($U.S./hour)
United States	253	5,678	22,443	15.45
Canada	27	574	21,259	17.31
W. Hemisphere*	450	1,000	2,222	n.a.
Brazil	153	418	2,732	2.55
Chile	13	31	2,406	n.a.
Mexico	88	248	2,818	2.17

* estimate
Source: World Bank, U.S. Department of Labor, and national sources.

resurgence of protectionism throughout Latin America and beyond. The Clinton Administration's commitment to free trade with Latin America is an important, positive policy for the region.

A Snapshot of the Americas

Table 20.1 shows a brief view of what the region looks like in broad indicators.

The first impression is the disproportionate weight of the United States. Even using the World Bank's International Comparison Program measures of per capita income, the discrepancy between North and South is still a factor of 4. Next, Canada, although rich in per capita terms, is not an economic giant compared to Latin American economies. In fact, Brazil is a close second. Third, the per capita and wage discrepancies are of a factor of 10. The exact number does not make much difference; the fact is that the gap will last for many decades. Studies of the pace of convergence among regions conclude that the per capita GDP gap between two regions shrinks at the rate of 0.02 percent per year. Even if that estimate is pessimistic in view of the increasing possibilities of integration—this is no longer the United States North and South, without communications—there is no prospect of a near-equalization in fifty years.

Trade integration today, as table 20.2 shows, is not very advanced. Two facts stand out in particular. First, Canada has virtually no trade

Table 20.2
Export Patterns: 1991
(in billions $US)

	Exporting Region		
	United States	Canada	Western Hemisphere
To:			
United States	—	95.6	57.6
Canada	85.1	—	4.0
Western Hem.	63.5	2.4	21.0
World	421.8	121.2	140.4
% of GDP (1989)	7.0	24.2	13.6

Source: IMF, *Directions of World Trade.*

link with Latin America. Surely only the special dynamics of a free trade agreement will change that. Second, intra-Western Hemisphere trade is very small. That raises the question of whether North-South integration will change substantially intra-Western Hemisphere trade integration. If regional schemes have failed, can a North-South deal do more? Third, not shown in the table, is the fact that much (in fact, more than half) of the U.S.-Western Hemisphere link reflects the special U.S.-Mexico relation. This immediately invites the question of whether direct neighborhood effects have a very special role that cannot be achieved by simple free trade.

Another point that emerges from the table is the relative closedness of the South as measured by the share of trade in GDP. This reflects substantially the closedness of the Brazilian economy. In part that is a characteristic of a large, diversified economy. But in part it is also a reflection of a very determined commercial policy in the past designed to keep out manufactured imports.

Benefits to the United States

The benefits to the United States are easily summarized. They come in two ways. First, Latin America is potentially a large market. This is already demonstrated in the context of Mexican trade opening—net exports to Mexico increased in five years by $10 billion. More is to come.

Equally important is the support for modernization and open societies that comes with close trade integration. The European Common Market brought Portugal and Spain to support democracy and speed up economic development. Much the same interest is served by U.S. integration with Latin America.

Even though there was success in the opening of Mexico, Latin America is still quite closed. One way to measure this is to look at imports per capita. In part, of course, they reflect the low level of income. But in part it is also a reflection of restrictive commercial policies. It is useful to bypass oil imports in countries such as Brazil. For that purpose, we can look directly at trade with the United States. The contrast between Chile or Mexico, who have opened up, and Brazil, Colombia, or Argentina, who still remain relatively closed, is striking.

The counterpart of this closedness is that there are important markets which, if open, would bring very substantial gains in productivity and hence in living standards in the course of trade reform.

Who Is Ready for a Free Trade Partnership

For some observers, a free trade agreement among unequals is not only a new idea, but also a bad idea. A common objection to a free trade agreement with Mexico, but even more so with other countries in the Americas, is this: they are not ready. "Not ready" means in this context that their economies are too unstable, their politics insufficiently settled, their standards of living too low—some or all of these. The argument has also been made from the South—Chile has argued that it *is* ready—whereas other countries in the region are not yet.

Superficially the argument is appealing, but in substance it is absurd. The response surely must be that the United States is interested in export markets and in regional stability. Trade is already taking place with these countries and nobody can possibly argue that existing trade restrictions, here or there, help make their economies or their societies function better. It can be argued, however, that more intensive trade and investment links will help promote freer societies, more stable ones and more pros-

Table 20.3
Imports Per Capita
($U.S.)

	World	U.S.
Argentina	244	69
Brazil	153	36
Chile	574	118
Colombia	172	65
Mexico	535	379
Venezuela	467	231

Source: IMF, *Directions of World Trade.*

perous ones. Hence, particularly for economies where much is to be accomplished—notably Brazil—the prospect of an FTA raises the ante and will enhance and speed up reform. Nobody is thinking of political union or EC-style deep integration, for which a very high level of community is essential. What is at stake is the removal of impediments to trade and investment.

It is clear that institutionalization of reform, the spreading of a modern business culture which ultimately is utterly incompatible with closed, politically opaque societies, is a fundamental U.S. aim and, indeed, a U.S. contribution to the region. Who needs it most are clearly countries like Brazil, not a country like Chile that has achieved it the hard way, but *has* made it. That is not an argument against free trade with Chile; it is an argument against singling out the most established and advanced economies for early treatment.

When Europe brought Portugal, Greece, and Spain into its fold, the purpose was to spread irreversibly democratic institutions and progress. That the venture was successful is beyond question. The same argument applies to Latin America, whether Venezuela, Peru, or Brazil be the case in point.

In selecting partners for an FTA, there ought to be a clear target on which no compromise should be allowed: anyone who wants to join must be ready to practice unrestricted free trade in goods, services, and investment with the partner countries by 2005. A successful FTA must make significant progress over and above what GATT has already delivered. Specifically that means three things:

- Elimination of *any* quotas or other non-tariff barriers.
- Full inclusion of *all* services in the liberalization process.
- Investment as an integral part of the liberalization effort.

How Will the South Benefit?

Assessments of the South's benefits range from big stakes to almost nothing. For Chilean policymakers, for example, an early free trade agreement is seen as an essential step in a growth strategy. For Mexico's policymakers, the passing of NAFTA by the U.S. Congress is an urgent prerequisite for progress in stabilization and modernization. For other countries, the urgency seems much less. In Colombia, the view is common that trade integration should proceed first with Venezuela and, after that training round, one might be ready for more. In Brazil, trade issues have not gone beyond a general approval of unilateral trade liberalization with little else as a trade strategy other than adherence to a GATT process.

Quantitative estimates of the trade benefits to Latin America are scarce. A study by Erzan and Yeats finds that the benefits would be quite minor. These authors conclude that where trade is not restricted by quotas, duties are low and hence trade is substantially unrestricted, at least in what regards primary producing countries. By implication, these countries would stand to gain little from a free trade agreement. For manufacturing countries, the presence of quotas and other non-tariff trade restraints would be more of an issue. But even these hindrances might be passing in the context of a successful Uruguay Round.

These minimalist estimates are worth knowing about, but there is no reason to believe that they give a realistic portrait of the effects of an FTA. In part, of course, the trade effects derive from the immediate removal of obstacles. In fact, however, the trade effects are much more sweeping when they come from an entire re-orientation of the region to become a modern, outward-oriented, and integrated part of the regional and world economy. In that broader sense, the move to an FTA represents nothing short of an upheaval.

A broader and more ambitious list of advantages includes the following: removal of trade impediments, guaranteed market access, more assured modernization, and improved access to foreign direct investment. We comment on each in turn.

Removal of Trade Impediments

The point has already been made that there are relatively few impediments to trade and relatively low tariff barriers except in hard-core protection areas. There is, of course, the need to make a distinction between nominal and effective rates of protection. The escalation of duty rates by stage of processing means that value added in manufacturing where material content is substantial exceeds substantially the nominal rate. But even so, these are not formidable tariff barriers by any stretch of the imagination. Still, getting exemption from these duties will yield a preferential advantage even for countries that already enjoy Generalized System of Preferences treatment.

Trade restraints by quotas and voluntary export limitations are the more obvious area where large benefits might be accomplished—textiles, steel, and leather footwear are ordinarily high on the list, as are cheap glassware and some agricultural products. There would be transition periods, but ultimately markets would open and with that, opportunities would expand.

Of course, as these industries are opened to intra-FTA competition, the arguments for protection become weaker and there is bound to be a parallel impetus for worldwide market opening. That diminishes the narrow benefits to the South, but from a global point of view it reduces the discriminatory effects, which is all for the good, more so if it lies a decade or two ahead.

Guaranteed Market Access

The status quo today is free trade and that is likely to continue. But there is no assurance that this will, in fact be the case. With the U.S. middle-class squeeze and falling real wages, there is substantial pressure to close off trade wherever it hurts. Thus, if there is a risk of a U.S. slide into protectionism, an FTA creates a regional umbrella that protects against extreme damage.

The presence of such an umbrella has important consequences for business strategy. Without the assurance of market access, firms would have to be conservative in their growth strategy and could not in fact bank on the U.S. market for their future. Being more prudent, they would limit their exposure and as a result their profitability. They would underinvest in trade expansion and hence the growth effects of modernization could be curtailed.

By contrast, with assured trade access, countries can take a regional view of their operation, merge across borders, and pursue a far grander strategy. That is where productivity gains become startlingly large and where the fixed costs of modernization are more easily amortized and hence more decisively incurred.

Modernization

Modernization is not a process that inevitably gathers momentum, moving forward with growing strength. Venezuela and Brazil have demonstrated how very precarious the process can be. It is therefore critical to muster all positive forces that strengthen the move toward modern, open societies and economies. One of these is clearly intercourse with the rest of the world. A free trade agreement creates a very powerful momentum and, arguably, a quite irreversible one. Institutionally, the provision of open access in goods, services, and investment opens up a country's ways of doing business to international competition and inevitably imposes international standards. People soon adopt and practice those standards themselves and require them of others. Traditional, inefficient, and opaque ways of doing business come into conflict with modern ones. Competition enforces the modern, international mode.

The modernization carries over in an important way to business-government relations. Cumbersome and costly regulation constitutes a burden to competition and will be thrown off. Arbitrary government intervention makes firms uncompetitive and must go. Soon governments will perform by international standards. A free trade agreement internationalizes an economy and in the process wipes out the hold of governments, monopolies, and restrictions on individuals' freedom and prosperity. This is a dramatic effect.

Table 20.4
Duty Levels (percent)

	United States	Canada
Raw Materials	0.2	0.5
Semimanufactures	3.0	8.3
Fin. Manufactures	5.7	8.3

Source: Economic Report of the President.

Foreign Direct Investment

Foreign resources in the form of direct investment serve several basic functions. First, they add to national saving in financing investment. Second, they give access to markets and technology, piggybacking on the scale or scope of the foreign investor. Third, they serve as a broad mechanism of business modernization.

It is clear that *some* foreign direct investment will go *anywhere*. But it is equally clear that steady and substantial flows require an institutionally more established situation. A free trade agreement provides exactly that. First, the specific provisions regarding financial services create an essential legal environment to assure foreign investors. Second, the assurance of institutional stability that comes with economic integration offers a special incentive for foreign investors to concentrate on a specific country.

The decision to locate in a particular region comes with two questions. What are production costs in the region? And what is the market access from that region? On both counts, a free trade agreement is favorable. On the cost side, import liberalization reduces production costs. On the market access side, it offers assurance that there will not be random or systematic reversal of opportunities to sell into a partner country market or specifically into the U.S. market.

What evidence is there to show that foreign direct investment has attracted a trade integration situation? Spain serves as a case in point. Measured as a share of Spanish GNP, these flows were small in the 1970s. Only with Common Market membership, in the mid-1980s, did FDI take off. By 1990, Spain received $11 billion in direct foreign investment, more than 2 percent of GNP. The evidence is not fully rigorous: in the absence of a Common Market link, some increase would have occurred because of Spain's modernization. But modernization itself is in part the result of joining the Common Market.

In sum, the South has far more to gain than the elimination of a few tariffs. In the process of historical change—as substantial as the shift to inward-looking economies sixty years ago—free trade with the North is a powerful help.

Three Concurrent Processes

In concluding, it is important to emphasize the complementarity of three approaches: GATT and the Uruguay Round, unilateral trade liberalization, and an Americas Free Trade Agreement. The first is a worldwide strategy. Each country in the region has important extra-regional interests and for that reason must be concerned that the *world* economy sustains open markets and broadens the opening of markets.

The Americas FTA is critical because it carries trade liberalization much further than can be done at the world level: the coverage of liberalization—goods, services, investment—is more substantial and the liberalization more complete. Being in is essential in order to avoid concentrated trade diversion effects.

Lastly, unilateral liberalization is important to avoid the costs of trade diversion when one is an importer. If Brazil, for example, has 40 percent tariffs and grants the United States or Mexico zero duty access, the scope for very costly trade diversion is substantial. The only remedy is to go quite far in the direction of unilateral liberalization. Since the FTA has a timetable of a decade, there is no need to rush in unilateral liberalization. But it is essential to let the FTA and the unilateral moves go hand in hand to minimize the unnecessary and undesirable trade diversion effects.

The three-pronged strategy as described here is favorable for the world economy. It produces more trade, less protection, and hence a greater scope for multilateral opening over time. No apologies need to be made for freer trade—unilateral, regional, and multilateral.

21

U.S.-Mexico Free Trade: Good Jobs at Good Wages

A free trade agreement with Mexico would represent a significant step in focusing trade policy on creating *more* and *better* jobs. Most of the work in improving the standard of living must come from education, skill building, and research, but trade policy can contribute by opening and strengthening markets for our export industries. Except in the case of Japan or some Asian countries, increased market access will inevitably require that we also must give in on remaining protection at home. More and better jobs therefore come at the price of more competition for protected industries, and they are sure to cause *some* losses of employment and wage pressure in uncompetitive sectors.

The controversy surrounding the proposed free trade agreement (FTA) with Mexico is misplaced. Free trade with Mexico cannot be a panacea for all U.S. problems, nor will it create "an economic and social disaster for U.S. workers and their communities" as argued by the AFL-CIO.[1] Any job losses are bad news at a time when real wages are depressed and employment is at best stagnant. But these issues must not become an argument for stopping a good move in trade policy. Even if trade liberalization inevitably causes some dislocation, that must not mesmerize us into maintaining the status quo for poor jobs. It is bad trade policy to keep workers and their children in poor jobs and even pervert protection to the point where we attract immigrants to perform this work. We should not let go of competition. Of course, displaced workers should get adjustment programs, skill building, and education to help them get into good jobs.

Labor opposes the FTA because opening, in its experience, focuses on Japan and developing economies that have participated in successive

Table 21.1
The United States and Mexico Compared: 1989

	U.S.	Mexico
GNP (Bill. $US)	5,461	226
Manufacturing	948	50
Population (Mill.)	251	81
Labor Force	124	30
Compensation ($US/hour)[a]	14.21	2.32

[a] 1989 Hourly compensation for production workers in manufacturing reported by the U.S. Bureau of Labor Statistics, Report 794.

GATT trade liberalization rounds without much visible effect on their openness, thus creating a sharply biased competition. Labor is right on that score and should urge remedies in our trade relations with Japan. But that has no bearing on the proposed free trade agreement with Mexico. The dramatic effect of opening measures in Mexico on our exports is already amply demonstrated by the experience of the past three years.

Trade and Employment Effects

Concerns about the effect of free trade on U.S. jobs focus on the low level of Mexican labor cost. Numbers such as 61 cents an hour are routinely cited. Of course, Mexican labor costs, as shown in table 21.1, are far higher than that, even if they are low by comparison with the United States. Moreover, even with these low labor costs, a move to free trade stands no chance of having major effects either on the U.S. economy at large or on manufacturing.

Puerto Rico, with an average wage of $5.70 in manufacturing, has not destroyed manufacturing in the continental United States, nor has the free trade agreement with Israel, where hourly compensation is half that in the United States.

Employment Effects

Three factors support the assertion that an FTA with Mexico cannot plausibly bring major harm and is very likely to be beneficial. First,

Table 21.2
Mexican Labor Compensation in Manufacturing ($U.S. per Hour)

	Skilled	Unskilled
Maquila	2.40	1.60
National	2.70	1.85

Source: Survey by Intergamma (a subsidiary of Hewitt Associates)

Mexico is very small relative to the United States. Any significant increase in Mexican exports (measured on the U.S. scale) would increase labor requirements and wages in Mexico dramatically and thereby squash competitiveness.

Second, although Mexican labor costs are low relative to those in the United States, these labor costs also reflect a low level of productivity, and in some areas such as textiles, the very low quality of output. The quality factor especially is a major obstacle to a dramatic development of Mexican exports.

Third, the United States is a very open economy. Competition from abroad is not a threat, but a complete reality. Protection continues only in a few sectors, not across the board in all lines of activity. Moreover, Mexico enjoys already a privileged position both as a result of the GSP and, more important, as a consequence of the maquila program that exempts re-imports from U.S. duties except for the Mexican value-added component. This combination of factors reduces the *extra* impact of U.S. trade liberalization to a few sectors and to a total effect that have simply no chance of amounting to much in terms of aggregate employment or output.

The maquila program has been cited as a major source of U.S. job losses in the 1980s, and an FTA is interpreted as a vast maquila program. But the fact is that the maquila program is quantitatively small—less than one-third of a percent of U.S. manufacturing GNP, and wages there are far higher than is commonly reported.

Table 21.3 shows the developments of U.S.-Mexican non-oil trade since 1986 and the employment implications. The swing in our net exports is $4,818 billion. A rough rule of thumb (developed by the Economic Policy Institute) translates an extra $1 million net exports into

Table 21.3
U.S. Non-Oil Trade with Mexico and U.S. Job Creation (Billion $U.S.)

	U.S. Exports	U.S. Non-Oil Imports	Net Non-Oil Trade Balance
1986	12,391	14,040	−1.649
1990	28,375	25,206	3,169
Net U.S. Job Creation: 1986–90			
30 Jobs per $1 Mill			25 Jobs per $1 Million
144,531			120,450

Note: 30 jobs per $1 million exports is the number used by the Economic Policy Institute.

thirty new jobs. With this benchmark, the swing in our trade balance with Mexico since 1986 means 144,531 *extra* jobs in the United States. Without the Mexican trade opening and recovery (and whatever caused Mexico to shift to a deficit), we would have 144,531 fewer jobs today.

This demonstration runs a bit counter to the folklore that Mexico is cutting our throat. Note that if one used a different benchmark, say twenty-five jobs per $1 million exports, we would have less job creation but still an impressive 120,450 extra jobs.

The focus on the non-oil trade balance is appropriate because the trend in the bilateral balance is the chief determinant of *net* job creation. To the extent that an FTA reinforces confidence in Mexico's modernization, as it already has started doing, capital that fled will return to Mexico and foreign direct investment will grow. The availability of external capital until now has been a severe constraint on growth and investment in Mexico.

With modernization reinforced by an FTA, lack of capital will largely disappear as a serious problem, and Mexico will resume trade deficits as appropriate for developing countries. Because the United States is Mexico's chief supplier, Mexican growth and deficits become a source of increases in U.S. employment. Assuming that Mexico runs a trade deficit of 2 percent of GNP, U.S. job creation over the next five years could be as high as 150,000. Even larger numbers are quite possible because an FTA gives us privileged access.

Table 21.4
Sectors with Significant Remaining Trade Barriers

	U.S. Employment (1,000s)	Hourly Compens.	High Trade United States	Barriers[a] Mexico
Agriculture	n.a.	n.a.	7%, *	11%, *
Automotive Products	992	21.51	*	*
Cement	20	n.a.	—	10%
Chemicals	835	18.19	—	15%, *
Energy Products	275	21.26	—	*
Electronic Equipment	2,000	14.51	2%	16%, *
Glass Products	143	14.52	22%	20%
Machinery and Equipment	110	15.33	3%	10–20%
Steel Mill Products	277	23.49	0.5–11%	10–15%
Textiles and Apparel	1,818	8.75	6%, *	12–20% *

[a] Figures report average tariff rates where these are high, and an * stands for some form of nontariff barrier.
Source: USITC Publication 2353, and U.S. Bureau of Labor Statistics data and author's estimates.

Sectoral Effects

An FTA will create more and better jobs, but in the process of doing so, some jobs are almost certain to be lost. Table 21.4 reports the key sectors where employment impacts can be expected.

The table shows that Mexico still has significant protection in key areas where the United States can, as a result, expect to score export growth. This includes specifically electronic equipment, automotive products, steel, and textiles. Textiles in fact are a key example of an industry that has already demonstrated its ability to compete very effectively in Mexico. In 1989, and more so in 1990, the United States ran a bilateral trade surplus with Mexico in textiles and apparel. The key to understanding this is to look at *quality*, not only at wages. In the quality perspective, the United States is to Mexico what Japan is to the United States.

Since the United States does continue to protect certain sectors with high duties and non-tariff barriers, an FTA would open these areas to

Mexican competition. Interestingly, the U.S. International Trade Commission identifies only horticulture and inexpensive household glass products as the areas where significant import increases must be expected. The explanation, once more, is that the United States is already substantially open to competition from low-cost countries and even more so to Mexico. In automobiles, for example, the maquila program offers Mexico the opportunity to compete in the United States.

To the extent that import increases can be expected in an area such as apparel, part of the extra imports will mostly displace sales by low-cost producers in Asia. In part, it will also reflect the result of U.S. textile exports to Mexico, which raises the quality of Mexican apparel to the levels required for the U.S. market.

The upshot of this discussion is that trade liberalization will give rise to increased imports, but that there is no plausible alarm scenario. Moreover, going beyond the particular loss of sensitive industries, trade creation induced by the FTA will produce new good jobs. It will cost primarily bad jobs or jobs that, in any event, are under threat from world competition.

Foreign Investment in Mexico

Investment in Mexico by Asian or European firms should not be considered an unqualified disadvantage of a FTA. Clearly, such investment will be motivated to a large extent by the desire to build up an export base to the U.S. market and, as such, seems threatening. But for the most part the goods come anyway, whether it be from Thailand or from Korea and Japan.

The penetration of our market by imports from Asia is already a fact; the only question is whether, at the margin, shifting the production from Asia to Mexico is in our interest. And here the answer is clearly yes. Mexican workers spend a far larger share of their income on our goods, and hence we have an interest in their having good jobs at good wages. It is understood, of course, that import content provisions would apply. Location of Asian plants in Mexico cannot simply be a means of circumventing U.S. trade restrictions by performing negligible assembly tasks in Mexico. The experience in Europe with certificates of origin demonstrates that while administratively cumbersome, it is by no means overwhelming.

The argument used for Asian producers goes in the same way for U.S. firms. Coproduction with Mexican labor is far better, from the point of view of U.S. labor, than losing an entire operation to Asia or other locations. In many industries, it is totally implausible today to produce goods fully with labor priced at the U.S. level; foreign production is far too cost competitive. Coproduction with Mexico represents by a wide margin the lesser of the two evils. In fact, the cost-reducing effects may well be important enough to allow higher U.S. wages and, at the same time, increased U.S. competitiveness at home and abroad.

Progress in Mexico

Democracy, workers' rights, safety, and environmental standards are obvious issues on the political agenda of modern, open economies. An FTA supports modernization in Mexico and thus nurtures these objectives. It will also help raise wage levels in Mexico back to their 1980 level and beyond. By contrast, trade restriction here must mean even more poverty there; poverty in turn fosters political radicalism, which is not in the American interest.

If we are seriously concerned about the standard of living in Mexico, and about democratization, we cannot escape the recognition that a thriving, open market economy will raise wages, create individual freedom, decentralize political power, and allow people to organize around local issues. If Mexico prospers, it will be in a far better position to take up costly but urgent measures on safety standards at the workplace and the environment.

Work standards and environment standards can obviously not become part of a free trade agreement; even in Europe where political integration is the object, social harmonization is on the political agenda, not an object of the 1992 regulations. But it is altogether plausible to foster cross-border union dialogue on the issue of safety standards. There is also an urgent need to reinforce regional and North American environmental policies. This should be handled separately from the FTA discussion, but at the same time. Agreements might be expected to phase in stricter Mexican standards by requiring new plants to abide by U.S. environmental standards, while existing plants might have twelve years to adjust.

In discussing standards abroad, we must not be tempted to make Mexican producers uncompetitive. The object is to spread prosperity at an affordable pace. It will take a long time before Mexico will look like the United States, but we can start making some headway.

Regional Concerns

If Mexico prospers, Central America will benefit. Mexican authorities already have started taking an active hand in the economic stabilization of Central America, and much more can be expected. The United States shares in this stabilization: enhanced political stability and security in the region and reduced pressure of immigration are clearly in the national interest.

The example of Europe deserves far more attention in our design of trade policy. The core countries of the Common Market have systematically reached out to the periphery to spread prosperity and stability. Bringing Spain, Greece, or Portugal into the Common Market is no different from an FTA with Mexico. And the discussion now with Eastern Europe serves much the same purpose. Unless the periphery has trade access, there will be no investment. Without investment, jobs will be poor and the pressure for migration enormous.

Mexico is recognizing these realities on its own border in the South, responding to the dramatic decline in living standards in Central America, notably in Nicaragua. Mexico has now started filling the leadership vacuum, helping stabilize the region. A rising tide raises all ships; a prosperous Mexico will be a powerful shock absorber for us and a great help in nurturing economic stability and prosperity in a region that is too close to neglect but, except for communist threats, too small to draw much of our attention.

No Going Back Now

At this stage, it has become very expensive to turn back on a free trade agreement. In Mexico, the idea of trade opening has become a cornerstone of the economic modernization strategy. The United States has every interest in Mexico's demonstration that with sensible policies, all of Latin America can return to prosperity.

In the postwar period, the United States has invariably favored an open world economy. Successive GATT rounds have opened markets, at least across the Atlantic. In Europe, on a parallel track to GATT, the Common Market has pursued an aggressive project of regional integration with unquestioned benefits. The United States has so far done little to exploit the parallel track. Free trade with Mexico offers an important market opening for the 1990s and beyond. The focus must shift from seeing trade as a threat to viewing it as an opportunity for jobs and profits.

Today the United States faces an unusual opportunity to implement an outward-looking trade policy with Mexico. Looking for modernization as the way out of a difficult economic situation, Mexico today is open to far-reaching trade reform. If we miss this opportunity, we are bound to fail at building an important Western Hemisphere trade and investment block in the 1990s.

Turning our back on trade opening means inviting a resurgence of protectionism not only in Mexico but throughout Latin America and beyond. Going back on the FTA with Mexico would send signals to the world economy far worse than did the recent failure of the Uruguay Round.

Note

1. This view was advanced by Thomas R. Donahue, Secretary-Treasurer, AFL-CIO, before the Senate Finance Committee on February 6, 1991: "The enactment of a free trade agreement with Mexico, as proposed by President Bush, would be an economic and social disaster for U.S. workers and their communities, and do little to help the vast majority of Mexican workers."

Appendix

Table 21A.1
U.S. and Mexican Hourly Compensation in Manufacturing ($U.S. per Hour and Index U.S. = 100)

	United States	Mexico	Ratio
1979–82	10.33	2.91	0.28
1983–86	12.70	1.88	0.15
1987	13.39	1.57	0.12
1988	13.85	1.99	0.14
1989	14.31	2.32	0.16

Source: U.S. Bureau of Labor Statistics.

Table 21A.2
Hourly Compensation in Manufacturing ($U.S. per Hour)

	1980	1989
United States	9.84	14.31
Canada	8.37	14.72
Mexico	2.96	2.32
Israel	3.79	7.69
Germany	12.35	17.58
Spain	5.96	9.10
Greece	3.75	5.48
Portugal	2.06	2.77

Source: U.S. Bureau of Labor Statistics, Sept. 1990.

22

U.S.-Japan Relations Fifty Years after Pearl Harbor

Pearl Harbor had economic roots, even if ultimately sheer nationalism took over. Today's economic frictions between the United States and Japan are the same as those that ultimately led to war. The U.S. Administration is trying unsuccessfully to paper over the conflict, and Japan unwisely takes comfort from the attitude. To talk straight now, bring about major changes, and thus avoid grave conflict later, form a better strategy.

In *The Causes of War* published in 1932 by the World Commission for International Peace, economic troubles foreshadowed grave risks in Asia: "In the present crisis in the Far East the underlying cause is obviously economic. Japan, with her surplus population penned in by restrictions on migration and impeded in her foreign trade, has reached a mood of desperation." Resentment of U.S. racism, as expressed already in the "Asiatic Exclusion Act of 1924" that limited Japanese immigration into the United States, added to the narrow economic motives for war. Harvard economist Richard Cooper believes that without the U.S. Smoot-Hawley Tariff of 1931, Pearl Harbor would not have happened. He argues that the tariff undercut the liberal faction in Japan, giving nationalist-militarist groups the upper hand. From there it was a short step to Pearl Harbor.

A revisionist view of Pearl Harbor may be comforting for Japan, but it is unpersuasive. Japan was at odds with world peace, just as Germany was. Their rearmament preceded the recession, and their aggressions shocked a world too frightened to resort to massive resistance early. They were insatiable: Pearl Harbor was for the Japanese generals what Munich was for Hitler. Germany today accepts and understands the guilt for making war and for the unspeakable genocide of Jews; Japan has yet to face up to history. Concerned with building a defense against communism in Asia, General Douglas MacArthur rushed to rebuild Japan. He chose to preserve Japan's deep roots, from Tokyo University to the Emperor, and thus ensured continuity. Rearmament and war were rejected, but the real issue—aggression—was hardly debated. Even today it is common to hear that "Japan was pushed too hard."

U.S.-Japan relations are not much better now than they were in 1931. A deep recession today would quickly lead to trade restrictions against Japan. No doubt, Japan would be indignant and truculent, looking for means to fight a trade and finance war. How come so little was learned? Why, fifty years after Pearl Harbor, is Japan still an outsider?

Japan goes through the motions of participating in world affairs. But missing is the commitment to help build a better world; Japan just stands by and waits to be told how much to pay and what is the bare minimum with which to get by. Japan has strangely been unable to find its way into the world community: it has lacked great leaders like Schuman, Pompidou, and Mitterrand in France; Truman and Kennedy in the United States; or Adenauer, Brandt, Schmidt, and Kohl in Germany. Shaped by the trauma of war, they built an open world economy where economic nationalism would not be again a cause of war. Economic causes do not justify aggression and war, but they create an easy ideology of encirclement and exclusion. They rally public opinion in aggressor countries unless a deep commitment to an international order provides a firm counterpoint. Japan has no strong links to a world system that it did not help build, and it has made few friends. Herein lies the risk of serious conflict.

Trade Conflicts

The growing economic rift between Japan and the West involves trade. Latent, no doubt, are envy, fear, and frustration on the part of Western economies that cannot rival Japan's astounding achievement. No surprise that they look behind the curtain to check whether all we see is straight and fair play. And it is not.

Four decades of trade liberalization notwithstanding, the Japanese markets for manufactures, for services, and for agriculture remain virtually closed. Manufactures cannot make their way into Japan, except when produced by Japanese firms abroad. The difficulty of access has nothing to do with special economic conditions of the Japanese economy nor with the shoddiness of foreign goods. It reflects a culture determinedly opposed to trade as a two-way street. That attitude is increasingly challenged by Europe and the United States. It is becoming more and more likely that it will lead to a major trade conflict.

The Western Perception

In merchandise trade and in services, it is exceptionally hard for European, U.S., or Asian firms to break into the Japanese market. Firms that have cultivated the market for a long time do sell and, because margins are extremely high, find themselves with a profitable business. But the number of successful firms is outnumbered 100 to 1 by those who have not been able to make it even if they try hard by international standards.

The episodes are more than telling. Security firms that ultimately manage to cut through bureaucracy and get registered in Tokyo find their bond issues boycotted. Manufacturers find it impossible to cut through the complexities of trade access. Service firms find it impossible to compete in public tender. The game is rigged, and it takes an age to make headway. By then Japanese competitors have in place the technology, innovation, or financial product that a foreign firm was trying to introduce.

Of course, there are messages to the contrary. Successful foreign firms operating in Japan sing an "all-is-well" chorus that is not really persuasive. We are told that U.S. firms are making profits in Japan. What is surprising about this? U.S. firms make profits everywhere; what is suspect is the need to even assert it. In fact, the very profitability of these firms has probably more to do with the closed Japanese markets, where margins are phenomenal, than with the achievements of the chosen few firms who have gained access.

The United States has responded to the perception of a closed Japanese market by challenging Japanese business practices in the context of the Strategic Impediments Initiative (SII). This involves negotiating an opening piece by piece. The procedure is noisy and not very effective.

The Facts

Japan tells us that most problems lie abroad: U.S. budget deficits and the poor quality of American goods are to blame. Or else, that Japan is not closed but must export manufactured goods to compensate for its lack of natural resources. Finally, that Japan may have been closed in the past, but liberalization is underway by leaps and bounds. These arguments either miss the point or run counter to the facts. The mechanisms that close Japan to outsiders are not clear—neither tariffs nor quotas play a role—but by any definition Japan is closed.

Manufacturing Import Penetration. By this measure, Japan is far out compared to other industrial countries. In Europe, the ratio is more than 10 percent of GNP. Even the United States, a far larger country, still has twice the Japanese import penetration ratio. Korea's import penetration in manufacturing is 18.7 percent—six times that of Japan. Of course, Korea is a developing country and hence the ratio might be high for that reason. But this would suggest that Japan might have had a high penetration ratio in the past. In Japan, manufacturing imports have moved between 1.5 and 3 percent of GNP, without much change for a quarter of a century.

GATT rounds of trade liberalization and major swings in exchange rates have done almost *nothing* to change Japan's openness. This evidence supports the view that Japanese protection is like an onion; it has multiple layers and the innermost are cultural, not the conventional restrictions in the form of quotas or tariffs.

Considering the entire range of non-oil imports, table 22.1 represents a dramatic portrait of Japan's situation. While Germany's import penetra-

Table 22.1
Comparative Openness: 1989 (manufacturing imports as percent of GNP)

United States	7.1	Italy	11.7
Canada	18.8	United Kingdom	17.9
France	16.8	Korea	18.7
Germany	15.6	Japan	3.1

Source: GATT and IMF.

tion increased steadily, that of Japan actually declined over the past three decades.

Intra-Industry Trade.   In open, developed economies, consumers have the advantage of choosing from a broad range of product qualities and varieties produced throughout the world. Given the diversity of consumer tastes and the specialization of firms, any country would both import and export consumer goods or capital goods in many categories. Intra-industry or two-way trade is the common experience of advanced countries.

The extent to which countries do pursue two-way trade is readily measured by an index that assumes a value of 1 when trade is completely two-way, namely, in a particular commodity group, imports equal exports. The index reported in the accompanying table assumes a value of zero when trade is a one-way street.

All three countries are resource poor. Korea and Japan have their geography and transport costs to the West in common; Korea is poor while Japan and Germany are rich. Whichever way we look at these data, Japan is severely closed to intra-industry trade. Any story of resource endowments, geographic location, or the state of development simply fails.

In Japan protection is at work, by an invisible hand. There is no other explanation for a value of intra-industry trade of finished manufactures in Japan of 0.33 versus 0.72 for each, Korea and Germany. A good spe-

Table 22.2
Intra-Industry Trade in Selected Manufactures (Index: One Way = 0, Two-Way = 1)

Category	Germany	S. Korea	Japan
Finished Manufactures	.72	.72	.33
Machinery & Transp. Equip't.	.66	.94	.25
Elect. Mach. & Apparatus	.89	.68	.27
Automotive Products	.71	.91	.17
Textiles	.90	.33	.36

Source: GATT, *International Trade.*

cific example is automotive products. Germany does have superior products and even so has intra-industry trade with a two-way index at 0.71. In Japan the corresponding number is an entirely absurd 0.17.

Japan does *not* practice two-way trade. Manufactured goods are produced and exported; they are rarely imported. To some extent, resource endowments influence the index. Clearly, a country without natural resources will be a net exporter of manufactures to pay for oil imports. Yet, the puzzle is this: why does Japan look so different than Germany? Germany does not have natural resources any more than Japan. Do Japanese consumers, unlike consumers everywhere else in the world, not like imports? Or are they still taught to save foreign exchange and favor home industry, as might have been plausible in the immediate postwar period? Or are there mechanisms we cannot see that plainly keep imports out? The skyrocketing of imports when liberalization does occur lends weight to this last hypothesis.

Remedies

Insistence on a radical, rapid, and complete opening of the Japanese market is now appropriate. It is not enough for Japan just to start catching up with other countries. Moving too late and too little means a path straight to trade conflict and beyond. Japan must make a real and determined effort to become a leading, active part of the world system. Japan must recognize that there are two ways to go. Either the country participates in a system of common goals and common responsibilities where the largest countries drive the initiatives and bear the burdens, or else Japan divides the world and builds its new Asian empire, based on confrontation and hostility to the West.

Dissatisfaction in America with its own performance and rising populism in response to the middle class squeeze will make America increasingly antagonistic. Therefore, the state of limbo cannot last; Japan must act.

It is tempting for America to set an agenda that Japan must accomplish: full market opening over the next decade or else face retaliation. But it may already be too late for such an approach. U.S. firms are fearful that in a confrontation they might not have access to Japanese components, U.S. business is reluctant to jeopardize access to technology, and our military even more so. We have become too dependent to make sanctions easy or even plausible. So the responsibility for a farsighted approach now rests with Japan.

In the 1930s, access to markets and access to raw materials were the issue, and with ineffective sanctions the aggressors drifted toward war. Just as in the 1930s, there are no plausible sanctions against large countries that do not play by the rules of the game. Unless Japan looks at the 1930s, at the arrogance of Pearl Harbor and the tragedy of Hiroshima, the country once again puts itself at odds with the world. The time is particularly appropriate for a major initiative: Europe is opening to the East to stem the tide of migration, and the United States is opening to Latin America. Japan needs to open to the world.

Japan's opening will lend strength to international peace. Of course, Japan's opening would be no panacea for what in the United States is understood as the "Japan Problem," which in truth must be called mostly our own U.S. problem—poor performance. But opening will relieve the growing tension, and will allow Japan to finally take a seat at the table and be a welcome member of the international community.

23

Trade with China: Add Bite to America's Bark

In June, the annual decision on whether to renew most-favored-nation (MFN) status for China comes up. President Clinton will have to determine whether China's record warrants continued favorable trade access. If not, he'll pull the plug—and risk a tantrum from China, not to mention a major setback for American exports and investments.

China is not a member of the World Trade Organization. As a result, the MFN privilege, which allows China the same deal on duties as everybody else, needs to be renewed every year.

Tempers run hot on this issue. China is a major trading partner—$21.4 billion worth of exports to the United States (or $56.4 billion if we include Hong Kong), and $14 billion worth of imports, according to International Monetary Fund statistics. Many multinationals in such sectors as manufacturing, services, and finance see China as their single most important market. They want to deal—no questions asked.

Opposing MFN status for China are a wide array of forces, including old-fashioned protectionists, companies hurt by China's refusal to enforce intellectual-property commitments, human-rights advocates, and right-wing cold warriors. They all want to use trade policy to try to force China to mend its ways.

The China dilemma is likely to become a big election-year issue. The President can make a deal or take a stand—whichever gets more votes. Senator Bob Dole (R-Kan.) can look principled or craven. Already, Clinton and Dole are squirming. Of course, the issues go far beyond

Originally published in *Business Week* (13 May 1996): 28. Reprinted with permission.

MFN and politics. The more basic question is how China integrates itself into the world community. So far, it has not done very well.

Slowly but Surely?

The prevailing policy in Washington has been to place its bet on transforming China from within by deepening trade relations, widening capitalism, and using the resulting economic progress as a nudge toward a peaceful posture and international cooperation. In other words, America is trying to foster an economic partnership that slowly creates an open, peaceful society.

But U.S. policymakers have forgotten that the late nineteenth century was also a great period of widening economic internationalism. Unfortunately, this globalism was followed by two world wars. Today, Russia's painful shift to a market economy is marked by demands for a return to empire. The United States plainly cannot take for granted that trade and free market economics are sufficient guarantors of democracy. It has to assert its principles and then back them up with strong trade and finance sanctions—and, if necessary, the exercise of force.

Today, the assumption around the world is that the United States is unwilling to back its interests. In fact, the United States appears not quite sure what its interests are. Policy, such as it is, revolves around increasing exports and making deals.

Endless Reruns

American instincts are to delink politics and economics domestically as well as internationally. Politics should not get in the way of the free flow of goods, capital, and ideas. The Administration has been on that track with China for two years. Every time MFN comes up, there is a heated battle—and every time, economics is chosen over politics.

But the decision to delink trade and politics should not be a foregone conclusion when it comes to China. For one, China does not delink. Whenever trade issues come up, China gives contracts to European or Japanese competitors to pressure Washington. To show displeasure with the United States, China recently gave Airbus Industrie a huge contract that Boeing Co. was expecting to get. Washington and Beijing are playing by a different set of rules.

There is also a wider issue. The U.S. government cannot afford to be seen as selling out to its export interests to the point that it sacrifices its global-security objectives. That would significantly cut into its standing as a world leader.

The solution is to put MFN on automatic pilot with a multiyear renewal. Let the United States give China MFN and avoid the annual haggling over renewal. But let Washington be smart about it: China gets MFN—but with a poison pill.

Washington should identify the key objectives in its China relationship. If China complies with these, MFN remains. If China fails, MFN is pulled automatically. That way, MFN status is China's to lose. In the meantime, let's get China into the World Trade Organization and Chinese trade issues out of the bilateral political arena.

V

European Union: Fantasies, Problems, and Impact

24

Euro Realities, Fantasies, and Problems

For nearly fifty years, Europe has been on a course of ever-broadening and deepening integration. For just as long, Germany has been building up a reputation as the foremost champion of hard money in the world. The DM, more respected than the BMW and Mercedes combined, stands as a monument of that effort. The proposed monetary union in Europe joins these two strands: Europe is to get German monetary integrity even as Germany accepts blending into Europe.

The Maastricht Treaty is the prenuptial agreement for this merger; on the way to consummation the doubts loom larger than sheer joy. Late in the game the questions come up of the benefits, the suitability of the partners, and the relations with those left out. Those questions are particularly acrimonious because the tight timetable destroys illusions, as does the poor economic performance of Europe. Europe has 18 million unemployed and nobody knows what to do with them. Moving forward is the answer from Germany's Chancellor Kohl; German industry and German banks agree: EMU is a must. As eager are the "social union" promoters who look to integration as a way to get on top of too much competition and too little social justice.

Questions about the merits of the scheme come as much from German monetary hawks (i.e., most of the population and most prominently the Bundesbank, which is about to lose its job), from obviously excluded bystanders such as Eastern Europe, or from benevolent spectators in the United States. The prospective partners who, financially speaking, live

Originally published in *World Economic Trends* (Trans-National Research Corporation), (July–August 1996): 25–40. Reprinted with permission.

from hand to mouth—France, Italy, Spain—are cheering glumly. They still believe that monetary union is a miracle cure for rotten public finance and a century of debased currency, but they are also wincing as they are weighed in for the race to Maastricht. And as all this goes on, Britain is searching its soul. Labor wisely is pro-Maastricht, in general, which is a safe and pragmatic strategy to tear the Conservatives apart; beyond that, let's see.

What is touted as the "century event" of Europe may have any of these fates: it may create a powerful and vigorous Europe, politically and economically cohesive and with financial strength that dwarfs the United States and the dollar; it might pass quietly and without much consequence, a nonevent; it may be blown away by financial markets even before it starts; it might restore prosperity in an all too clammy Europe; or, it may die on the hands of Maastricht-bean counters who apply the tests and find the partners unfit to consummate the union. What is the most likely course? EMU will happen, it will not be the end of European currency troubles and, most assuredly, it will not solve Europe's prosperity problem. Euro fantasies make EMU a panacea, or at the minimum a pivotal step, for making Europe something wonderful: politically, culturally, economically, socially, and financially. Do not hold your breath.

EMU in Perspective

The enlightened postwar agenda, driven by the United States but bought into vigorously by France and Germany, was this: anything that would keep Germany from making war on France, dragging the whole world into these recurrent conflicts, seemed a splendid idea. And it was. The early and narrow agreements around the Marshall Plan, Coal and Steel Union, and the European Payments Union, which restored regional trade, all created a pattern of cooperation and common institutions that broke the ice and set a pattern. Later, the move to a Common Market brought about a major identity boost for Europe and a growth boost at the same time. One more round, the completion of the "internal market" in 1992 sought to transform Europe into an integrated and competitive market of the kind the United States represents so strikingly. That process is well underway.

No surprise that after the optimism-boosting hit of "Europe-92," there had to be an encore, and that is the setting in which common money came to the agenda and the infamous Maastricht hurdles were set out. Europe was to get a common money as one of the steps to go beyond the nation state and into an irreversible deepening of a Europe without boundaries. The trade integration measures and removal of impediments to cross-border activity measures, although beneficial, are ultimately non-controversial; they merely amount to removing government restraints on trade and economic activity. They fall short of a breathtaking move to free trade, although in a segmented and restricted market they are welcome. Can the same be said of the next step, European Monetary Union? Here skepticism is appropriate: the costs of getting there are big, and the economic benefits from being there are minimal. The scope for disappointment is major.

Yet, in the past few months European Monetary Union has moved from an improbable and bad idea to a bad idea that is about to come true. High unemployment, low growth, discomfort with a welfare state that is no longer affordable—all these factors find their outlet in a desperate bid for a common money, as if a common money could address the real problems of Europe. On the contrary, the hard work to get there, meeting the famous Maastricht criteria, is adding to the burden of an already mismanaged Europe. The battle of Maastricht may become remembered as one more of the really useless battles in European history.

European integration, at the outset, was a historic move. Its purpose was to bring Germany and France together and thus avoid the recurrent wars of a century. European integration went further: a Common Market, an internal market with no obstacles to trade in goods and services and free movement of people, and next monetary integration on the way to full union. Even as that agenda is being implemented, the circle of candidates gets wider, disenchantment gets bigger, the contradictions become more apparent. Chancellor Kohl of Germany has recognized that unless he drives EMU hard, right now, the concept will lose support and it will just become a bad idea that fell by the wayside. But Kohl is not alone. The French, too, want EMU. Their reason is surely not to build bridges that avoid future conflict—Germany and France by now are as tight as the United States and Canada. The reason is that no French minister of Finance dares go to bed not knowing where the franc is in the morning. Monetary union will allow them a good night's sleep, the first in a decade. And then there are all the other candidates who try to get a bit of credibility for policies that do not quite make it without membership: Ireland, Belgium, Scandinavia, Italy, and Spain.

By April 1998 the key membership decision will be made; by 1999 currencies are locked to each other, irrevocably; by 2002 there is only the Euro. That will not be the end of the story; the question of who is in and out is open, and frustrated relations between the two groups will jeopardize much of the gain of a common money.

Will It Really Happen?

EMU now is almost surely happening. Over the past few months, a decisive change has occurred. The question of whether EMU will happen is no longer asked; even Buba chief Tietmeyer invariably says "when" not "if." The reason for the increased assurance that EMU is about to happen is, no doubt, the French success in toughing it out on the budget —winning the standoff with strikers, pushing through much of the proposed budget cuts. That is what impressed Chancellor Kohl in Germany and gave him the confidence that Germany and France can do it together. On the French side, too, there was a test. The French understood that budget cutting was necessary, Maastricht or not. New was the success in pushing interest rates below the German levels, thus demonstrating that in the EMU context France can be a hard currency country.

Just in case, it is worth asking where the problems for actual passage to EMU might come from. There are three ways in which EMU can go wrong. First, technically it becomes impossible and the bean counters just say no. Second, a speculative attack takes out France. Third, it becomes a political liability, is put back on the shelf, and becomes history.

On the technical side the issue is how to meet the Maastricht criteria. Germany and France are within sight (see table 24.1), and so are a few small countries. Italy is definitely not by any definition. How far then can the criteria be stretched? In some politicians' view, particularly in Italy, this will all become grand political negotiation, and the criteria will be interpreted "flexibly." Not so. In Germany, EMU is a tough issue: at stake is gambling away stability, and that is something no politician will do lightly. Moreover, and this may ultimately be decisive, both the German Parliament and the Bundesbank have a final say on whether the criteria for various participants (including Germany?) are satisfied. Clearly, Italy cannot make it. But can France? If the current poor growth performance stretches into 1997, budgets will look even worse than the present forecasts. Some fudge—deficits are cyclical, structural deficits are already good and getting better—is acceptable; big fudge in a situation of weakening resolve is quite impossible.

Much of the attention now focuses on the final set of exchange rates at which currencies are to be locked in January 1999. If there is any prospect of an initial devaluation, say by France, speculative attack is a foregone conclusion. A speculative attack spoils the appetite for EMU. It either means a bitter and prolonged fight with high interest rates and recession or it means giving in, allowing a depreciation and thus reducing the partners' enthusiasm for going ahead. In Europe there are too few jobs; taking them away by competitive depreciation is not part of the script even when the event is forced by a speculative attack.

The political problem comes in the simple form of 1998 elections in both Germany and France. If the economic situation of 1997 is poor, if the budget cutting now under way translates into yet weaker growth, or if Maastricht gets a bad name, one or the other of the players may drop the hot potato. More likely than not, Chirac the eternal opportunist will be tempted to make the turn. Yet, that is not easy. If Germany turned away, its currency would strengthen and its bond yields would drop in response to the perception that the hard DM will stay and debasement has been avoided. If France, by contrast, drops out, the conclusion can only be that the country lacks the resolve. It is a short step from there to a speculative attack and a collapse of the franc. France looks good only as long as there is an expectation that the Teutonic ECB will run its monetary affairs.

On the German side there is, of course, also a political issue. But so far the opposition has kept away from opposing EMU, and it is likely that this will remain the case. The only way things can go wrong is if the public at large gets scared that money is about to go *kaput*. In that case, the ball is in Kohl's court to become inventive—postponement, extra effort?

Thus, EMU is on unless economic performance between here and late 1997 is even poorer than now expected. The working assumption is that Germany and France are within the allowable range for fudge.

Problems on the Way

There remain key problems on the way to a common money. Most importantly, there is virtually no country with a budget that makes the Maastricht criteria, including Germany and France, the two key countries. As a result, all of Europe is plunging into budget cutting, all at once, with the likely outcome of a slowdown. True, the budget cuts are appropriate even without EMU, but their timing, size, and coincidence will cut into growth, raise unemployment further, and add to the cost of EMU before it even starts. Monetary authorities have shown no disposition to accommodate. They have their own agenda: hold tight to the last moment, help shape the right attitude for the new Central Bank. The combination of overly tight monetary policy and determined budget cutting suggests a tough time ahead for Europe.

An even more important issue is the question of what happens to those who cannot or do not want to be part of the club. Britain has shown a deep aversion to being in. British pragmatism stops at inflation targeting as the common bond, and joining the monetary *Burschenschaft* is too much. Then there is Italy with its undervalued currency. France wants Italy to be in so that further competitive depreciation becomes impossible. But once Italy is in, with an appreciated currency, the country is soon back on the ropes, just as in 1992. The question of the "outs" comes down to a simple question: what can be offered to Britain and Italy to join the club? Unlimited, unconditional defense of their currencies by Germany is a good enough reward for Italy. Predictably, Germany is utterly unwilling to take that offer, leaving France sulking in the wings. Everybody is waiting and hoping that Italy and Britain, the soft currencies of 1992, will make it a point of pride to show that they are European, that they are willing to be hard currency countries, that they will do the pushups necessary to join. Do not wait for Britain; the Labor government has as much trouble with the Social Charter as it does with the ECB.

If EMU is a foregone conclusion, there are nevertheless a few interesting questions to be asked. First, who are the "ins" and "outs," and what is a better place to be? Next, what is wrong with EMU, and are there important *economic* benefits from EMU at all? Further, is EMU a natural first pass at abandoning sovereignty? Finally, what can we expect from the new European Central Bank (ECB)? Here is an attempt to provide some answers.

Who Is "In"?

Ritual cleansing is underway throughout Europe. Everybody is trimming budgets, hoping to make it or at least impressing markets that there is a good chance. Who will in fact make it?

Without Germany and France, there will not be an EMU. For Germany, EMU is a political step reflecting the deeply held belief that stabilizing Germany requires an irreversible link to France; nothing else matters in this context. Nobody loses sleep over Greece, Portugal, or even Italy and Spain. But assuming that France and Germany are the founding members, how will they structure the debate around fulfilling the Maastricht criteria and where will they draw the line between the "ins" and "outs"? The present position of debts and deficits, on a narrow reading of the criteria, has nobody in. Nobody is perfect, not even Germany. If it is not the debt ratio that is too high, it is the deficit ratio. Moreover, optimism is pervasive about the 1997 recovery. Without that, everybody's deficit numbers will look far worse, and the prospects for making the 3 percent hurdle, even approximately, must be written off. It is questionable whether politicians can afford to let the market toss around these questions for the next two years. Far more likely is the scenario where a practical decision is made now, perhaps implicitly, and that working assumption is carried forward.

The assumption has to be that France and Germany are moving forward, together with a small group. They will lay out a demanding three-year program of fiscal adjustment, which puts them by 1998 *below* the Maastricht targets. That will serve as a justification for fudging a bit up front.

Who else will get to fudge the numbers? Belgium decidedly cannot unless the public debt is written off, but who has the courage to take such

Table 24.1
Financial Outlook for 1997

	Debt	Deficit	Inflation
Belgium	131.1	3.7	1.7
Denmark	56.9	3.7	2.5
France	56.9	3.7	1.3
Germany	62.4	3.6	1.5
Ireland	80.3	2.6	2.4
Italy	124.8	6.4	2.9
Netherlands	78.2	2.7	1.8
Portugal	70.7	4.2	2.7
Spain	79.8	3.1	3.0
United Kingdom	62.0	3.7	2.5

Note: Budget deficit and debt as a percent of GDP.
Source: OECD *Economic Outlook*, June 1996.

an extreme step? Without debt surgery, the simple fact is that Belgium has twice the maximum indebtedness, in wild defiance of the treaty. Of course, there is an interesting precedent. In 1926, in the midst of over-indebtedness and a funding crisis, Belgium gave bond holders, in a forced consolidation, the national railways. There are plenty of public enterprises in Belgium; might there be a repeat? Belgium is a Northern European darling and hard money partner, and that ought to call for some special efforts.

Off the list for immediate consideration is surely Italy. Italy has a problem with *both* debt levels and deficits (not to mention inflation and long-term interest rates). It is difficult to believe that all this can pass German scrutiny; it is also inconceivable that Italy can clean up in time. The conclusion is that Italy will not make the first wave. But Italy is a big European country. More important, German and French industry definitely want to put Italian competition on a short leash, effectively excluding competitive depreciation. But the answer is, they cannot.

The overriding issue in the "ins" versus "outs" debate is surely this: monetary union is like marriage between partners with *very* different asset positions; naturally, prenuptial arrangements are the rule and must be followed closely. The passion is gone; the agreements last. German bondholders rule supreme since they have the most to lose. France has always oscillated between hard and soft money, but Germany has a long-standing tradition built around the coalition of bond holders and the Bundesbank. Chancellor Kohl would make a big mistake if he threatened the bondholders, the savers, the people with more fear than memory of a debased currency. For that reason, we can be confident of two points. First, Italy will not be in because to German bond holders (rightly or wrongly), Italy is the incarnation of monetary delinquency. Second, if there is fudging to be done for Germany and France (where credibility does allow some fudging with the timetable), the same cannot be done for countries who have a bad fiscal reputation.

If There Are "Ins" and "Outs," Which Is the Better Place to Be?

Surely, for Italy being out is the better position. The French are all tied up in knots over Italian competitiveness and the fear that yet another round of competitive depreciation might come along. They are willing to make deals to help Italy come on board. Of course, the key for Italy to make exchange-rate commitments is an offer from Germany of "unconditional, unlimited intervention" in support of the lira. Hell will freeze over before that comes about. Yet, Italy stands to gain from professing interest in EMU membership; it helps in the inevitable budget fight, which has nothing to do with Maastricht. More important, it helps bring down interest rates and that helps the budget.

If Germany and France do go at it alone, and if as expected there are "outs," we should be confident that there will be a structured process to bring the "outs" on board in due time. But, because Germany will not offer exchange-rate guarantees, much of the burden will fall on the "outs" who have to lay out their convergence programs and do the work. There is little here that is free. The pressure is under way for the "outs" to declare themselves: Italy is expected to make much more important efforts at consolidating public finance. Britain is being threatened with the prospect that EMU means finance moves to Frankfurt unless Britain is plausibly part of the club. As EMU gets under way, the pressure on the "outs" will increase. They are as essential to the success. If they are indifferent or picky, like Britain, raise the ante; if they are financially tainted like Italy, push harder.

The issue of being out is particularly difficult for Eastern European countries. They are on the way into European Union (free trade and all that), but on the financial side they are especially weak. Is their situation even worse? If EMU were an integrating device, then it would be critical not only to be in, but in early. Since the benefits are, in any event, overdone we need not worry too much. On the contrary, with the Euro as a new currency, a very interesting option emerges. Why should a country like the Czech Republic or Poland not adopt outright the Euro as its national currency just as Argentina has, effectively, gone on the dollar? Such a move would deal with financial instability, but it would come at the cost of losing the exchange rate as an adjustment tool.

EMU Benefits and Problems

Whatever persuaded political leaders in 1991 to single out money as the key integration vehicle, money is a poor choice. Money at its best is *a*political, and that is what the ECB will accomplish.

Leaving aside any of the political benefits from integrating moneys, are there narrow economic gains to be reaped? EMU is quite unlike the all-important customs union and the brilliant scheme of completing the internal market. Those were dramatic initiatives of integration that carried incentives to make the European market, desperately uncompetitive and segmented as it was, into a large single unit. The imagination was carried by the experience of the vast and highly competitive U.S. market and the initiative was both bold and worthy. EMU has little of that.

The expected benefits in the integration area are two. One is more convenience in transaction by avoiding cumbersome money changing and reduced costs in making payments. The other is reduced volatility in currency rates, to zero in fact, and a resulting increase in the willingness to trade and invest across intra-European borders.

A single market does *not* mean integration of the means of payment. A Euro in Barcelona does not have the same meaning as a Euro in Berlin. The U.S. experience points the way. In the late nineteenth century, even though the United States was an integrated monetary area, a $100 check on California received in Boston could be worth anything between $95 and $105, depending on the rate at which checks cleared. Before the creation of the Federal Reserve at the beginning of this century, there was no *par clearing*—flexible rates between various cities and huge bank charges, more so the less competitive the local market for exchange. Membership in the Federal Reserve system carries as a benefit the use of Fed member banks, free of charge, and Fed wires for transfers. The burden is the requirement of clearing all checks at par. It is true that there will be a transfer system akin to Fed wires for the group of member countries, but little has been said about par clearing so far. Whether a tourist can save a few pesos is utterly uninteresting, but whether business saves 3, 4, 5 percent that are currently appropriated by oligopolistic banks is all-important. Interestingly, par clearing could be done even in the current system. It has to do with denying banks large and variable margins on check clearing; it has nothing to do with exchange rates! Obviously, Brussels is reluctant to take on the banks—more so if they are aware of the furor created by this issue in the context of the Fed creation—and is interested in creating a retail constituency for an exaggerated view of the benefits of one currency.

As to currency volatility, there is a very nasty issue to contend with. Will there be more volatility between "ins" and "outs" than in the current regime? If so, is it possible that the minor gains in extra stability of the DM-franc rates is more than offset by the increased volatility of rates to the outside? If so, trade integration may be captured by the "ins" at the expense of the "outs" and of the rest of the world, from Eastern Europe to the United States. For Europe, the volatility issue is overdone in any event. There is little evidence that currency volatility, small as it has been, is an impediment to trade. As a result, reduced volatility between the "ins" will not change much the landscape of trade and investment in Europe. In the meantime, though, it can be used as a scare factor for countries like Britain to be in or to be really out.

There is the further question of whether, governed by one money, Europe will just do better. The French view is emphatically positive: if Italy cannot devalue anymore, they can not steal French jobs. Ergo, one money is great. Of course, that is an extraordinary fallacy. At issue is the *real* exchange rate, exchange rates adjusted for costs. If the nominal exchange rate cannot change, but for equilibrium the real rate must change, expect wages and prices to do the work. The French may be right to believe that it is far more difficult to make adjustments by deflation rather than devaluation. But that is small comfort.

In countries with highly flexible wages, the exchange-rate regime makes no difference. In countries where labor markets do not function well, flexible rates are all-important. European monetary integration heads straight for the weakest spot. The greatest criticism of EMU lies precisely here: if there is one market in Europe that functions awfully, it is the labor market. Yet, as EMU abandons exchange-rate adjustments, it moves precisely to the labor market the task to accomplish adjustments in competitiveness and relative prices. Without wage flexibility, the adjustment process is frustrated, and stress on output and employment (and pressure on the Euro to inflate) will predominate.

The overriding cost of an integrated monetary area is that nominal exchange rates disappear as an adjustment mechanism. If a region goes into decline, say because its exports become obsolete, deflation has to take the place of devaluation. If a region goes into boom, say because it has superior research and education, and results in superior trade performance, inflation takes the place of appreciation.

Exchange rates as an adjustment tool have a good history (Mexico and Latin America notwithstanding). Forcing adjustment into the labor market (again, the poorest performing of all markets in Europe) is bound to be a very unsuccessful strategy. In backward regions, unemployment will accumulate together with social problems and complaints about the benefits of integration. Abandoning exchange rates as a tool requires putting something else in place; the promoters of Maastricht have carefully avoided spelling out just what that might be. Competitive labor markets is the answer, but that is a dirty word in social Europe.

EMU and Sovereignty

The creation of European Monetary Union is not a natural part of a process of trimming sovereignty in favor of a broader European process; it is not a first step, with foreign policy and defense naturally following soon. On the contrary, depoliticized money is the ambition everywhere around the world. Accordingly, creating an independent central bank in New Zealand or Chile is mostly the same as creating an ECB. Money must not be democratic or else it is bad money; for that reason, as is the case in Germany, money must be taken out of the hands of legislators, whose horizons are short and whose motives are suspect, and has to be entrusted to conservative managers with long horizons, accountable only for the quality of results achieved.

In the ECB setting, money management is removed from national authorities, even where it is already institutionalized in an appropriate way, as in Germany, and is simply moved one layer up to a Europe-wide level. For many European countries that is the only way in which the Central Bank can be liberated from political influences—move it out of town, literally. In others it is merely a lateral move from one independent body, which currently shadows Germany, to another, which subsumes Germany. But the point is, good central banking is *apolitical* and the more it is so, the better it gets. That is what the ECB is all about. And that is why it is not a transfer of sovereignty but a Europe-wide abdication of sovereignty over the issue of money.

This is, of course, quite unlike defense or foreign policy, which are intrinsically political. In this area, the issue is how to reconcile conflicting national objectives, views, traditions, or cultures. In the area of money, we all want the same, stable money. In defense and foreign policy, we broadly want peace (most of the time), but that is where agreement ends. Hence the transfer of sovereignty means giving up something real and precious; giving up nationally (mis-)managed money is just kicking a bad habit! The difference could not be bigger.

What to Expect from the ECB?
Italians dream that the ECB will make their life easier than the Buba now; for Germans that is the nightmare that keeps them awake. The fears are unjustified; on the contrary, the new central bank is certain to establish itself at the outset as an immediate continuation of the Buba, the current pillar of European monetary orthodoxy.

This result is assured by the narrow rules of the game, but even more so by two other facts. First, once people are on the board of a Central Bank, in the spotlight of public attention, they immediately turn conservative. It happens routinely to Federal Reserve members and it will happen just the same to those new ECB board members. In fact, in the nomination process, governments will be scrutinized for the choices they make. A lightweight nomination backfires by creating a bad impression and by being certain to carry no weight in the new institution; by contrast, an important personality, distinguished in monetary management and conservative as is called for by the appointment, will be well-received and bound to be influential. With these considerations in mind, there will be serious attention rather than routine patronage in the appointments. The ECB is likely to be an assortment of conservative people.

But that is not enough. The chairman of the new board is all-important. With no precedent in place, the chairman charts the course. If, as now seems likely, Wim Duisenberg of the Netherlands Central Bank heads the ECB, the assurance of all-out hard money is written in stone. After all, it is Duisenberg who has on occasion expressed the fear that Germany could turn soft! It is Duisenberg who shows irritation to the point of anger when challenged on disinflation beyond the reasonable.

It is obvious the ECB will be off to a "good start," if that is measured by holding interest rates high and inflation low. The trouble is this: Europe by that time may be in deep trouble. Budget cutting on an accelerated pace combined with tough central banking from here to January 1999—Tietmeyer's farewell will not be gracious—and beyond spell trouble. Most unfortunately, central banking in Europe does not buy into the concept that budget cutting requires accommodating monetary policy. That means Europe from here to 2000 cannot expect much growth. Europe's new money, far from creating prosperity, may in the end be blamed for a period of poor performance.

A lot of criticism focuses at present on the simultaneous fiscal trimming in Europe and the attendant risk that Europe will fall into recession. That charge is wrong in two ways. First, Maastricht is a wonderful excuse for doing what needs to be done anyway. Europe has vast deficits, high debt, an unaffordable and inefficient public sector, and an equally bad welfare system. Moreover, Europe has vast unfunded public liabilities. Sharp restructuring of public finance is necessary, Maastricht or not. If Maastricht is a good excuse, let's use it. Moreover, fiscal trimming need not beget recession. On the contrary, if the central banks accommodate by easing monetary policy, growth can go on harmoniously and unimpeded. Of course, if central banks misread their role, deficit cutting winds up with a debacle and EMU will be blamed for it.

A Better EMU

In setting up the Maastricht criteria, policymakers focused on avoiding pollution of the central banks' objectives by the weakness of member countries' fiscal positions. High debt and deficits, in this perspective, are an invitation to monetization and "inflating away" of fiscal problems; in the extreme, treasuries go right to the Central Bank to be accommodated. The separation of treasuries and central banks is entirely appropriate. As important is the emphasis on fiscal adjustment, if only because of the vast unfunded pension liabilities that are now on the horizon. But it is also true that the precise reasoning that screens out high debt and deficit countries—they are a threat to the integrity of the ECB—can be used for high unemployment countries. In high unemployment countries, plausibly, policymakers will turn to the Central Bank to seek help—a bit more money, a few more jobs! The incentive problem is just the same as inflationary accommodation of jobs, for inflating away debt is like inflating away unemployment. Neither may work, but the attempt or the expectation of an attempt will be outright counterproductive.

The implication, surely, is that EMU should include an explicit unemployment threshold. Countries with more than say 6 percent structural unemployment cannot be members. They first have to undertake the structural and macroeconomic policies (including freeing up regulations, reducing excessive benefits, etc.) so that unemployment comes down to levels that are not a threat to the ECB.

If Maastricht were structured that way, it would bring about a transition phase of a supply-side revolution. Countries would be falling all over themselves creating jobs by deregulation instead of destroying jobs by taxation. Unfortunately, even though the logic is impeccable, Europe's good economics does not go all the way to the labor market.

Europe as the Weak Link

At a time when Europe is facing reality—abolishing the welfare state, reintegrating millions of unemployed into a normal working life, deregulating statist-corporatist economies, cultivating the supply side, integrating the East—the experiment with a new money is a bad idea. Per se, the new money creates insignificant benefits at best, but it adds crisis

potential, it frustrates adjustment, and it displaces pragmatic cooperation. Viewed from outside, a common money is an experiment that is
deeply misdirected. All energy and political capital are required to make
the important reforms in the real economy; assurance of even harder
money—or money at least as hard as today's DM—are out of place. They
make Europe one of the weak links in the world economy.

Outside commentary, especially from the United States, is routinely
written off as sour grapes. Back in the 1980s, Europe moved to monetary
integration to create a counterweight to a financially unstable United
States. But Europe also built a deep economic union, challenging the U.S.
hegemony in the world—eat your heart out! It does not quite look that
way from here. The United States did emphatically approve of the European customs union and the internal market even if they meant trade diversion away from the United States. The view has always been that
anything that avoids European wars is a good idea. Common money is
not a threat to the dollar. Imagine that the dollar goes down as a result
(note, the United States is financially stable, with lower debts and deficits
than Germany); then all it means is that the United States is more competitive and Europe less. That is not exactly a U.S. problem!

Instead, the U.S. fears about EMU are these: it could become a really
gigantic screw-up and whenever that happens, Europe gets into political
trouble and that is always expensive for the world. Of course, Europeans
with their rose-tinted Euro-glasses do not see that prospect. The U.S.
skepticism comes from seeing that tying up currencies just forces the adjustment into other directions: high interest rates and high unemployment. Having seen that story when the dollar got overvalued in the
1960s, the United States has never found excitement in fixed exchange
rates. Watching the recurrent currency crises in Europe in the 1980s
merely reinforces the prejudice. The United States has substantial flexibility both in wages and labor market institutions. With such arrangements it is conceivable to enter fixed exchange rates. Europe, having
neither flexible wages nor functioning labor markets, already has mass
unemployment. EMU will only add to it on the way there, once the system is fully trapped in fixed rates across vastly divergent countries. If
there was ever a bad idea, EMU qualifies.

25

EMU: Will It Happen, Will It Not, and What Difference Does It Make?

European Monetary Union (EMU) is almost certain to happen in the next decade and, quite likely, on schedule starting January 1, 1999. (At this point, our bet is 65 : 35 in favor of timely EMU.)

The anti-EMU sentiment may already have peaked in part because of Chancellor Kohl's decision to run for another term, and his restatement of commitment to timely EMU. In part, European economies are on the upswing, and with this comes a more positive view of European initiatives.

Timely EMU is, however, not a foregone conclusion. Two stumbling blocks need watching. First, Chancellor Kohl is far behind in the polls, and even an upswing is unlikely to change the difficult atmosphere. If the opposition singles out EMU as a campaign issue, Kohl may be forced to declare "stability first" and ditch EMU.

Even if Kohl strongly supports timely EMU, he may run into problems because of Italy, Spain, and Portugal. In German public opinion, these countries are not considered "serious" partners even though on inflation and budget data they bring the same results as Germany. If they, and notably Italy, are unwilling to accept late entry, EMU may well be an overriding liability.

Finally, a generalized fudging of numbers is under way to bring all potential member countries at least close to the 3.0 percent of GDP maximum deficit. The debt criterion has already been moved aside, using a Maastricht Treaty formulation that waives the hurdle if "enough" progress is being made in the direction of a 60 percent debt ratio. The fudging and neglect of the debt criterion open the possibility that a

Excerpt from a paper written with Francesco Giavazzi of Bocconi University.

decision to move ahead will be challenged in the German courts or rejected by the German parliament.

Suppose EMU Does Not Happen in Time

If EMU does not happen in time, what are the consequences? We firmly expect that the maintained policy is to ultimately have the EMU—this is a political project and as such it has wide support even if the modality and timing create problems. Accordingly, the authorities will be sure to structure a plausible timetable that puts matters off for say two years, not six. We also would expect an EMS-style cooperation agreement to limit the fallout: an EMS-2 is already in place.

It is a mistake to believe that a breakdown of the strict timing of EMU would immediately lead to bad policy among the usual suspects. Around the world, bond markets have become the disciplinarians of policy. Maastricht may have been a good excuse for making major strides— and strides were made, notably in Italy—but without Maastricht the same and perhaps even more would have happened simply because the countries that are fiscally most vulnerable are especially vulnerable with respect to interest rates. Hence, quite independently of Maastricht, they would have been forced to make their peace with the market. The bureaucratic insistence of the Maastricht Treaty has unfortunately obscured this important mechanism.

In the meantime, while the back and forth about EMU happening goes on, there is a predictable impact on the dollar: EMU is associated with a strong dollar. That is the case at least until it is clearer as to who is in and out and what the ECB looks like.

Back to Assuming EMU Happens in Time

The decision to go ahead will be made formally during the weekend of May 8–10, 1998. The last word rests with the European heads of state— ironically, in a meeting that will take place in the United Kingdom and will be chaired by the prime minister of Britain, an unlikely member of the EMU. If the decision is affirmative, the immediate question arises as to what the conversion parities will be. If parities are announced—for example, the present central EMS parities—there is an issue of how to defend them between May and December, and how to avoid last-day jumps in rates. An eight-month window of volatility and scope for mistakes opens up.

If EMU happens, it will include France and Germany. But initially it may well leave out some countries, say Italy. What transition arrangements are likely to limit the consequences? The most plausible arrangement is to guarantee the Italian exchange-rate band conditional on Italian monetary and fiscal performance. Not easy and not uncontroversial! That is the kind of deal that broke down in 1992.

EMU brings with it a common monetary policy. This raises two questions. First, will the *Euro* be a good or bad money? We conclude that the EMU, without question, will be a hard money. In the past, Europe has followed the Buba, and the Buba has looked after Germany. In the future, the ECB will have to look after Europe, whatever that means. Second, how will monetary policy be conducted? At present, there is a dramatic difference in the channels of transmission of monetary policy as well in the responsiveness of inflation (expectations versus demand pressure) to monetary policy. The task to develop a monetary policy will be a time-consuming experimental task, and that may mean trouble.

In the bargaining to accommodate German opposition to a perceived "soft" EMU, the *Waigel pact* has gotten out of hand. There is now in place a mandatory, stiff penalty system that strikes deficits in excess of 3 percent of GDP even when these are cyclical. (The downturn must exceed a full 2 percent of GDP to get a waiver.) This system will force countries to bring down their deficits toward zero just to avoid the risk that a slowdown brings big penalties. The mechanism is fraught with conflict: if German inflation leads the ECB to raise interest rates and that slows Italy's economy, the Italians pay the penalties over and above the increased budget deficit that comes from higher rates affecting debt service and activity. (This is, of course, a replay of German unification in the early 1990s.) The Maastricht criteria have proven a headache, and the Waigel pact with its righteous and inadequate provision for cyclical factors is far worse.

A single money takes away exchange rates as an adjustment mechanism. In fact, the exchange rate has played no role for countries like France or the Netherlands for already a decade. Possibly, though, the creation of a common money has as a chief benefit the ability to highlight the extraordinarily poor functioning of labor markets. Even though European unemployment exceeds 10 percent, there is a consensus of official agencies that little room exists for noninflationary expansion! Now structural adjustment should move to center stage, but without a crisis there appears little disposition for that move.

The creation of a European money introduces an asset that is potentially a rival for the dollar. With ultimately large and broad markets in Euro assets, world diversification of portfolios will favor this asset at the expense of a present overloading in dollars. At the same time, of course, there is the emergence of a supply of assets in Euros so that the balance is far from obvious. Finally, cross-border diversification (including into dollar assets) is still only a small way to completion. On balance, there is no presumption of a strong Euro, weak dollar world. In fact, if the Euro were to prove strong, European employment problems would be worsened and that would feed back to monetary policy.

The Euro will force a totally unexpected degree of competition on European banking systems. Today markets are segmented and repressed with banks, institutionally by regulation and by currency denomination, that have very substantial captive business in lending, in deposits, and in distribution of securities. The Euro will hasten a competitive restructuring of the banking sector that is overdue in any event. Since some national banking systems are exceptionally weak, this will not go without strain.

Today European financial markets are oriented along country lines— French bonds, French stocks. With the creation of a Euro capital market and with a disappearance of national policies as a dominant factor in security valuation, a massive restructuring is certain to emerge. Stocks, for example, will be priced by industry and within industry, not by country. Bonds of countries, local governments, or companies will be priced on a credit quality basis.

The EMU will make the European Union the single largest financial market in the world. It complements the customs union and internal market initiatives to create a vast market without borders. Since the starting point, notably in finance, is a segmented and financially repressed set of economies, the change is formidable. Even if the EMU does not happen, the forces of competition now under way will accomplish much of this integration. A common money, however, will speed up the process dramatically.

With EU expansion to the East, the Euro will become increasingly the money of Eastern Europe, including in those countries that may not join and today rely substantially on the dollar. What the dollar is to Latin America, the Euro will be for Eastern Europe. Argentine-style currency board schemes around the Euro are highly plausible. The implication would be a shift in international finance and the dollar.

No Return?

The lack of flexibility that comes from the absence of exchange rates, a joint monetary policy, and stringent fiscal rules is rife with conflict. Is this not an invitation for a breakup? Indeed, EMU may disintegrate exactly as the Bretton Woods system did. If for some country the outcome involves too little discipline on inflation and too much exposure to shocks that could be offset by flexible rates, then opting out becomes attractive. Weak countries cannot do this since they would face a formidable confidence penalty. Strong countries can, as Germany did in leaving the dollar in the early 1970s. But that is not easy: a single currency is very different from a system of fixed exchange rates. Abandoning the Euro will be much more difficult than giving up Bretton Woods. Moreover, European Union increasingly is a political project.

And the UK?

We firmly expect the new Labor government to join the EMU the moment the project looks good. There is division in Britain, but there is also a presumption that being part of various European ventures has been highly productive. Once EMU enthusiasm comes on, Britain will join, and that may be as early as 1998.

Implications for CitiBank

The transition to a monetary area will create a vast new financial market; the pieces are there today, but financial repression and lack of cross-border competition are stifling opportunities. Whether EMU happens or not, a European financial market is coming and its size will be huge.

Table 25.1
Comparative Size (billion $US)

	GDP	Stock Market Capital-ization	Debt		Bank Assets	Total
			Total	Public		
EU(15)	8,427	3,779	8,673	4,814	14,818	27,270
United States	7,254	6,858	11,008	6,712	5,000	22,865
Japan	5,144	3,667	5,326	3,450	7,382	16,375

Source: IMF.

Basically everything in European finance will undergo a restructuring comparable to what has been under way in the United States. Market shares will be severely challenged, and the new distribution is likely to be far away from the preset one simply because the national factor, with the Euro and deregulation, will have become far less significant. In this Schumpeterian process, everything will be up for grabs: consumer banking, corporate banking, underwriting, distribution of securities, *Euro*-trading—all will get a Euro-structure. The benefits of a wide and deep European capital market have been widely advertised by the proponents of a single market and the Euro; the fallout of the competition has received scant notice so far.

The perception of this competition happening is just sinking in, but no players have positioned themselves to be the main actors. The Euro market is surely the next battleground for international banking. Anyone who does not play a key role there cannot possibly aspire to be among the top world players.

The French government has mandated that all markets have to function in Euro as of January 1, 1999. This strategic move lays out a claim for Paris as a financial center and forces French financial institutions to position themselves early to prepare the ground and stake out territory in the new market. The opposite risks being the case for U.S. institutions, where skepticism about the Euro translates into procrastination. This is surprising since the transformation of Europe into a U.S.-style financial market ought to give U.S. institutions a special expertise and advantage in operating in that environment.

26

If the Franc Falls, So Will Europe's Dream of a Common Currency

While Germany runs its tight-money strategy, the rest of Europe is on the receiving end, with one currency after another weakening in the knees and collapsing. Now it's the franc's turn. The French government has vowed not to yield: that however fierce the attack, it will keep the franc glued to the mark.

But other governments have made the same vow, to no avail. Their currencies have gone soft, and so will the franc. And when the franc has gone, those few remaining will be on the line: Denmark's and then Belgium's, until no currency is left in place but a lonely, strong, overvalued mark. Dreams of a common money will be shattered; bitterness and recrimination will take their place.

Few countries have withstood the hard-currency test since exchange-rate turmoil struck in September, when the French and the Danes were voting on a common European currency. The lira went down at the slightest probe; the pound sterling fell after $35 billion was lost in a futile defense; and Sweden practiced astronomical interest rates for a few months, then threw in the towel. France will follow suit, before the Mar. 21 election or just after.

The conventional wisdom is that Europe's widening slump and the currency crisis are the fault of the German Bundesbank, known to currency mavens as "Buba." And the immediate reason for the turmoil would seem to be Buba policy. If German interest rates were low, every-

Originally published in *Business Week* (29 March 1993): 18. Reprinted with permission.

body would have low rates—German rates plus a little bit. But since German rates are high, everybody else's are high—Germany's plus quite a bit—and that's too much to take, if it lasts.

"Not Just Yet"

Now that the currency pressure and high interest rates have been on for almost half a year, everybody wants relief. Nobody has any patience left for the Buba's "not just yet" attitude. As currency defense has become the routine, growth has evaporated. Last year was poor for business; this year is worse. Next year barely promises recovery—and that's the optimistic scenario.

Should we blame the Bundesbank for all this? For some the answer is obvious. After all, it sets interest rates that nobody can match for any length of time, and it has turned its own inflation fight into a Europe-wide slump. It is the pressure of mounting recession, not the credibility of the central bank that has brought down recent wage settlements to 3 percent or just above.

But the 1993 wage round is not over until May. Giving up now would mean that inflation will linger on, as will slow growth. Later in the year, once moderate wage settlements establish a safe prediction of low inflation for 1994, the Buba can declare victory and cut interest rates to 5 percent from more than 8 percent and open the doors for growth. Rather than accept a truce, the Bundesbank is right to fight on until inflation is quite dead.

France may understand the German game plan, but it is counter-productive from a French perspective. France feels it can't wait, and it has a point. The French need low rates now, to call off the speculators and the doubters. The franc is not overvalued: inflation is less than in Germany, the external balance shows a surplus, public finance is sound. But France is a Latin country, and that means the currency is always suspect (speculators like to take a bite, just to see if the coin is solid). And if one speculator hangs around, so will all. And if they all attack a currency, who's to say they can't bring it down?

Preposterous Plans

The answer for Europe is not a premature end to inflation-fighting in Germany. The answer must be an ambitious, joint commitment to currency cooperation. If the finance ministers in Germany and France declared their agreement to defend a fixed parity whatever the cost, the massive deterrence of such an accord would make the franc as good as the mark in a split second.

The blame for the franc crisis cannot be put on the Bundesbank, which has to fight inflation until it is dead. The responsibility must be placed on the politicians in Germany and France, who have been unwilling to say which parities deserve all-out support. The leaders have ignited the speculation by passing absurd monetary-integration schemes linking some currencies with no prospect of stability—those of Italy or Greece, say—to some of the hardest in the world. Maastricht, the European monetary-integration project planned for the end of the decade, has suddenly moved forward and is knocking at the door. If there is to be monetary integration between Germany and France, leaders on both sides must now underwrite the franc.

If the franc is allowed to fall, so will any prospect of monetary union between Germany and France. The French won't forgive the disgrace of the defeat, and the Germans, while they may gloat at having the hardest coin, will have missed the opportunity to create firm Franco-German cooperation. In the 1970s, France's Válery Giscard d'Estaing and Germany's Helmut Schmidt boldly created a scheme of monetary integration that was nothing short of a political masterstroke. In the next few weeks, leaders in these two countries must return to that Franco-German accord for inspiration.

27

Why the Mighty Mark Is a Sitting Duck

This will be the year when the mighty German mark comes under attack. Making big money by shorting the German currency will be like shooting fish in a barrel.

Forecasts for European growth in 1994 aren't optimistic—moderate growth of 1 percent at the very best. But that's an average, and it's misleading. Paradoxically, those countries that devalued because they couldn't stand the heat of the tough German monetary policy will do well. The rest are on the ropes, especially Germany itself.

In the late summer of 1992, speculators took on the soft European currencies and pounded them until the links with the German currency gave way. Major devaluations—28 percent for Spain, 22 percent for Italy, and 16 percent for Britain—were the result. Far from doing irreparable damage to the financial reputations of the devaluing countries, the speculators did them a huge favor: along with a major gain in competitiveness, interest rates came down sharply. In an otherwise stagnant Europe, these countries' export sectors are paragons of growth and prosperity.

So the soft-currency countries are the winners. The countries that were on the currency speculators' hit list in 1992 have now turned into strong prospects for growth, while those with the toughest central banks and hardest currencies are heading for another recession. France and Germany may enjoy taking pride in their undefeated currencies, but their economies are failing to take off. Budget problems, a continuing obsession

Originally published in *Business Week* (7 March 1994): 30. Reprinted with permission.

with tight money, and a devastating loss of competitiveness keep them grounded. In the face of ever-rising unemployment, already 12 percent in France and headed upward, business confidence remains stagnant or worse.

Few Hours

Germany's problems go beyond those of an ordinary downturn. It is not just that the federal budget is tightening even in the midst of a recession. Far worse is the problem of restructuring an overweight and overpaid industrial sector. With the average factory worker's pay and benefits at $24 an hour—compared with $15 in the United States—German industry is uncompetitive. Not only are wages too high, but the Germans work fewer hours than those in other major industrial powers. Without overtime or multiple shifts, even machinery there gets more time off. The early eighties cachet of masterful engineering and unquestionable quality is no longer enough. Quality has become another commodity—even the Americans can do it. Moreover, one can buy two Americans cars for the price of a similar German one. Even if the first one breaks down, forget it and use the second one.

For a time, the crisis in German industry was masked by a series of surprises that kept order books filled. First, up to 1985, the grossly overvalued dollar allowed Europe to sell virtually anything, no questions asked. Then came the boomlet of Europe '92—with its great expectations, confidence, and talk of the advent of a European century. Even before the bubble burst, on top of an already overemployed European economy, came German unification. Thanks to a $100 billion-a-year West German fiscal expansion to bring East Germany into the modern economic world, demand for German goods skyrocketed.

Sinking Together

Today, those booms are history. The dollar has collapsed, and U.S. companies have restructured to compete. Europe is in recession, German unification by now is disillusioning and troublesome—certainly no consumer spree. In addition, those competitive devaluations of the soft-currency countries have cut into German exports and rendered the German domestic market vulnerable to foreign competitors. Little surprise, then, that German companies have hastened to downsize—that forbidding American euphemism for payroll reduction. Hitherto, eliminating jobs has been taboo in Germany. Now, there is a rush to press forward with restructuring, and scarcely a day passes without news of a major cutback: 10,000 workers here, 20,000 there. Only the unemployment office works overtime.

For Germany and those countries with currencies linked to the mark—France, the Netherlands, Belgium, and Austria—1994 will indeed be the Year of the Dog. Unemployment will rise, confidence will fall; a double-dip recession is the most likely course. The problem is worsened by a monetary policy caught between the risk of recession and a collapse of the currency. To keep the mark from plunging against the dollar, or at least to keep it treading water, interest rates can't come down. But the longer they stay high, the deeper the drop in confidence.

German interest rates must come down a lot, sooner or later. U.S. interest rates are on the rise as the economy moves toward full employment. As the differential between the two rates narrows, the mark will become the currency speculators' next target. Selling marks short becomes the gamble of the year. The good news is this: the sooner the speculators make their killing, as in 1992, the sooner Germany and Europe can turn to easy money and growth. That seems sure to happen in 1994, so growth can follow in 1995.

28
Europe's Money: Implications for the Dollar

The decline in the U.S. net international creditor status, the sharp loss in international competitiveness, and the relative decline of U.S. financial institutions, both in terms of size and stability, all mark a watershed for the dollar as the dominant asset in world finance. Monetary and financial integration under way in Europe point clearly to a new world financial scene where a European asset will emerge that is at least rival to the dollar, if not dominant. Integration in Europe promotes this new asset by a three-pronged approach: the creation of an integrated financial area, monetary integration, and the creation of a Europe-wide payments mechanism.

If European integration gives rise to a well-regulated and inflation-stable asset, and if U.S. financial performance continues to deteriorate, then there will clearly be problems for the dollar, and these difficulties will exacerbate the difficulties of adjustment in the U.S. economy in the 1990s.

European integration in the area of money, finance, and the payments mechanism are far from accomplished. The details are not even decided, and the question of the accompanying political integration remains unresolved and controversial. But even so, pragmatic progress in the direction of integration has been under way for a decade and is irreversible. The attraction of this area of financial stability for the periphery is clearly indicated by the recent decisions in Finland, Sweden, and Austria to adopt EMS-pegged exchange-rate regimes. With the growth in intra-European

Testimony before the Subcommittee on Domestic Monetary Policy, U.S. House of Representatives, July 25, 1991.

trade, finance, and politics, the central role of the dollar in world finance is being eroded.

If this prediction is correct, a number of questions emerge. First, what are the costs to the United States (if any) of losing monetary hegemony? The conclusion here is that the costs are unlikely to be important. The chief reasons are two: U.S. institutions do not have an exclusive franchise on doing dollar-denominated business, and U.S. dollar-denominated liabilities today are interest-bearing, so that the gains from their issue are insignificant. In other words, nobody is doing us a favor by holding our debts.

The second question is: do we need special policies (and which) to cushion the fall from supremacy? Specifically, should the United States try to forestall the course of events by a major international currency proposal? The answer here is emphatically no. We should stay with flexible exchange rates and avoid ending up with an overvalued currency as a result of a misled emphasis on having a hard currency.

Dollar Dominance

The predominant position of the dollar in world finance is represented by its use as a "vehicle currency." Trade is invoiced in dollars; world trade is financed with dollar credits; dollar balances are held by corporations worldwide; dollar instruments are held by official agencies, by banks abroad, and by institutional and individual investors. Cross-border lending, sovereign and private, is dollar-denominated. Dollar cash serves as stable money throughout Latin America, in Poland, in Asia, and in the underground worldwide.

It is clear that none of these functions is performed *exclusively* by the dollar. Some trade is invoiced in yen or in DM or even in sterling. Credits for trade financing or cross-border lending do also take the form of DM or yen loans. But even today, after dollar weakness and nearly twenty years of floating exchange rates and an increasing net debtor status for the United States, the dollar predominance remains. In part, it is merely a reflection of the relative size of the U.S. economy. The United States is by far the largest economy in the world. The closest rival, Japan, does not come close to offering competition.

Table 28.1
Economic Size (share of world GNP)

Industrial Countries		Developing Countries	
Europe	29.6	Africa	2.2
Japan	15.3	Asia	7.2
United States	27.1	Europe	6.0
Canada	2.7	M. East	2.6
		L. America	5.7
		E. Europe	1.6
		USSR	4.0

Source: IMF, *World Economic Outlook.*

Moreover, the U.S. capital market is wide open to cross-border transactions without control or red tape; exchange controls have never existed in this century; clear legal processes apply in a U.S. jurisdiction; competition and efficiency make for low transactions costs. No other financial market has the sheer size, the variety of instruments, the degree of competition, and the international openness. Hence the predominance. The closest rival, Japan, cannot offer these advantages. There is not only its much smaller size, but also clannish restrictions on competition, especially by foreigners, exchange control until very recently, and uncertainty about Japan's long-term role in relation to the Western world. These factors stand in the way of the confidence required for a major international role of the yen. That is not to say that Japan does not have deep pockets, but it does limit the role of Japan's capital market and the yen as an international asset.

Europe's Competition

A poll of 1,036 European business leaders conducted in 1988 showed that 86 percent (ranging from 60 percent in Germany to 98 percent in Italy and France) favored a common currency. A majority of those queried (from 52 percent in Germany to 87 percent in France) favored a currency unit that represents an average of the EC currencies, such as the ECU, rather than a single currency.[1] The Delors Report (14–15) has pushed the discussion much further, defining the issues and the agenda:

A monetary union constitutes a currency area in which policies are managed jointly with a view to attaining common macroeconomic objectives. As already stated in the 1970 Werner Report, there are three necessary conditions for a monetary union:

• the assurance of total and irreversible convertibility of currencies
• the complete liberalization of capital transactions and full integration of banking and other financial markets
• the elimination of margins of fluctuations and the irrevocable locking of exchange rate parities

The first two of these requirements have already been met, or will be met with the completion of the internal market programme. The single most important condition for monetary union would, however, be fulfilled only when the decisive step was taken to local exchange rates irrevocably.

The developments in Europe open up genuine possibilities for a competitor to the dollar. Over the past decade, Europe has evolved into a hard currency region, centered on the deutsche mark. The initial commitment was mostly a device for Germany to avoid sharp appreciation relative to its chief trading partners. For the weaker currencies, the EMS was a means to cut inflation by a tough stance on exchange rates.

Realignments in the EMS have become increasingly infrequent and membership, formal or informal, has been spreading. Until 1986 there were basically annual realignments involving most currencies. Since then there have only been three realignments and none in the past eighteen months. Thus exchange rates have became far firmer.

A further development in this direction has been the narrowing of margins in the EMS. Countries like Spain that had no specified margins adopted commitments, countries like Italy that had wide margins have narrowed them, and ambitious countries like Belgium have narrowed their margins to less than 1 percent. Countries outside the community, notably Scandinavia and Austria, have started pegging their currencies to the EMS. The fact then is that Europe has become a center of gravity and that the stable DM-franc relation is the center of that emerging block.

Against this background further institutional integration is now being planned. This integration falls into three areas:

• *The creation of a common European money managed by a European Central Bank.*   So far there is only a system of fixed exchange rates. But the transition to the more ambitious scheme is already quite far advanced.

The blueprint for a Central Bank is ready, and the intergovernmental conference to change the EC Treaty is scheduled. The chief question concerns the exact timing, or the exact preconditions, for the move from the current informal fixed rate system to a single money. We return to this issue below.

• *The need for par clearing.*   Having a single money does not in and of itself deliver an efficient payments mechanism. The experience in the United States prior to par clearing makes that clear. A well-functioning payments mechanism requires that checks across borders clear at par within a specified time period. Today checks in Europe take an extraordinary long period to clear, and the fees at which conversion is effected are extortionary. As a result, the payments mechanism is cumbersome and an obstacle to trade. Par clearing is certainly going to be a byproduct of common money, and it may even come before, as an aspect of the internal market. Once par clearing takes place, European money becomes, of course, a highly useful money.

• *Under the heading of the "internal market" program, cross-border liberalization of financial services is taking place.*   It is expected that increased competition will reduce dramatically the transactions costs for all kinds of financial transactions, from insurance and underwriting to interest costs on consumer loans. Among the efficiency gains to be derived from the internal market, the improvement in financial efficiency counts for two-thirds of the benefits.

With the financial integration will come inevitably the creation of new financial assets that exploit the large scale of the new European capital market. The creation of a European commercial paper market and of a broad market for public debt will not take long. Because of the economic size behind the market, and the competition allowed and encouraged, the assets are bound to be rivals to dollar-denominated securities. And the markets that emerge will be important competitors to U.S.-located financial markets.

The European Transition

A full European financial integration is not easy to achieve. Politically it is attractive, but economically, although divergences have narrowed, they do persist. Monetary integration is often interpreted in terms of the loss of independence of monetary policy and the creation of joint monetary institutions. But realism requires one to recognize that there is no longer independent monetary policy in Europe. The only question is whether exchange rates are or are not fixed. And that has little to do with monetary policy, but is rather a question of wage behavior and fiscal policy. With capital movements fully liberalized and exchange margins shrinking, monetary policy will have to carry even more of a burden, at an even higher price to public finance.

In most European countries, the scope for significant monetary independence has basically vanished. Exchange-rate expectations are governed by accumulated imbalances and loss of competitiveness, by political squabbles about who "makes" inflation and who "suffers" from it, not by short-run monetary policy. Monetary policy only serves to postpone exchange-rate crises, but it does so at an important cost to the budget. For most EMS members, monetary policy has basically become an instrument for managing the balance of payments, and only in the center country, Germany, is it devoted to setting the EMS inflation trend. Even in economies where there is no crisis in sight, there is invariably a concern for realignments in the system, and hence the possibility of any particular country staying with the average rather than with Germany. That in turn requires a level of interest rates that includes a premium for the remote risk of a depreciation.

Once it is recognized that monetary independence is gone and that exchange-rate realignments are costly, one can ask why countries would not go ahead and abandon the pretense altogether. In most cases the obstacles cited merely postpone, and without much justification, the necessary adjustments and the move to fixed rates. But that answer does not apply with equal strength to all EC countries. Some, like Greece, Portugal, or Spain, are far out of line with the rest and should therefore receive separate and differentiated treatment that may stretch over a number of years.

A more rapid implementation of a firmly committed exchange-rate policy is likely to be put in place for the core countries. To avoid the fiscal costs associated with exchange-rate uncertainty, governments in soft currency countries can pressure for increasing exchange-rate fixity. They can immediately discard exchange-rate margins altogether. This would signal a much stronger commitment to fixed rates. The strategy is attractive because it is already widely believed in Europe that monetary policy is no longer effective, except to provide financing for the external balance. European monetary policy is made in Frankfurt and any independence is not only an illusion, but is also expensive in terms of domestic debt service.

There is no need at this stage for any joint institutions to manage European money. Central Bank consultation, as it has occurred in the past two or three years, can assure continuing efforts at disinflation. But exchange-rate fixity must become more believed and for that purpose governments must take on bigger *actual* commitments. The more governments put at stake, the more credible their policy. The only issue is how to manage the transition. That problem will be just as difficult two, three, or five years from now. It will always be inconvenient to give up an option. But because governments retain the option, capital markets retain the risk premium. Recognition of this fact should lead governments to take the radical steps required to move within a short time span—less than a year—to a fully fixed rate.

In this spirit, the Netherlands, Denmark, or France should to fix their exchange rates *without any margin* to the DM. In the case of Italy, the occasion should be used for redenomination to eliminate the excess of zeros and achieve a simple 1 : 1 relation. How is such a system implemented? Three institutional arrangements of the payments mechanism help impose the fixed rate.

First, economic agents in the core group that has adopted zero margins should be allowed to write checks in any of the core group currencies. Second, banks in the core group countries must clear all checks at par, independent of origin or denomination. The provision of par clearing was an essential innovation associated with the Federal Reserve system. The fact of a currency area, already prior to the creation of the Federal Reserve, was not enough to create fixed rates between various cities. Third, central banks organize a core-group clearing system. These arrangements assure that rates are in fact fixed at par. The only departure would stem from confidence crises.

Once a pragmatic fixed-rate system has operated for a while, the transition to an institutionalized monetary system is far easier than it appears today. The point of describing the transition is to argue that this is where the problems are, not in the design of the institutions that ultimately protect the stability of money.

Costs to the United States

What are the costs to the United States of competition from a European money and an efficient European financial market? The costs come in several ways:

• The world demand for U.S. currency and bank balances held in dollars will decline, at least relative to a trend without these European developments. That implies a fall in the demand for the U.S. monetary base and hence a loss of seigniorage revenue.

The creation of a usable European money will divert demand away from dollars as the universal second (or first) hand-to-hand currency. Of course, in Latin America the dollar will still serve that function, but presumably much less in Asia or in Europe itself. Also as a store of value, for households in politically or economically unstable countries or for the underground, dollar balances now have competition.

It is very difficult to know just how much of the U.S. currency is held today abroad. It is even more difficult to know how much of a diversion toward the EMU might be expected. In the 1980s, the revenue from seigniorage was on average 0.37 percent of GNP for the monetary base and 0.32 percent of GNP for currency. Thus one is not talking of really big numbers. As a guess, with the development of an EMU, the seigniorage revenue might fall by 0.1 percent.

There is the additional question of a once-and-for-all shift out of U.S. currency into the ECU. For better or worse, such substitution never occurs from one day to the next, but rather follows a logistic curve. Thus an overnight collapse of demand for U.S. high-powered money is unlikely. In any event, total currency outstanding is only $250 billion. Suppose that one-third of that demand might be affected by currency substitution toward the EMU and that it were to decline by 50 percent; that still only represents a fall in demand of $31 billion. In terms of asset market shocks, that is a rather small magnitude. Table 28.2 shows the U.S. net external position to put the numbers in perspective.

There has traditionally been a concern with the possibility of a dollar overhang, especially in respect to foreign official holdings of dollar assets. The right view to take here is that the difference between corporate treasurers and the managers of foreign official reserve holdings has become minor. Both are out to make profits and weigh interest differentials

Table 28.2
U.S. Net Foreign Investment Position (billion $)

	1980	1990
Net U.S. Position	333	−412
U.S. Assets Abroad	922	1,764
Direct Investment	385	598
Foreign Assets in the US	542	2,176
Official Assets	176	370
Direct Investment	124	466

against capital gains or losses from exchange-rate movements. There is no overhang—today interest rates are just high enough to make official and private investors hold the outstanding stock of dollar securities. But, of course, these positions are by no means frozen. Safe-haven considerations might overnight lead to a massive shift into dollar assets. By contrast, loss of confidence in U.S. monetary management could bring about a flight out of U.S. assets in no time. There is no special concern for foreign official holdings of dollar assets if only because they represent today a small share of U.S. external liabilities.

• The second area where a U.S. loss might occur is in relation to the risk premium charged on dollar-denominated assets. Portfolio holders diversify their holdings to reduce risk. They will charge a premium for securities of which there is a larger quantity outstanding than belongs in a maximally diversified portfolio. If the creation of a European money creates an asset that reduces the demand for dollars, then an increased premium will be charged for holding dollar assets. The dollar area for which using dollars is the natural habitat will therefore experience an increase in the cost of capital. To some extent, this can be avoided by issuing EMU-denominated claims, but that will not be convenient for everybody. Hence some loss. Just how much is hard to know. Models based on portfolio diversification suggest a fraction of a percent. In the aggregate, that represents a substantial transfer away from the issuers of dollar denominated claims.

The reduced cost of capital has implications for banks that operate substantially in the EMU mode. Their privileged access to capital allows them to compete more effectively for good loans. The resulting improvement in their portfolios feeds back favorably to improve yet further their cost of capital. U.S. financial institutions whose habitat is the dollar will, as a result, experience a deterioration in their capital market position.

The reduced capital costs and the reduced costs of all financial services and transactions increase the competitiveness of European firms relative to those in the United States. Working in a more efficient financial system, and possibly in a more stable one, simply means higher competitiveness.

• The third area where losses will occur is in financial services. To the extent that U.S.-located financial industries have a privileged franchise for dollar business, the creation of rival assets and rival centers will cause a loss. The extent of this loss is hard to judge. In the first place, U.S. financial firms will actively participate in the European and worldwide business. But even so, the financial liberalization works primarily to increase the scope for European-located institutions.

• The fourth area involves the question of how the United States will be seen as a provider of stable money. It is one thing to have a rival; it is another if that rival produces a superior money. It is quite possible that in the 1990s there is a European money *and* that this money is like the DM and hence far better than the dollars. This kind of consideration could lead to a once-and-for-all shift away from the dollar. Such a shift in turn poses the question of how to respond to such a shift.

As a positive effect of European money, we can count the fact that this provides Eastern Europe with a plausible alternative to their own money. This will avoid Latin American-style hyperinflation and the accompanying social and economic problems.

How to Make the Best of It?

For the United States the chief question is what exchange-rate policy to adopt in the face of these European developments. There are two choices. One is to move aggressively for a system of fixed exchange rates, on a parallel track with the European monetary unification; the other is to maintain flexibility of rates as an important cushion.

In the fixed-rate option, as Europe is moving closer together, the United States is not allowing the North Atlantic gap to widen, but rather urging a narrowing in the style of Bretton Woods. This would require coordination of monetary policy between the European Central Bank and the United States. All the dilemmas of the 1960s would reemerge, more so if the United States has problems with growth and gets caught between the objectives of competitiveness and price stability. The greatest risk is that the fixity of exchange rates locks the United States into a level of competitiveness that is incompatible with growth. That risk is more realistic once budget cutting gets under way. Today's level of the dollar is far from competitive as an engine of growth.

The alternative is managed flexible rates. The managed part would involve accommodating shifts in the demand for *money* by coordinated, sterilized intervention. This is precisely the kind of sterilization required when current substitution is the issue. Beyond that accommodation of money demand shifts, exchange-rate policy should be such as to sustain full employment. That means a substantially improved budget, low real interest rates, and a cheap dollar. It would be a serious mistake to make the dollar extra hard at the expense of full employment. Such a policy would not last and would merely imply even higher interest rates and worsening problems of financial institutions.

Europe's money represents moderate bad news for the United States. The spillover effects to the United States in terms of direct losses in seigniorage or in business opportunities are clearly present, but as clearly are not really dramatic. The larger costs come from the appearance in world business and politics of a dynamic Europe and a staggering United States. The European developments therefore make it even more important to bring a cure to our basic problems—deficits, education, productivity, financial stability—that is best done by attacking the basics, not by opting for a hard exchange rate.

Note

1. These data are reported in "European Business and the ECU" published by the Association for the Monetary Union of Europe, Paris, October 25, 1988.

29

Fifty Years Deutsche Mark

Fifty years ago, on June 20, 1948, German monetary reform put an end to the Reichsmark, and pervasive liberalization turned stifling economic repression into a miracle of growth. Today, even as hard money celebrates its fiftieth anniversary in Germany, this is also the end of the Bundesbank as monetary leader of Europe: the Buba is dead, long live the ECB. Europe is at a crossroads just as significant as the 1948 decisions giving rise to the deutsche mark and the Buba.

Nobody knew in 1948 that the bold removal of price controls and the introduction of a new money could not make things much worse than the prevailing state of affairs: a war economy with controls and black marketeering, pervasive shortages, collapsing production, and a profound loss of confidence. Decontrol and monetary reform were an act of faith. Who could be sure that hyperinflation would not emerge, once again, as it had in the 1920s? U.S. General Clay, conscious of the risks, told then economics minister Ludwig Erhard: "Mr. Erhard, my advisors tell me your boldness is crazy." And Erhard replied: "General, my advisors say the same." The rest is history: the economic miracle was built on free market economics and on five decades of uncompromising pursuit of price stability.

The Record

The Buba has sustained price stability like no other central bank. If in Germany a DM's purchasing power of 1948 is down today to just a quarter, the purchasing power of a dollar is as little as 15 cents; Britain,

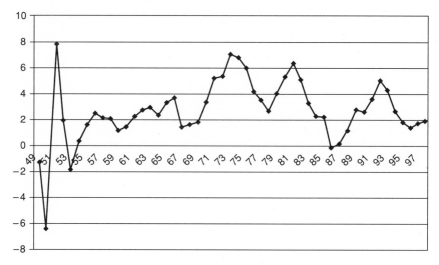

Figure 29.1
Germany: Inflation 1949–98

Italy, and France have done far worse. Even though the record is enviable, it is a lot less stellar than might appear. Over the past fifty years German inflation averaged 2.7 percent, not the 1 or 1.5 percent that has always been proclaimed as the goal. In only fifteen of the past fifty years was inflation actually in the blessed corridor between zero and 2 percent. (See figure 29.1.) Still, the record is enviable.

Of course, there is always an explanation: fixed exchange rates on the dollar in a world of overexpansion is the story of the 1960s, two oil shocks in the 1970s, and the unification shock at the beginning of the 1990s. Each is a good excuse for extra inflation and, in each instance, the Buba determinedly extinguished the fire. Could they have done better in terms of price stability? No doubt, but not without even higher unemployment. Sheer toughness would not have paid off in higher credibility and hence better results.

With a determined central bank, why has there not been all-out success? Surely the answer has to do with unions and the welfare state, of which Germany has an inordinate share. The Buba sets its money growth; the welfare state and the unions determine the split, and it always comes out as too much inflation and too little economic growth. One of the lessons of Buba history is surely that it takes two to foster credibility and performance: a tough central bank and a competitive economy.

The Legacy

Over the past fifty years, the Buba has written the primer in central banking. Three central points emerge: a stubborn message of a commitment to price stability, not day-by-day necessarily, but clearly as a trend. Next, monetary aggregates as the key commitment to price stability. And third, an untiring insistence on communicating to the public over and over again what the Buba can and does promise—price stability—and what it cannot bring about, such as full employment, high growth, and quick prosperity.

The ECB will do well to stay away from monetary targeting; even the Buba could barely hold up the myth of a stable relationship between money and prices. In fact, they took liberties in a way a tightly scrutinized ECB will not be able to. In the new EMU, there is no presumption of stable aggregates, more so as a deep process of financial restructuring creates an altogether different menu of monetary instruments. Like everywhere else, inflation targeting should be the conceptual framework and interest rates the key instrument.

The ECB will do well to learn from the Buba that political independence can only be gained if the public trusts the central bank more than the politicians do. (Remember the Buba staring down poor Waigel on the gold issue.) The Buba achieved that result by decades of thoughtful communication wherever the occasion arose, close to citizen groups from savers to bankers or scholars, by building a constituency in support of hard money. A traumatic monetary history gave the Buba a great backdrop against which to invoke the fears of inflation, but that does not diminish the accomplishment. This precedent will be hard to match. The Euro is repugnant to just about anyone in Germany, from economics professors to housewives, the aged and the clergy. The EMU is the creation of haggling and compromise, a political ambition more than a good idea in support of hard money. The ECB starts with a credibility deficit and therefore needs to make its case to the people; otherwise, the politicians will get to it.

Beyond the DM and the EMU

At the solemn ceremony in Frankfurt's Pauluskirche on June 20, more will be celebrated than just half a century of hard money in Germany. There is cause to celebrate the worldwide acceptance, at least on the part of central banks, that inflation is no answer to the problem of unemployment, not even in the short run. There is no European or American central banker or treasury official who has not at one point or another been driven to near-despair by the Buba's stubborn insistence to stay its course. They all have come on board. But convergence is not enough.

Today Germany and Europe are at the same crossroads they were in 1948—lack of confidence, lack of dynamism, and mass unemployment. Monetary stability enshrined in the ECB is not enough; financial stability from the Waigel pact does not complete the picture of a path to full employment and a dynamic economy. In 1948, the liberal model served well for reconstruction, job creation for millions of displaced persons, and rapid growth until the 1970s. The self-satisfied assembly that will the celebrate fifty years of hard money and convergence, from Kohl to Schroder, Lafontaine, and their status-quo European partners, needs another message from the same history book. Beyond the Euro, Erhard-style reforms are essential for another economic miracle in Europe.

30

Scenarios for Europe

It will take a while and it is not quite clear how we will get there, but a decade from now Europe will call the shots in the world economy. In the 1970s, the oil producers were at the top of the heap—it was just a few years before they would fully own the world. A decade later we were all on the verge of paying rent to the Japanese. Their discipline and saving earned them top grades, and their bubble wealth was buying them every piece of overpriced real estate around the world. And just now, or until a few weeks ago, the United States was tops with technology and top valuations and just being awesomely cool. It is obvious that now Europe's turn is coming. But the United States will get fat and lazy, asset prices will meet reality, the finance franchise will wear thin, and not saving a penny (even with a balanced budget) will become a problem. That is Europe's opening, first with a strong currency and ultimately with a deep restructuring of an economy that has as many problems today as it has genuine opportunities for tomorrow.

Nobody looking at the U.S. economy of the mid-1980s would have discerned the makings of a zero-inflation, balanced budget, full employment, and big time boom economy. The Japanese were talking about a lack of U.S. quality and technology, the Europeans were bemoaning the lack of saving, and U.S. gurus were looking offshore for magic recipes for superior corporate governance and management. In the same way, just now, it is hard to discern in Europe the very makings of a world champion. For those believing in the market, there is just plain too much socialism, from Jospin to Lafontaine, and there is too much corporatism everywhere. And then there is Brussels, which is all too easily seen as big government in the making, captured by every lobby that looks to limit competition.

But there are clearly other forces at work. European companies are furiously restructuring to reinvent themselves as global players. Governments everywhere have no money and hence are on the sidelines in shaping market developments. Brussels has, at least for now, a furiously anti-statist and pro-competitive commissioner in the person of Karel van Miert. More important, even the last person is getting the message that the government won't be able to do much for him and that it is getting time to look after himself. These new forces will put Europe at the top, not with a dramatic revolution, not in a year or two, but surely over the decade to come, piece by piece.

The Euro may play its part in all this. The big payoff on the Euro is, of course, in the capital market. Reinforcing financial deregulation and internal market measures that allow cross-border competition, the Euro creates the basis for a single-denomination European capital market of a potential size and depth comparable to the United States. It will move from the dull bank-based financing structure (almost as bad as the post office being your investment banker) to big-time debt markets and markets for corporate equities that offer transparency for the mismanaged or sleepy European companies. Capital markets are good at kicking butt, and that is just what European corporate giants need. The capital market also favors come-from-nowhere upstarts, and that is essential in Europe, where status quo has been the rule and Schumpeterian creative destruction the big taboo.

Europe has two great problems: pervasive regulation and inefficiency, including big and intrusive government on one hand and mass unemployment on the other. Ultimately these two formidable problems are also the key to Europe's shot at world championship. Abandoning a mindless welfare state where some people work and pay taxes so that other people can sit at home offers a prospect of years and years of high and noninflationary growth. There are at least 8 million people who can and should work. Deregulation and downsizing of government add the market environment in which new opportunities are opened up and new businesses will be formed everywhere. For every civil servant that loses his job and gets out of the way, two new jobs will be created by the market.

Europe is emerging from a decade of convergence: tight money, tight budgets, tight everything. True, that has created the financial environment in which European Monetary Union was a serious proposition rather than an irresponsible elopement. But now the time is ripe for a big deal: a Europe-wide major tax cut paid for by the very prosperity that it creates. Accompanied by jettisoning the welfare state, such a bid for prosperity creates the environment in which growth and change can go hand in hand.

VI
A Latin Disease? Or Triangle?

31
The Latin Triangle

In the process of inflation stabilization, the hardest part is how to handle the currency. When monetary and fiscal policy are turned sharply toward restraint, real appreciation of a flexible exchange rate is almost inevitably the result. That helps stabilization, but it builds up its own problems in due course. In a managed stabilization involving a pegged rate, incomes policy, and indexation, real appreciation emerges as a consequence of an excessive reliance on the exchange rate as a nominal anchor. From real appreciation it is not a far distance to overvaluation and from there, ultimately, to an exchange market crisis. For the most part, currency crises are not accidents. The question is why governments follow this hazardous road.

This chapter reviews the stabilization experience in three countries—Chile, Mexico, and Brazil—to elaborate on the emergence of overvaluation and determine what might have led governments to opt for the risks that they incurred.

A Framework

A starting point for the political economy of exchange rates is provided by placing the exchange rate in two contexts. The first is the link between the exchange rate, the standard of living, and internal and external balance. The second considers the exchange rate in the inflation process.

A link between the standard of living and the exchange rate comes from the real or consumption wage. The price of imports, for simplicity, is equated with the nominal exchange rate, E. Let the money wage and home prices in terms of the consumption basket be W and P. The home

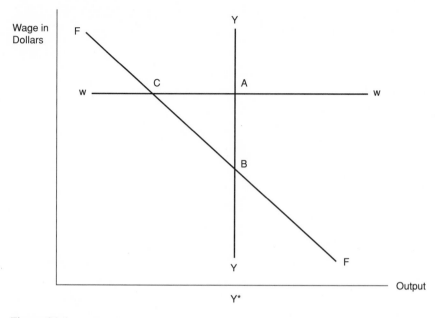

Figure 31.1
The Latin Triangle

price level is a function of import prices (E) and domestic output prices, which are equal to unit labor costs (aW). Thus we obtain a direct positive relation between the wage in dollars W/E and the standard of living. Real wages in terms of the consumption basket $(w \equiv W/P)$ can only rise if wages rise in dollar terms. In terms of domestic goods, given labor productivity, real wages are given.[1]

$$w = W/P(aW, e) = \varphi(W/e; a) \tag{1}$$

The consumption wage is a central political variable. In figure 31.1 we show the line ww along which there is social peace. Any level of the wage in dollars that is lower leaves labor dissatisfied and is tantamount to strikes, riots, or political unrest more generally.[2]

There are two more relations to be considered: along YY there is full employment. Any level of output below Y^* means unemployment, any higher level represents an excess demand in the labor market. There is also the external balance, FF. Points to the right and above FF show deficits: output and/or the level of wages in dollars is too high so that there is a trade deficit. Below and to the left of FF there are surpluses.

The typical political economy situation is one where the three schedules do *not* intersect, leaving us with the Latin triangle ABC. There is no equilibrium that balances the external accounts, achieves full employment, and at the same time leaves labor satisfied. Introducing a political constraint in the labor market thus creates, not surprisingly, overdetermination. Thus at point A there is full employment and social peace, but there is deficit on the external front. At point B external balance prevails with social peace, but there is unemployment. Finally, at point C full employment and external balance are assured, but social peace is not because the real wage is too low.

Suppose now some shock happens, political or economic. The target wage w rises, and the challenge is how to reconcile constraints and aspirations. The answer is to borrow (point A). The country runs policies to achieve a high level of output and a high real wage. External finance pays the bills. This may take the form of aid or of borrowing in world capital markets. One way or the other, disequilibrium is postponed.

The action only starts getting interesting when the money runs out. At some point adjustment becomes necessary. Moving to point C by devaluation is one answer. But the moment that happens, strikes and riots break out, wages adjust for the devaluation, and the economy moves back toward point A, but of course with a devaluation-inflation spiral that goes nowhere.

The alternative is an attempt to reduce spending, contract output, and move to point B. In this strategy, real wages are protected, but employment is not. Point B won't last long since the misery of unemployment creates its own political backlash. From there, sooner or later, the move is to point C. Output and employment do rise, but now the politics of real wage reductions come in. There is an extra complication in that the short-run response of output and employment to real wages may well be negative. True, a cut of wages in dollars raises competitiveness, but it may well reduce spending. There are income and substitution effects: lower real wages mean lower real income, and that reduces domestic demand. It may be more than offset, though not in the short run, by the substitution effects that shift demand toward domestic goods. Thus the move from A or B is highly dubious as a political proposition and hence will be postponed to the last minute and beyond.

One complication bears noting. As the economy stays at point A and postpones adjustment by drawing on external financing, it builds up debt. That creates an extra burden and an extra source of vulnerability. Accordingly, over time the FF schedule actually shifts down and to the left: it takes increasingly competitive wages or lower spending levels to create the surpluses that finance external debt service. Accordingly, a period spent at point A means that ultimately the sustainable real wage (point C) becomes much lower.

The framework shows why exchange-rate economics is so much a political theme. In a classical study of devaluation crises, Cooper (1971) found that finance ministers who preside over a devaluation almost universally fall: they end the dream, they create a mess. Of course, that conclusion is wrong; they are the unfortunate ones who are caught at the tail end of a period of economic mismanagement. Of course, often they themselves are responsible for building up the problem.

The inflation-depreciation linkage provides the other ingredient for our political economy setting. Inflation is a problem; reducing inflation is hard if there are no volunteers. The exchange rate becomes the seemingly costless option for pioneering disinflation. Slowing the rate of depreciation relative to the prevailing rate of inflation not only helps slow down inflation, but is outright popular since it raises real wages. Of course, it is a grave mistake not to look down the road and ask how the resulting overvaluation will be undone. More often than not, there is a currency crisis at the tail end of this story.

The inflation process is made up of wage increases, rises in public-sector prices, and exchange depreciation. In any significant inflation context, there are important elements of indexation. Thus wage inflation will be indexed to price inflation but will also depend on the level of unemployment. Public-sector prices will tend to be indexed and the exchange rate may or may not follow an indexation rule. As a result, the link between inflation and depreciation involves an accelerationist Phillips curve:

$$\Delta \pi = \alpha(e - \pi) + \lambda y \tag{2}$$

Here π is the rate of inflation, e the rate of depreciation of the currency, and y the output gap. The equation states that inflation accelerates whenever depreciation runs ahead of inflation or when output exceeds potential. If there is no output gap and the real exchange rate is constant, inflation is constant. To close the model we would need the determination of output. Here the real exchange rate and the real quantity of money as well as fiscal policy enter as determinants.[3]

The unpopular way to bring down inflation works on the demand side. The standard IMF program would reduce the growth rate of domestic credit, money growth, and hence spending. The sharp rise in unemployment would then translate into reduced wage inflation and ultimately lower inflation. All this is very unattractive. By contrast, trying to bring down inflation by slowing the rate of increase in public-sector prices is very popular. But it translates immediately into increased budget deficits. That is too obvious a problem. The same is true for attempts at price control. Here, too, the backlog is obvious. That leaves the exchange rate as the option.

Slowing down the rate of exchange depreciation reduces inflation in a number of ways. First, the direct impact on import prices of consumer goods and intermediate goods shows up in reduced price inflation and comes back from there, via indexation, as reduced wage inflation. But there are also extra effects: competition from lower inflation of import prices forces reduced inflation on domestic producers. Expectations of declining inflation foreshadowed by the reduced exchange depreciation spreads to forward-looking price formation. Through a variety of channels, reducing depreciation works to reduce price inflation just as Eq. (1) above suggests.

Over time, depreciating at a pace below the rate of inflation has two implications. First, inflation falls. Second, steadily the *real* exchange rate appreciates. When the disinflation objective is accomplished, a new problem has been created in the form of a substantial overvaluation. The counterpart of real appreciation is an external deficit and/or a domestic recession. If the overvaluation is financed by external borrowing and offsetting domestic fiscal expansion, unemployment may be negligible, but the deficit will be huge (point A in figure 31.1). If the financing is not there, domestic recession mirrors the external overvaluation (point B in figure 31.1 above).

One way or the other, bringing down inflation is *not* the end of the story; rather, it is the beginning of the next cycle. The surprise is that over and over again, governments take the course of seemingly least resistance: inflation is enemy #1, never mind overvaluation. Some case studies will bear out this proposition.

Case Studies

In this section, we report three case studies: Chile at the end of the 1970s, Mexico in 1990–95, and Brazil, still in the making. The cases have a few points in common: an effort to stabilize inflation in the context of a broader package of reforms. The programs share in particular two features: a trade opening process and renewed access to international capital markets.

Chile

Following the coup, the Pinochet government increasingly found its way to a comprehensive model of reform implemented by the *Chicago Boys*. The budget was balanced; privatization and deregulation, including trade opening, were to improve economic efficiency. Inflation stabilization was a paramount objective. By 1977 much of this had happened, growth was coming on big time, and an economic miracle was in the making. But inflation stubbornly continued, albeit at a far reduced rate.

In line with monetarist thinking of the time, the "law of one price" gained adherence among policymakers. In their thinking, there was a vicious circle of inflation and depreciation: depreciation took place in order to avoid a loss in competitiveness. But depreciation in turn raised prices and wages, which called for yet another round of depreciation and so on. It seemed plausible to stop the process by just halting depreciation, once and for all. In a highly competitive, open economy the impact on prices could only be this: a dramatic, immediate stop of inflation. Moreover, if expectations mattered, the fixed exchange-rate strategy—now we would call it a nominal anchor—could not fail but to stabilize the prospect of stability.

Table 31.1
Chile: Macroeconomic Indicators

	1977	1978	1979	1980	1981	1982
Growth	9.9	8.2	8.3	7.8	5.5	−14.1
Inflation	64	30	39	31	10	21
Curr. Acct	3.7	5.2	5.4	7.1	14.5	9.2

Note: Current account deficit as a percent of GDP.
Source: Dornbusch and Edwards (1994).

Accordingly, in 1978 the government moved to a fixed exchange-rate policy: 39 pesos/$U.S. forever.[4] In a dictatorship, "forever" has a more plausible ring than in an unstable democracy. Hence the experiment got under way with every expectation of success. And successful it was, for the time being.

Economic growth stayed high throughout 1978–80 and inflation came down substantially, though not to levels near price stability. An important reason for the slow phasing down of inflation was the presence of mandatory, backward-looking wage indexation. Even as the government fixed the exchange rate, it gave wage increases of 30 percent per year. Not surprisingly, price inflation was not very different. The Law of One Price was not working tightly.

Figure 31.2 shows the real exchange-rate index. It is apparent that a huge real appreciation developed. In terms of Eq. (2), with $e = 0$, the inflation process is such that the rate of real appreciation is equal to the rate of inflation, dampened by a cyclical factor. With inflation initially high and a boom on top, real appreciation was rapid and cumulatively very substantial. That process continued until the collapse in June 1982.

The impact on the real economy took a while. In part this reflects the impact of real appreciation on demand. The *Diaz Alejandro* effect was at work, that is, the income effect of real appreciation at the outset more than offsets the substitution effect. Accordingly, real appreciation starts off by being expansionary in terms of aggregate demand. Moreover, it is also very popular since it means increasing purchasing power. The opening of the economy reinforced that effect: quotas and tariffs were gone so that imports were cheap on account of both liberalization and

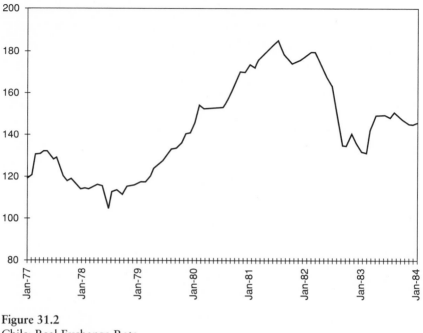

Figure 31.2
Chile: Real Exchange Rate

real appreciation. Not surprisingly, the current account increasingly showed the effect of the disequilibrium prices. But with a near-balanced budget, who was to think of the deficit as anything but a reflection of a vigorous miracle economy?

An important complication of the overvaluation strategy played itself out in financial markets. Those who believed that the fixed-rate strategy would last had an interest in borrowing offshore, in dollars, and thus avoiding the high domestic interest rates. Those who did not trust the policy had an interest in borrowing at home in pesos. In an environment of financial deregulation and major bad loans on the books dating back to the 1970s, real interest rates became extreme. And the higher they became, the worse the loans, and the more adverse selection was the rule. Not surprisingly, when the currency ultimately crashed, so did the banking system.

An overvaluation never goes away quietly.[5] Overvaluation and the attending financing requirement involve a vulnerability. Exactly which event ultimately undermines the strategy is wide open. In Chile's case, it was the international debt crisis. But that is not to say that a soft landing was around the corner had it not been for that crisis. Policymakers like to explain that everything was all right, had it not been for this or that unpredictable event. But overvaluation ultimately falls by its own weight; not all news is good, so that it is mainly an issue of time before a sufficiently unfavorable event breaks the strategy.

The end of the first Pinochet stabilization was a deep recession, a massive real depreciation, and a full banking crisis. It meant starting all over again. A decade later the next stabilization had shown itself to be extremely successful. One of the pillars of that period was to keep the real exchange rate competitive at all times.

Mexico

After the mid-1950s, for a period of twenty years, Mexico held on to full convertibility and a fixed exchange rate. The performance was exemplary in terms of discipline. But then, with oil outrun by aspirations, exchange-rate mismanagement started and has continued for the past twenty years. Specifically, the exchange-rate experience of Mexico has been closely associated with the political cycle. In the run-up to both presidential election years 1976 and 1982, the real exchange rate was overvalued and a currency crisis followed, and the same happened in 1994.

Our interest here is in the most recent episode, the overvaluation of the first half of the 1990s and the collapse of 1994–95. The Salinas administration took office in 1988, even though the economic team had been in place already during the previous sexennio, though one layer down. Disinflation had been a process under way since 1987 when, at its peak, inflation was well above 100 percent. The strategy for disinflation was the *pacto*, an incomes policy package that quite essentially matched the Mexican corporatist political model: labor (i.e., the PRI unions represented by Don Fidel Velásquez, aged 97), business, and the government met periodically to lay out ceremoniously an agreed strategy for wages, prices in the private and public sector, and the exchange rate. The agreements assured that there were no backward-looking indexation effects to dominate the disinflation program.

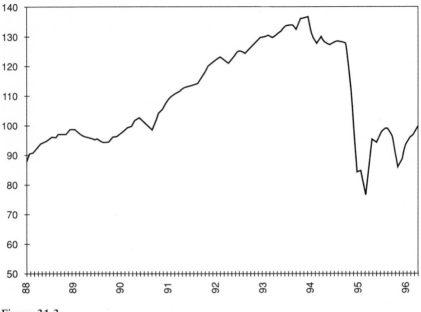

Figure 31.3
Mexico-United States: Relative Price Levels

On the surface, the strategy worked well—between 1987 and 1994, the inflation rate came down from 130 percent to only 7 percent. But the strategic ingredient along the way was the exchange rate. The real exchange rate (measured by Mexican wholesale prices in U.S. dollars) appreciated steadily. The formal arrangements for the exchange rate varied: prefixed, fixed, a band. The central fact, though, is that depreciation steadily lagged behind inflation and, accordingly and mechanically, the real exchange rate appreciated.

Mexico, just as Chile, had undergone a major program of deregulation, restructuring of the public sector, and aggressive trade opening.[6] As a short-run effect of these measures, growth was slowed down and the external deficit, reinforced by real appreciation, became very substantial. But with the budget balanced, how could the deficit be anything but a sign of vigor and dynamism? Interestingly, unlike in the case of Chile, investment had not increased at all, but that did not stop observers from talking about deficits generated by high levels of capital goods imports.

Table 31.2
Mexico: Macroeconomic Indicators

	1990	1991	1992	1993	1994	1995
Growth	4.4	3.6	2.9	0.7	3.5	−6.2
Inflation	30	19	12	8	7	52
Budget	−2.2	−0.3	1.6	0.7	−0.7	1.0
Curr. Acc't	−7.5	−14.8	−24.4	−23.4	−28.8	−0.7
% of GDP	−3.0	−5.1	−7.4	−6.4	−7.7	−0.2

Note: Budget as a percent of GDP, current account in $US billion and % of GDP.
Source: Bank of Mexico.

The government was clearly aware of the large real appreciation. But the availability of virtually unlimited external capital and the political timetable made a shift in strategy unpalatable. Disinflation at any price!

The strategy of keeping depreciation below inflation was kept up right into the election year. And even when political problems foreshadowed weakness, including massive capital flight by wealthy Mexicans in the aftermath of the Chiappas uprising and the Colosio assassination, the strategy was kept up. More than that, monetary strategy was enlisted to keep up the facade with full sterilization of the reserve losses. The Mexican government pretended that there were no problems, and the always gullible foreign lenders mostly bought the story.

The strategy finally collapsed in the transition to the new government and in the midst of year-end balance sheet cleaning by foreign investors. The new government contemplated devaluation and, it is rumored, the wealthy Mexicans got a first helping of the reserves. The rest is history— a massive collapse of the peso and a meltdown. In Mexico, just as in Chile, the banking system that had gotten involved in the betting on the peso went bust. That cleanup is worth $30 billion or more and continues.

Brazil

The central macroeconomic institution of Brazil, ever since the stabilization of the military government in the 1960s, was indexation. Everything was indexed—the exchange rate, wages, public-sector prices, asset yields. As a result, and because Brazil is a large, relatively closed, and above all

Table 31.3
Brazil: Macroeconomic Indicators

	1992	1993	1994	1995	1996*
Growth	−0.8	4.2	5.7	4.2	3.0
Inflation	1129	2491	941	23	12
Curr. Acc't	1.7	−0.1	−0.3	−2.6	−2.1
Budget.	−2.2	0.2	0.5	−5.0	−2.2

* Forecast. Current account and budget as a percent of GDP.
Source: IMF and J. P. Morgan.

inward-looking economy, macroeconomics could be quite stable even in the face of extreme inflation. In fact, it almost seemed as if Brazilians were enjoying the experience of a hyperinflation, But, of course, economic performance deteriorated. The official reason, ex post, is inflation. But that is not the whole story. An important part is misgovernment both under the outgoing military government and under the democratic governments of Presidents Sarney, Color, Itamar, and Cardoso.[7] This is not a fine point: after inflation is gone, there is a lot of work to be done to get the economy in shape.

In the transition to the new government, in 1994, then Finance Minister Cardoso embarked on a strategy of abolishing inflation with an ingenious monetary reform. A new money, the *Real*, was phased in and the old hyperinflation was out; in the transition a unit of account that shadowed the dollar was used to get around backward-looking indexation. Once the Real was introduced in July, at 1 : 1 on the dollar, it was allowed to appreciate on the U.S. dollar, thus strongly reinforcing the impression of a hard currency and of an end to inflation. No surprise, the enthusiastic publicly elected finance minister was to become the next president. No surprise, he was attached to the disinflation miracle and the hard Real; indexation of anything was out of question. No surprise, finally, that he got trapped in a major overvaluation.

At the outset of the stabilization, in mid-1994, the Real was allowed to appreciate in nominal terms. That, of course, strongly reinforced the real appreciation coming from minor ongoing inflation. Over time, with inflation at an annual rate of more than 15 percent, real appreciation

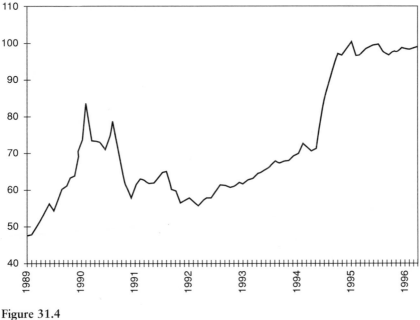

Figure 31.4
Brazil: Prices in $U.S.

cumulated to a significant level. Two years later, real appreciation came to an increase of prices in dollars of more than 50 percent. Effectively, the authorities had shifted to a "flexible" exchange rate, but that meant essentially a rate of depreciation mostly in line with inflation. The accumulated real appreciation was maintained.

Brazil's overvaluation is showing on several fronts. First, Brazil is *very* expensive. The resulting trade problem is being handled by import duties and quotas and by export subsidies. That is a pragmatic solution to offset overvaluation, but of course it results in conflicts with trading partners. On the side of growth, the extremely high level of real interest rates in 1995—more than 50 percent—caused a slowdown. Now interest rates are being reduced, as far as possible. While foreign capital is coming, there is some hope, but how long will capital keep coming, especially if neighboring Argentina starts to disappoint? If interest rates have to be raised, growth and banking problems spell the end of a successful stabilization.

Brazil has a tradition of disregarding foreign experiences and more so foreign advice. That has often served the country well. The strategy is being followed once again. Just as in Pinochet's Chile or Salinas's Mexico, priority is given to Cardoso's political vision: a second term. Keeping inflation down is essential and to accomplish that, the currency needs to stay hard. If that means high interest rates, so be it; if it means the banking system gets worse, so be it; if it means protection, so be it. The strategy will last until further notice: high reserves, a relatively small external deficit, and pragmatism suggest that a Mexican-style collapse is unlikely. But even in Brazil, not all news is always favorable. A vastly overvalued exchange rate in a country that has opened up trade and relies on nervous external finance—direct investment accounts for less than 10 percent of the financing—can become a problem.

Why?

We have reviewed three experiences of overvaluation. Two ended disastrously, on another one the jury is still out; there is every reason to be optimistic, except experience. Why do governments choose a strategy of currency overvaluation?

A first pass at this question is that they do not. A plausible argument is that there is a distinction between real appreciation and overvaluation; they look the same, but the former is an equilibrium increase in a relative price while the second is a disequilibrium phenomenon. When a government stabilizes and reforms, prices inevitably improve the long-run outlook for the use of productive resources. If a country were a firm, the stock price should rise. Is a real appreciation not just the equivalent?

The analogy goes far and surely supports some real appreciation. But even here it is tricky. True, asset prices should rise, but the real exchange rate most closely resembles the wage in dollars. A major restructuring and opening up in the first place frees up labor and therefore requires a fall in the equilibrium wage in dollars. Only when investment creates new jobs (in part as a result of reforms, in part in response to increased profitability induced by a real depreciation) can wages in dollars start rising. To use the stock market analogy further, a major corporate restructuring that introduces new technologies, brings about outsourcing, and reduces waste surely warrants a rise in the stock price, but it does reduce the demand for labor and hence would be accompanied by a fall in the equilibrium wage—stockholders get more, wage earners get less.

Governments, and the market, do not recognize this distinction. Over and over again, trade opening and restructuring are used as reasons for real appreciation simply because they represent reform and reform is good. A further mistake in this direction is the misreading of productivity growth. It is frequently argued that there is no overvaluation because productivity growth is high. The argument almost suggests that after measuring competitiveness by the price level in dollars, productivity growth is used as an extra adjustment. But, of course, productivity growth finds itself into prices and is not an extra. A further reason why governments go wrong in this direction is that they mismeasure productivity growth: the available numbers refer to gross output per worker, not value added. Thus, when restructuring and outsourcing become important, the difference between gross output and value added opens up in a major way. The demonstration of dramatic reductions in relative unit labor costs, as claimed for example in Mexico, is hard to reconcile with sharply increasing prices in dollars.[8] The most likely explanation is a significant overestimate of productivity.

A separate line of explanation focuses on a misreading of both the facts and the circumstances of crisis. In any one of the episodes discussed, the country in question stands high in comparison to its history: reform is undertaken, the right steps are being taken, money is plentifully available from abroad. This necessarily introduces an element of delusion. If capital inflows are huge, who could think of depreciation to sustain competitiveness? Reform addresses competitiveness, and the rest is a story of the capital market. Finance is dominant, continuity is the only thing foreign investors demand: keep playing the same music so that more money comes; if money keeps coming, where is the risk?

The misreading takes place on both sides of the market. Investors are overconfident that they are well informed and liquid: as a result they stay until midnight, expecting to get out on the very last train. On the borrowing side, this behavior induces the illusion that investors have no doubt, that their loyalty is total, and that adjustment is in no way urgent. When, suddenly, an unanticipated major piece of bad news emerges, investors pull out, the market crashes, and the economic team has lost the gamble. In Brazil today, that prospect seems totally unlikely along the way. It is rejected vigorously by everyone concerned: preposterous! The same was true in Chile, and the same was true in Mexico.

A third point concerns inflation. Governments over the past decade have bought massively into the view that inflation is all-important in public opinion. Bringing down inflation is the magic crusade. In part, it is what capital markets want to hear to keep the money coming. In part, it is the most visible sign of a reform strategy. It is definitely what the public really cares for, however mysterious the reason as seen by economists.[9] Moreover, central banks do their part. In the increasing quest for independence, inflation fighting is important and a hard currency helps. Reinforcement from foreign official institutions can always be counted on.

Finally, governments inevitably adopt a sequencing in their policies. The sequencing involves, importantly, the political timetable. Importantly, disinflation and overvaluation fit into that scheme; devaluation must come afterward, at worst once reforms are complete, but hopefully the issue will somehow just go away. Of course, the issue does not go away and the crash ultimately is very costly. Shortsightedness or procrastination is therefore an important ingredient in mismanaged exchange rates. In the end there is a vicious circle: when overvaluation has become significant, ultimately there has to be a devaluation. But it is well established that a devaluation is a political disaster.[10] So why risk a devaluation?

Notes

1. To fix ideas, one might think of the P-function as Cobb-Douglas in import and domestic prices.

2. The relation might also be a function of the level of output. In that case, at higher levels of output, real wage vindications might be higher and in depressions labor might settle for less.

3. See Dornbusch (1980, 1993) and Rodriguez (1978, 1982).

4. See Edwards and Cox-Edwards (1987), Corbo and Fischer (1994), and Dornbusch and Edwards (1994) for a discussion of the Chilean experience.

5. See Goldfajn and Valdes (1996), who examine a large set of overvaluation experiences.

6. On the Mexican experience, see Dornbusch, Goldfajn, and Valdes (1995) as well as the extensive references given there.

7. The last military president, a cavalry man, will be remembered for proclaiming: "If inflation were a horse, I would long have dominated her."

8. See Bank of Mexico (1995), pp. 141–158, which contains an elaborate presentation of the productivity theme.

9. Shiller (1996) reports surveys of inflation attitudes. His finding is that the public in Germany, Brazil, and the United States views inflation as reducing the standard of living.

10. See Cooper (1971) for a documentation of the fall of finance ministers in the aftermath of currency depreciation.

References

Bank of Mexico. (1995). *The Mexican Economy: 1995*. Mexico City: Bank of Mexico.

Cooper, R. N. (1971). "An Assessment of Currency Devaluation in Developing Countries," in G. Ranis (ed.), *Government and the Economy*. New Haven: Yale University Press.

Corbo, V., and S. Fischer (1994) "Lessons from the Chilean Stabilization and Recovery," in B. Bosworth, R. Dornbusch and R. Laban (eds.), *The Chilean Economy. Policy Lessons and Challenges*. Washington, DC: Brookings.

Dornbusch, R. (1980). *Open Economy Macroeconomics*. New York: Basic Books.

———. (1993). *Stabilization, Debt and Reform*. Englewood Cliffs: Prentice-Hall.

Dornbusch, R., and S. Edwards. (1994). "Exchange Rate Policy and Trade Strategy," in B. Bosworth, R. Dornbusch and R. Laban (eds.), *The Chilean Economy. Policy Lessons and Challenges*. Washington DC: Brookings.

Dornbusch, R., I. Goldfajn, and R. Valdes. (1995). "Currency Crises and Collapses." *Brookings Papers on Economic Activity*. No. 2.

Edwards, S., and A. Cox-Edwards. (1987). *Monetarism and Liberalization: The Chilean Experiment*. Cambridge: Ballinger.

Goldfajn, I. and R. Valdes. (1996). "The Aftermath of Appreciations" NBER Working Paper No. 5650. Cambridge, Mass.: National Bureau of Economic Research.

Rodriguez, C. (1978). "A Stylized Model of the Devaluation-Inflation Spiral." IMF *Staff Papers* 24 (March).

———. (1982). "The Argentine Stabilization Plan of December 20th." *World Development* (September).

Shiller, R. (1996). "Why Do People Dislike Inflation?" NBER Working Paper No. 5539. Cambridge, Mass.: National Bureau of Economic Research.

32

Mexico—The Folly, the Crash, and Beyond

The 1994–95 crash was not the first crisis in Mexico and probably is not the last one either. Mexico has a record of being fundamentally mismanaged—too much borrowing and too little saving, too little competitiveness, too much government, too little transparency, and an unbelievable denial of reality. Of course, it takes two parties to create a crisis: as in every other instance, an overeager capital market supported the unrealistic assumptions of the Mexican strategy. Every crisis, though, has a new angle; the replay is almost the same, but not quite.

The penultimate crisis came as recently as 1982, when Mexico's finance minister came to New York to reveal that he could not pay the bills and most of Latin America soon followed. The present crisis has much the same origins as the preceding ones: irresponsible lending by overconfident, overeager creditors, and on the Mexican side major currency overvaluation. What is new is the exact detail of poor debt management and overlending. Then it was bank debt. This time around it was called Tesobonos, but the principle is the same.

Waves of excitement in supplying developing countries with capital are not unprecedented. It is worth bearing in mind the historical record so as not to lose perspective on the fragility of the financing of large current account deficits. The distinguished Harvard economist Frank Taussig (1928), writing on the eve of widespread debt defaults to comment on the collapse of Latin credit at the time, describes the usual sequence of events:[1]

The loans from the creditor country begin with a modest amount and proceeds crescendo. They are likely to be made in exceptionally large amounts toward the culminating stage of the period of activity and speculative upswing, and during that stage become larger from month to month so long as the upswing continues. With the advent of crises, they are at once cut down sharply, even cease entirely ... A sudden reversal takes place in the debtor country's international balance sheet; it feels the consequences abruptly, in an immediate need of increased remittances to the creditor country, in a strain on its banks, high rates of discount, falling prices. And this train of events may ensure not only once.

The overconfident investors who, as in every previous crisis in Latin America, thought there was another El Dorado with extraordinary returns in dollars year after year, were disillusioned beyond belief.[2] The very investors who for a year on far more than one occasion received personal assurances that this would never, never happen became the most extreme protagonists in selling Mexico out.

At the time of the 1994–95 crisis, it was tempting to argue that ultimately interest in lending to Mexico and the region would return, but only when assets were dirt cheap. Investors would first lick their wounds and curse their fate. Then they would need to see what Mexico would do to rebuild its image. Just as in real estate, there is always another boom; it just does not come in time to bail out the current holders of the hot potato. In fact, though, the return of capital was surprisingly rapid. Super high interest rates and the strengthening of the peso (and analogies with Turkey's quick turnaround) brought money back in no time. Far from disillusioning emerging market investors, the Mexican near-meltdown had little lasting influence; the emerging market finance is here to stay and grow. Of course, a large part of the confident return may be the U.S.-IMF bailout of Mexico. Much of the background to that operation remains to be disclosed. It may have little to do with protecting Mexico, but with the protection of widespread U.S. investors in various emerging market funds and much more with huge off balance sheet positions of some New York institutions.

The crash of the Mexican peso is just one more example of the cycle of exuberant optimism followed by collapse and bottomless skepticism in Latin American finance. As long as the music goes on, more and more ignorant investors are pulled in. And with the prospects so bright, more and more promoters raise capital to take investors for a ride on the bubble. The crash of the peso has ruined investors' bonuses and it has also dealt a major setback to Mexico's prospects.

Preview

In the end there is always a crash, but it takes much longer than one thinks and then it happens much faster than one would have thought. A country that only a moment ago was basking in the glory of reform and prosperity falls straight into bankruptcy. Investors feel cheated, economic prospects turn bleak, and the hunt is on for the whodunit—an incompetent finance minister who played the wrong music and thus sapped confidence, foreign investors who pulled out and left the country high and dry, or the previous administration that left behind an awesome legacy. A post-mortem is instructive. In the case of Mexico, the responsibility lies squarely with former President Carlos Salinas and his obsessive preoccupation with inflation.

Following a borrowing spree in the late 1970s, Mexico last crashed in 1982. Debts to commercial banks around the world went into default; the peso was devalued over and over again in an attempt to gain a trade surplus to meet the demands of creditors. But even as the currency went down, inflation exploded. That vicious circle of inflation and depreciation came to a peak with inflation well above 200 percent. Under the pressure of events, reform and stabilization became the central objective. Much good was done: privatization, trade liberalization including NAFTA, deregulation, and budget balancing including fiscal reform.

Somewhere along the way, external confidence recovered, money started coming, external deficits ballooned. With easy access to financing and much of the domestic agenda accomplished, reducing inflation to U.S. levels became the central preoccupation. Depreciation of the currency was kept far below the rate of inflation; that helped slow inflation, but it also meant an increasingly uncompetitive trade position. At the outset that could be rationalized by renewed access to world capital markets and the rewards of a reformed and stabilizing economy.

The trouble is this: somewhere along the way a U-turn must come to restore competitiveness; otherwise, the currency ultimately goes over the cliff. By 1993, Mexican producer prices had risen *in dollars* by over 45 percent compared to prices in the United States. An overvaluation of at least 25 percent could be discerned. Growth slowed down (except for election year spending), real interest rates were extremely high when measured by rates on commercial bank loans, and the external balance shifted toward a massive surplus. All the symptoms of a troubled financial situation were in place. Clearly the peso had become overvalued, but Mexican leaders refused to acknowledge the facts and foreign investors were lulled into holding on to exposed positions. Superior fiscal performance was, of course, a strong point in explaining why Mexico was quite uniquely attractive. Of course, that was not enough.

Exchange-Rate-Based Stabilization

In the 1990s, Mexico continued an ambitious reform process that had already started during the de la Madrid administration. The key aspects of reform were a settlement of external debt with a Brady Plan, deregulation and trade opening, and privatization. Even though much of reform today has become suspect and is said to be tainted with corruption, the major accomplishment in economic modernization should not be disregarded. Mexico did take a large and important step toward an open and competitive economy. President Salinas, and his cabinet, deserves lasting credit for the vision and courage.

Accompanying the reform process was a major effort to establish financial stability. The key features of that process were two: balancing the budget and bringing down inflation. Table 32.1 shows the rate of inflation of the CPI (over the preceding 12 months). In the early 1990s inflation peaked near 30 percent, a rate far too high for comfort, and budget deficits of 5 to 10 percent at the end of the 1980s were by all accounts excessive. An all-out effort to secure financial stability was called for.

As Table 32.1 shows, fiscal consolidation was swift and substantial. On the inflation front, the progress was no less. In looking at the disinflation, it is helpful to use a summary formula that expresses the inflation rate in terms of past inflation, the acceleration that comes from real depreciation (or the deceleration induced by real appreciation), the acceleration deriving from increasing real public-sector prices, and the impact of the output gap in stimulating higher margins or real wage claims:

$$\pi = \pi_{-1} + \alpha(e - \pi_{-1}) + \beta(p - \pi_{-1}) + \phi y; \qquad \alpha + \beta = 1 \qquad (1)$$

Table 32.1
Macro Indicators

	1990	1991	1992	1993	1994	1995
Growth	4.5	3.6	2.8	0.6	3.5	−6.9
Inflation	29.9	18.8	11.9	8.0	7.1	52.0
Depreciation	14.4	7.3	2.7	0.6	8.3	90.2
Budget	2.8	0.5	−1.6	−0.7	0.1	−0.1
Curr. Acc't	−3.0	−5.1	−7.4	−6.5	−7.9	−0.3

Note: Current account and budget as a percent of GDP.
Source: Bank of Mexico.

where π is the rate of inflation, e the current rate of depreciation, p the current rate of increase in public-sector prices, and y the output gap. The problem in disinflation is that there is no volunteer to start the process. Wages tend to be indexed, explicitly or implicitly. Public-sector prices follow the rate of inflation or else there is a risk of widening deficits. The exchange rate must offset the prevailing rate of inflation or else there is a loss of competitiveness. Finally, a recessionary squeeze of real wages or margins is unpopular. Thus, inflation yesterday becomes inflation today.

Incomes policy is one way to cut through the inflation cycle. If all wages, prices, and the exchange rate at some point started to decelerate, all together, inflation would be down without cuts in real wages, real appreciation, or declining real prices in the public sector. Mexico did well with that strategy on the mid-1980s, but increasingly the *pacto* strategy became strained—there was too much wage inflation and too little currency depreciation. Inflation did come down steadily—by 1993–94 it had fallen below 10 percent. But at the same time the real exchange rate appreciated steadily, reaching an all-time high in late 1994. The real exchange rate is measured here by Mexican wholesale prices in dollars relative to the U.S. wholesale price level.[3] As always, there is a question as to an appropriate base period. Surely, the peak level of competitiveness in 1987 is not suitable. But by the same token, an all-time high real appreciation must be explained. Our contention is that the reform measures called for real depreciation, not real appreciation. If that is correct, the issue of base period or measure of real appreciation misses the basic point.

Exchange-rate-based stabilization goes through three phases. The first one is very useful and perhaps even indispensable. In this short phase, exchange-rate pegging helps bring about a stabilization. It achieves some concrete stabilization objective and creates results, and hence confidence. Moreover, the first phase often benefits from an initial undervaluation that creates a cushion for real appreciation. Even so, this phase cannot last very long because much of what is done here is in fact borrowed: it is to be validated by policy improvements down the road. The more that is borrowed, the less the prospects that it can be repaid, namely, that the stabilization will last. In the second phase, increasing real appreciation becomes apparent, and is increasingly recognized, but it is inconvenient to do something. The reluctance to act in part involves the very realistic issue of what exactly to do. Not doing anything is easy; doing something is much harder. Not surprisingly, this phase lasts quite a while, and it feels good since an overabundance of capital inflows suggests that something is being done right. Finally, in the third phase, it is too late to do something. Real appreciation has come to a point where a major devaluation is necessary. But the politics will not allow that. Some more time is spent with denial and then, sometime, enough bad news piles up to cause the crash.

Mexico's exchange-rate story of 1991–94 follows very much that pattern. In 1992–93 the question of excessive real appreciation and overvaluation was increasingly discussed. But with no concrete ideas about another strategy, and no wish to give up on disinflation, nothing was done. And then the election year of 1994 came in sight. Last opportunities to do something in 1993 just went unused, and then 1994 was there and doing anything was completely out. But the bad news on the political front did come and the rest is history.

In 1993 a devaluation was still a possibility; certainly President Salinas considered it as an option in the spring of that year, or at least he privately said so. But soon the government had political priorities that conflicted with reality, and perhaps even fooled itself that the problems would go away or the financing would become easier. The rest is history: reserves were run down to unmanageably low levels, debts were dollarized, maturities were shortened—just keep the music going so nobody finds out that the emperor has no clothes. Of course, these very steps to try to squeeze an extra year of life out of a moribund strategy help explain the extreme severity of the following crisis.

Mexico's policymakers rationalized that real appreciation was unproblematic: NAFTA would bring direct investment and trade opportunities. Deficits were large now but would be small in the future and, in any event, money was no object since investors had fallen in love with Mexican stocks and T-bills. Overvaluation turned problematic when the upcoming 1994 election brought with it the possibility of changes in economic strategy or a show of weakness of the official party.

Indeed, politics turned nasty (Chiappas and the assassination of a rival candidate and more) and that caused some eyebrows to be raised. But no day passed without fresh assurances to the investors that all was well: the peso would never be allowed to fall. The foreign loans kept coming but at higher interest rates. High interest rates and lack of competitiveness increasingly strangled growth. No growth and a gigantic external deficit —almost 8 percent of GDP—made for a classical prediction: the peso would yield, sooner or later. Continuity and credibility babble can hold off problems only so long.

Yet, President Salinas held on to the strategy of no waves—politics first, reality later. The myth of a super-performing Mexico was kept alive; criticism was not allowed, certainly not from cabinet members who hoped to get the magic nomination to be the next holder of absolute power. Chilean Dictator Augusto Pinochet had put himself in the same position in the late 1970s. Just as Pinochet and his cabinet were impervious to common sense in currency matters, Salinas also thought that with enough manipulation and censorship he could keep the peso afloat. Ultimately, both turned out to be very wrong and in a strikingly similar manner.

With Chiappas, the crisis might not have happened. But that is unlikely, since there is always *some* extraneous event that makes the glass run over, and if the currency is badly out of line, it does not take much. But why now the seemingly bottomless drop of the peso? The analogy here is with a bank run. Mexico dissipated its reserves in an attempt to sustain various levels of the peso. Nobody wants to be caught as the last one out or the first one in; investors left en masse.

Mexico's per capita income today is still 5 percent less than it was in 1982, at the time of the last crisis. The easy money is gone, and real income will be falling further. Salinas's brilliant reforms were about to put Mexico on the path of prosperity; his utterly misguided currency experiments instead plunged the country into economic and possibly political turmoil.

Massive selling, redemptions in funds, and forced liquidation with price collapses chasing year further redemptions marked the immediate collapse period. Markets simply vanished. The financial chaos, the sheer lack of a market, the inability in early 1995 to raise even a few hundred million dollars in new credits conjure up the image of a gigantic fraud— Mexico had never reformed, there was no substance, the other shoe (whichever that might be) was about to drop.

Of course, that is an extreme and totally unwarranted assessment of where Mexico has come. A better analogy is with a company where the engineers have developed great technology, the workers have done a special job in raising productivity, and the salespeople have excelled in developing markets. Yet, in this rendition, while nobody was watching, the CEO and the CFO were playing the markets, speculating in currency and rigging up a gigantic loss that overshadows all the gains made in the years of reform. Mexico had sort of an Orange County problem, to draw an analogy with recent financial scandals in the United States. Moreover, whoever is in charge of financial supervision in the international system closed an eye to what was going on.

Reform without Growth

The interesting question in analyzing the latest Mexican collapse is just how it was possible that government persuaded itself that there was no problem. Of course, the truth may well be that the cabinet was fully aware of the problem but simply insisted on getting through the election, into a new government, and coping with issues later. But it is also possible that in the isolated atmosphere of Mexican government, denial of reality was dominant.

The most striking fact of Mexican performance that should have aroused attention was surely the lack of growth. In the period 1985–94, Mexican output grew at an average rate of 2 percent. Labor force growth over that period was at least 3 percent. Accordingly, informality rose on average over the whole decade. In the more recent period, 1990–94, growth averaged 2.6 percent per year, still below the growth of the labor force. By 1993, growth had basically vanished. The election year brought back growth, driven by a significant and targeted fiscal expansion. But clearly the government could not have taken that to be anything other than election pump priming.

The basic contention is that the lack of growth—not the current account or the real exchange rate taken in isolation—is the evidence of an overvaluation problem. Even though the lack of growth ought to have caused alarm, the government was confirmed in its prejudices by two important propositions. First, Mexico was experiencing high productivity growth and hence surely had no competitiveness problem. Second, the modernization and reform ought to imply an increased valuation—in the stock market and in the real exchange rate—not an overvaluation.

The Productivity Issue

The OECD, of which Mexico is a member, does not report productivity data for the Mexican economy. The reason is the absence of reliable employment data. But the Mexican government does report productivity in manufacturing and the central bank makes much of the major *gain* in competitiveness implied by the data. Specifically, a Bank of Mexico (1996, p. 282) series based on relative unit labor costs shows a loss of competitiveness of only 7 percent between 1990 and 1994: III. This contrasts sharply with the data reported elsewhere. The reason is an average growth rate of productivity reported as 5.7 percent per year.[4] This rate exceeds the rate Japan experienced in its best years, 1960–73.[5] There are a number of reasons to be suspicious. First, employment is poorly recorded, at least in the judgment of the OECD. Second, it is not obvious that the distinction between gross output and value added is consistently applied. At a time of significant growth in outsourcing, this difference is critical.

But even if the numbers were accurate, there are two further caveats. First, many firms can learn to live with virtually *any* exchange rate. They just become more capital intensive. Of course, it is not the case that the economy, as opposed to firms, can do this. The labor redundancy that emerges needs an answer. In Mexico, output has barely grown at the rate of labor force growth; thus, if productivity growth was significant, labor market conditions must have deteriorated year after year for many years. The point then is that competitiveness has to do not only with firms, but with an economy's ability to have full employment. In Mexico, that was patently not the case.

Trade Liberalization and the Real Exchange Rate

Another critical issue in the overvaluation discussion is trade liberalization and deregulation. The argument is often made that reforms warrant real appreciation. But this is an inappropriate identification. Reforms have two features. On one side, they lead to a more efficient use of resources; on the other side, they free resources. The former justifies higher stock market valuation (or higher real wages), while the latter begs the question of where resources will move. If wages and prices were *fully* flexible, liberalization would be accompanied by a fall in wages and prices in dollars.[6] The resulting gain in competitiveness would create demand and hence employment. In the absence of wage-price flexibility, a real depreciation is required via devaluation. It is instructive to look at Argentina's experience just now. Massive unemployment is the counterpart of dramatic restructuring, including in the public sector, and of trade liberalization. Wage-price flexibility is not working fast enough—there is only ever so slight deflation. Since the exchange rate cannot be used, an extended period of muddling on seems to be the likely course. In Mexico, by contrast, the exchange rate could have been used as a counterpart to reform and as a way to translate it into a high growth experience. Of course, real depreciation would not only solve the employment issue. It would also help on the external side in containing the trade deficit induced by trade liberalization.

Alternative Hypotheses

This chapter has argued that overvaluation is the reason for the Mexican crisis of 1994–95. Alternative hypotheses have been advanced and are at least plausible.[7] One highly visible contention has to do with Mexican credit expansion in the election year. In the face of reserve losses, Mexico's central bank fully sterilized, while development banks kept up a significant expansion in credit. Too much money, motivated by the election year, is in this view the central contention. There is no question that central bank policy helped promote and presumably aggravate the crisis. It is right to believe that high interest rates could have avoided the crisis then and there. But it is also likely to be true that an extended period of high interest rates would ultimately have raised credibility questions: growth was becoming insignificant except for credit creation, and election year spending and nonperforming loans were rising steadily. High interest rates could have affected the timing, but they could not have undone the overvaluation. Of course, in expanding demand and widening the external deficit, the credit policy of the central bank and the development banks contributed to the extent of the crisis. The same is true of the debt management strategy in the form of dollarization and shortening of maturities. They were part of a desperate game to get beyond the election, and they suggest just how aware the administration was of the underlying unsustainability of their policies.

In summary, Mexico's reforms should have set the country off on a path to high growth. The failure is not due, of course, to the reforms. Overvaluation was the key mistake. Bad credit policies and mismanagement of debt were important aggravating factors. Thus the lesson is: don't overvalue. Just as in Argentina now, sound credit policy is not enough when there is a substantial overvaluation!

Postscript: Crawl Now or Crash Later

One would have thought that the severity of the recent experience might have taught Mexican policymakers a lesson—stay far, far away from an exchange-rate-based stabilization. Yet, precisely that same strategy is being pursued yet again. By late 1996, of the huge real depreciation of 1995, much less than half is left. Even in the face of more than 20 percent inflation, monetary policy kept the peso flat for an entire year rather than depreciating at the pace of inflation. The peso is said to be a "flexible" rate, but in between interest rate and aggregate policy Mexico manages to keep the peso, keep the capital coming, and risk preparing yet another instance of overvaluation. It is early to express that concern, but it is the appropriate time since correction of the course remains easy. It is difficult to expect that inflation can fall rapidly below world trends sufficiently to bring a remedy. The experience with real appreciation reported by Goldfajn and Valdes (1996) shows clearly that large overvaluations have little chance of a mild end.

Countries with 15–20 percent inflation per *year* should not belittle inflation; they must see its control as one of a number of priorities, and they should view it as a process of five or even ten years. Accepting the right perspective on moderate inflation is important because otherwise severe recession, super high real interest rates with resulting banking problems, and currency overvaluation with the risk of a collapse might be the result rather than the dramatic success hoped for on the inflation front.

Chile offers an excellent example of good policy. Over the past decade, the country has had an average inflation of 17 percent. At the outset it was 30 percent, in the early 1990s it was still double digit, and today, ten years later, it is down to 7 percent. The average growth for the ten-year period was 7 percent. Chile's approach has been exemplary, particularly in the past few years when the central bank has refused to overreach and squeeze inflation down to the fashionable 2 percent of the industrialized countries. Chile's policymakers recognize that strong growth, modernization, and integration in the world economy are not held back by 6, 10, or even 15 percent inflation but could be seriously hampered if overambitious disinflation created a macroeconomic problem.

The central lesson in stabilizing inflation is that it is very perilous indeed to use the exchange rate for anything but a very transitory, initial consolidation effort. The exchange rate cannot carry most or even much of the burden of stabilization. Nor can monetary policy do the job all by itself. Fiscal policy and competition both do a very substantial portion of the work.

The concern for inflation is altogether appropriate, but single-mindedness is not. In the face of moderate inflation, growth also must be part of the discussion. It is not correct to argue that there can be no growth in the presence of inflation, nor is it right to state that even moderate inflation is a detriment to growth. In a cross-section of growth rates for a large group of countries with inflation in the range of 5–20 percent, it is hard to see any evidence of a relationship between inflation and growth. In the absence of a cost in terms of growth foregone, that suggests a more gradual disinflation strategy is acceptable.

Of course, it might be argued that the only stable inflation is zero inflation. That is the kind of dogmatic posture that has no empirical foundation. For the past decade or more, countries have been at work reducing inflation or at least containing it. Countries with moderate inflation rates, such as Chile, have perfectly well managed to achieve *gradual* reductions without either compromising the credibility of that strategy or sacrificing growth. On the contrary, the fact that inflation was steadily—over twelve years—falling but growth was strong throughout made the program a textbook case of successful inflation fighting. Mexico's case, by contrast, is a series of failures and blunders as a result of half-baked ideas about credibility, inflation kills, and the like. Chile today is a low inflation country. Mexico is once again back to intolerably high inflation. The right message is that inflation must come down and that there is never room for complacency; that is not the same as inflation reduction first, growth later. Comparing Mexico's and Chile's per capita GDP over the fifteen years leaves no question. Mexico's currency experiments have been expensive, and if there is one more building up, who needs it?

Notes

1. See Taussig (1928, p. xx). See also the wider discussion of international lending following the default of debts in the late 1920s reported in Cardoso and Dornbusch (1989).

2. More broadly, Kindleberger (1989) reviews the history and atmosphere of financial crises.

3. There is a further discussion of the particular measure of competitiveness below. Suffice it to say here that we stay away from consumer prices to avoid capturing the various subsidy removals for consumer goods associates with the budget correction.

4. Average real wage growth over the period is reported as only 1.8 percent. See Bank of Mexico (1996, p. 290).

5. See Maddison (1991) p. 275.

6. See Dornbusch (1973) for the analytical demonstration.

7. Note in particular Bank of Mexico (1995, 1996), Blejer and de Castillo (1996), Calvo (1996a, 1996b), Calvo and Memdoza (1996), Cole and Kehoe (1996), Gil-Diz and Carstens (1996), IMF (1995a), Morgan (1996), Lustig (1995), Mancera (1995), Masson and Agenor (1996), Roberts (1996), Sachs, Tornell, and Velasco (1996), Santella and Vela (1996), and US (1996).

References

Andrews, David, and Shogo Ishii. (1995). "The Mexican Financial Crisis: A Test of the Resilience of the Markets for Developing Country Securities." International Monetary Fund Working Paper, International Monetary Fund, December.

Bank of Mexico. (1995). *The Mexican Economy.* Mexico City: Bank of Mexico.

———. (1996). *The Mexican Economy.* Mexico City: Bank of Mexico.

Blejer, Mario I, and Graciana del Castillo. (1996). "Deja Vu All Over Again? The Mexican Crisis and the Stabilization of Uruguay in the 1970's." International Monetary Fund Working Paper, International Monetary Fund, July.

Calvo, Guillermo A. (1996a). "Capital Flows and Macroeconomic Management: Tequila Lessons." Unpublished manuscript, February.

———. (1996b). "Why Is 'The Market' So Unforgiving?" Unpublished manuscript, University of Maryland.

Calvo, Guillermo A., and Enrique G. Mendoza. (1996). "Mexico's Balance-of-Payments Crisis: A Chronicle of a Death Foretold." Working Paper in International Economics, No. 20, Center for International Economics, Department of Economics, University of Maryland at College Park, March.

Cole, Harold L., and Timothy J. Kehoe. (1996). "A Self-Fulfilling Model of Mexico's 1994–95 Debt Crises." Staff Report #210, Research Department, Federal Reserve Bank of Minneapolis, April.

Dornbusch, Rudi. (1973). "Tariffs and Nontraded Goods." *Journal of International Economics.*

Gil-Diaz, Francisco, and Augustin Carstens. (1996). "Some Hypotheses Related to the Mexican 1994–95 Crisis." Serie Documentos De Investigacion, Banco de Mexico, Direccion General De Investigacion Economica.

Goldfajn, I., and R. Valdes. (1996). "The Aftermath of Appreciations." NBER Working Paper No. 5650.

Gonzalez-Hermosillo, Brenda. (1996). "Banking Sector Fragility and Systemic Sources of Fragility." IMF Working Paper, International Monetary Fund, February.

Hanke, Steve H. (1996). "Currency Board for Mexico." *Central Banking,* Volume VI, Number 4, Spring.

International Monetary Fund (1995a). *World Economic Outlook*. Washington, DC.

———. (1995b). *International Capital Markets*. Washington DC.

Kindleberger, Charles P. (1989). *Manias, Panics, and Crashes: A History of Financial Crises*. New York: Basic Books.

Lustig, Nora. (1995). "The Mexican Peso Crisis: The Foreseeable and the Surprise." *Brookings Discussion Papers in International Economics*, The Brookings Institution, June.

Maddison, Angus. (1991). *Dynamic Forces in Capitalist Development: A Long Run Comparative View*. New York: Oxford University Press.

Mancera, Miguel. (1995). "Don't Blame Monetary Policy." *Wall Street Journal*, January 31.

Masson, Paul R., and Pierre-Richard Agenor. (1996). "The Mexican Peso Crisis: Overview and Analysis of Credibility Factors." International Monetary Fund Working Fund, International Monetary Fund, January.

Morgan, J. P. (1996). "Mexico's 1994 Crisis and its Aftermath." *Economic Research Note*, Banco J. P. Morgan, S. A., April 5, 1996.

Roberts, Craig. (1996). "Mexico: Don't Blame Salinas for Zedillo's Mistakes." *Business Week Economic Viewpoint*, March 4.

Sachs, Jeffrey, Aaron Tornell, and Andres Velasco (1996). "Financial Crises in Emerging Markets: The Lessons From 1995." *Brookings Papers on Economic Activity*, 1, 147–198.

Santella, Julio A., and Abraham E. Vela. (1996). "The 1987 Mexican Disinflation Program: An Exchange Rate-Based Stabilization?" IMF Working Paper, International Monetary Fund, March.

Taussig, F. (1928). *International Trade*. New York: Macmillan.

33

Another Peso Disaster May Be Waiting in the Wings

You'd think that the 1994 economic crisis would have taught Mexican policymakers a lesson: stay far away from currency overvaluation or risk financial meltdown. But no. The same strategy that led to that disaster is being used again. Instead of being allowed to float lower, the peso is being held artificially high to attract foreign capital and combat high inflation.

If market forces had their way, a country with high inflation would see its currency depreciate. Otherwise, the country would become uncompetitive in world markets, export growth would slow, and imports would explode. Foreign trade would then become a drag on growth. This is precisely what happened to Mexico last time, and it is happening again today.

By conventional purchasing-power parity measures, Mexico's competitiveness today is only about 20 percent better than in 1993. Over the past year and a half, its competitiveness has been shrinking rapidly. Indeed, it is barely enough to keep the economy expanding. It is definitely not sufficient to spark high growth and job creation.

Why can't Mexican authorities keep their country competitive by allowing the peso to depreciate at the pace of inflation? One answer is that an overvalued currency attracts foreign capital. Mexico's industries may be going under from loss of competitiveness, but its bonds are popular because of high interest rates set by the Bank of Mexico. The result is a cycle of high interest rates, imports of capital, and further over-

Originally published in *Business Week* (25 November 1996): 26. Reprinted with permission.

valuation of the peso. The ensuing erosion of competition then gnaws at economic growth and employment.

Obsessive

It would be better to be less obsessive about fighting inflation and to seek long-term solutions to generating domestic capital. Why is this so hard for policymakers to accept, especially given Mexico's recent disastrous experience?

There is a second reason for the high-peso strategy. An overvalued peso lowers import costs, thus slowing inflationary pressures. With inflation in check, workers will accept slower increases in wages, again curbing inflationary forces. From a perspective of inflation fighting, holding the exchange rate works. But this seemingly virtuous circle hurts international competitiveness and trade. An overvalued peso means that Mexican exports become increasingly expensive and imports get cheaper. This is what has been happening over the past year. The trade advantage from the 100 percent devaluation of the peso in 1994 and 1995 has been dissipating month by month. Mexico's big trade surplus is beginning to shrink fast and will soon disappear.

A third reason for a high-peso strategy focuses on financial balance sheets. Mexican banks are the walking wounded, and corporations are not much better. The best cure for both of them is low interest rates. But how can an open, high-inflation economy such as Mexico's have low rates? The answer is to have rates that are moderate relative to Mexican inflation. That means relatively high nominal rates, but zero real rates. That still gives Wall Street returns of 25 percent until further notice and allows Mexico to start growing again.

Half-Baked

Mexico's central bank has demonized inflation to a point where it cannot cut loose from its own rhetoric. There is plenty of evidence that extreme inflation—20 percent per month—is devastating for growth. But more relevant is the overwhelming support for the contention that moderate inflation of, say, 20 percent per year, does not interfere with growth.

True, it would be better to have none. True, it should be brought down over time. But it is not the single overriding issue. Growth, jobs, and political stability are just as important, and they do not thrive when competitiveness is sacrificed for balance-sheet manicures.

So Mexicans wait for their overvalued peso "to be hit again" in the foreign-exchange markets while the internal policy debate revolves around half-baked ideas about credibility. The prospects for strong growth are bleak. The standard line of central bankers and hard-money gurus—zero inflation is the only stable inflation—is just not true. Countries with moderate inflation around the world have managed to achieve gradual reductions without either compromising the credibility of that strategy or sacrificing growth. Countries such as Finland, Japan, and Switzerland, which took the zero-inflation propaganda too seriously, are now flat on their backs. Mexico must cut loose from the fiction and get back to life. It's time for Mexico to have a new team in the central bank. The present crew shows no signs of learning from the past, understanding the present, or preparing for the future.

34

Brazil Has Run Out of Excuses

Is Brazil headed for trouble again? Two years ago, it finally brought inflation under control. Then, Finance Minister Fernando Henrique Cardoso, who accomplished the feat, was swept into the Presidency. Then, there he sat, doing nothing further. There has been no action on balancing the budget, privatization, decentralizing the state, social security reform, or administrative reform. The excuse? They are "politically difficult."

Brazil, so goes the refrain, is unique among emerging economies. It is a true democracy, and how can anyone expect a democracy to make difficult decisions? Dictator Augusto Pinochet could make them in Chile. Alberto Fujimori could after a coup in Peru. Carlos Salinas de Gortari had a clear path in one-party, autocratic Mexico. But Brazil is democratic, and things just can't be rushed. And why rush, since inflation is under control? Well, because the stabilization of Brazil's inflation is less of a miracle than the government claims. In most other countries, a major effort in fiscal discipline is part of an anti-inflation strategy. Not in Brazil. Instead, Brazil overvalued its currency and sharply raised its high real interest rates. Last year, real interest rates averaged over 50 percent, and prices in dollars have risen over 40 percent since the stabilization plan began.

The cost of this policy is heavy: a bank crisis and low economic growth. The government is stepping in with bank bailouts. Meanwhile, big wage increases are making industry uncompetitive. The budget deficit

Originally published in *Business Week* (10 June 1996): 24. Reprinted with permission.

has reached 5 percent of gross national product, and the public debt has doubled in a single year.

Long Wait

There was a time when Brazil moved ahead. In the two decades prior to 1980, Brazil had one of the highest rates of growth in per capita income in the world. True, inflation was always a problem, but indexation kept it from becoming an obstacle to growth and financial stability. As in Latin America and Europe, the shift to democracy made sound economic policy much harder. But that was a decade ago, and excuses are wearing thin. Where Asian per capita income has doubled in the past 15 years, Brazil's has gone nowhere.

Brazil is a large, inward-looking country. It has always done things its own way, often with success. Lessons from abroad are invariably written off as irrelevant. In the past, Brazilians might well have claimed that the strategy served them well. But that is patently not the case today. Losing a decade and a half of income growth is subpar performance by any standard.

For now, overly eager foreign capital, attracted by high interest rates, is helping to keep the show going. Foreign exchange reserves are high, and the currency is stable. But some foreign investors are much less impressed. These investors are wary that the "miracle" is fading and that the bill for procrastination will soon come due. Once capital pulls out, there are few options. Raising interest rates further would stop growth completely and promote even wider bank failures. Letting the currency go means giving up inflation control.

Meltdown

Brazilian policymakers, basking in the admiration of the press and the public, misread their situation. They underestimate the internationalization of their economy and their dependence on external capital. Either the government starts reform with big and eager steps, or they should expect major trouble. There won't be an exact replay of Mexico, but even half that experience would be a dramatic setback. It is hard to predict the timing of meltdown, but that makes the prospect no less real and the need for reform no less urgent. The Mexicans didn't hear any criticism until the markets crashed, and Brazil is enjoying the same reticence. The trigger for financial trouble may come from outside Brazil. A rise in global interest rates or a dip in global stock markets will be enough to sour Brazil's financial prospects. It is equally true that aggressive reforms can take Brazil out of the danger zone and make it a dynamic country of the future.

Brazil isn't the only mismanaged economy in the world, but it is unique in that its elite thinks the country is doing well. They should be concerned about stabilization and reform for reasons far beyond financial stability. Brazil has one of the worst income distributions in the world, and poverty levels in the north are comparable to the most backward countries in Africa. President Cardoso has a special responsibility. He is immensely popular. He is an accomplished communicator and a superior intellectual. He can make Brazil take the medicine and set it on the right path—or he can do nothing and be another leader who failed to take responsibility for Brazil never taking its rightful place on the world scene.

35

Argentina's Monetary Policy Lesson for Mexico

Ever since Argentina got its new currency in 1991, a dramatic change has taken place. In the 1980s Argentine output shrank almost 0.5 percent per year; in the past six years annual growth has been in the 5 percent range. Argentina is the only country that today enjoys both price stability and vigorous growth.

Over the years, Argentina has experimented with both good and bad monetary policies. Now even casual observers can see that hard money is the hands-down winner.

With this evidence, it's instructive to compare Argentina's story with the experiences of other countries in the region that have fiddled with currency experiments but, lacking the discipline brought about by a law, have not been forced to recognize the importance of fiscal and structural reform. The Argentine Convertibility Law gives the country no choice but to adjust prices and competitiveness to the currency.

"Argentineans are always in trouble about their currency," *Bankers Magazine* wrote in 1889. "Either it is too good for home use, or as frequently happens, it is too bad for foreign exchange. Generally they have too much of it, but their own idea is that they do not have enough. The Argentineans alter their currency almost as frequently as they change their finance ministers. No people on earth has a keener interest in currency experiments than the Argentineans."

A few years later Finance Minister Ernesto Tornquist put Argentina formally on a gold standard, limiting the issue of money to the holdings

Originally published in the *Wall Street Journal* (28 February 1997): A15. Reprinted with permission.

of the treasury, thus stabilizing currency. That's when Argentina became, for a while, one of the leading economies in the world.

"In consequence of this law, gold poured into the treasury in quantities which far surpassed the most optimistic anticipations," according to "Economic Development of the Argentine Republic in the Past 50 Years," published by Banco Tornquist in 1919. "The monetary circulation increased correlatively, business increased in unlooked for degree and the economic development of the country presented the notable success which has attracted the attention of the whole world."

Argentina did well with its internationalism until, in the 1930s, the light was switched off on free trade and stable money around the world. Along with the rest of Latin America, Argentina went for protectionism. That set the stage for Juan Perón to add populism and labor unions; from there it was downhill both for monetary stability and the standard of living. Per capita income stagnated; inflation increased; periodic half-hearted attempts at stabilization and reform yielded to whole-hearted moves to nationalize production and print more money. Capital fled the country; soon Argentinians paid their taxes like Italians—hardly at all —and formed unions like the British—with a vengeance. In the early 1980s, only some 3,000 people paid income tax and the big question was why so many did. Unions divided their time equally between working and striking. Hyperinflation was the inevitable last stop of this debilitating process.

After some half-hearted measures to stop hyperinflation failed, President Carlos Saul Menem and his uncompromising new finance minister, Domingo Cavallo, introduced the Convertibility Law in 1991. At the outset, hard money meant just recognizing the facts: the dollar had become Argentina's de facto money. The law established a firm rule: fixed parity with the dollar, the dollar as legal tender, no issue of local currency except when backed 100 percent by dollar reserves in the central bank, and no financing of the Treasury by the central bank.

Hard money provided the cover for the urgent reforms: privatization, restructuring of the public sector, and elimination of pervasive subsidies. Moreover, the monetary regime withstood tough tests during the Mexican peso crisis.

True enough, Argentina has high unemployment—the immediate counterpart of drastic restructuring and liberalization—but no politician would dare touch the rule; in Argentina everybody understands that tinkering with the monetary rule means going back to hyperinflation. The old answer of public works is fortunately out of date. The remaining strategy involves deepening flexibility and productivity, and adopting a tax structure that favors employment rather than taxes.

Since hard money has been a political and economic success for Argentina, who is in line to emulate the experience? Believe it or not, Mexico. A move onto a fixed dollar parity would offer relief from the six-year cycle of devaluation and collapse that coincides with presidential terms. Halfway into the current cycle, the government has just spent its way to winning the forthcoming congressional elections. For the presidential election in 2000 we can expect even more politics and less economic stability. Mexico can change all that by going on a dollar-based system.

Argentina's currency board-like arrangement would be ideal for Mexico, except for one small problem: credibility. Mexico remains suspect and hence must take more drastic steps.

In order to address this, Mexico should go one step further and get rid of the peso almost completely. Specifically, the entire banking system should operate in dollars. That way any fears of junking the currency board or of yet another devaluation would become impossible. This rather radical reform would establish an unprecedented level of confidence. The argument on the other side—that this is politically impossible, nationalism won't permit it—is outdated.

Mexican per capita GDP today is still where it was in the mid-'70s. If Mexico cannot manage a competitive exchange rate, it must get rid of its exchange rate. On a dollar system, wages and prices would quickly converge to U.S. levels, the official system of wage fixing (known as the *pacto*) would fortunately become impossible, risk premiums in credit markets would shrink, and the credit market would come back to life. The loose cannon—the peso—would be rendered harmless.

Whatever it does in the monetary area, Mexico is on probation for years to come. The U.S. cannot do much to help Mexico along—such proposed reforms as monetary union and a Mexican seat on the Federal Reserve Board are inconceivable. But the best chance to make headway is to use a system that is known to have worked well elsewhere. As Argentina's experience shows, stable money is the beginning of economic prosperity and political stability. Mexico needs both and has the prospect of neither. After too many experiments, hard money now, before the next devaluation, is the safest way.

36

How Not to Safeguard South Africa's Democracy

When majority rule swept into power in South Africa, the victorious broad coalition hoped that the self-imposed embargo by foreign investors would give way to a return of investment, with beneficial effects for both economic growth and the availability of foreign exchange. Multilateral institutions would do their utmost to help accomplish a soft landing for the critical democratic effort, with billions in International Monetary Fund and World Bank money. The timing was right: world economic growth promised to turn up, and with a troubled dollar, gold prices were doing well.

Unfortunately, things haven't turned out that way. The budget deficit is large—running to at least 6 percent of gross domestic product. The immediate influx of foreign capital didn't materialize, so foreign-exchange reserves are already depleted. Foreign investors, leery of a situation in which potential profits aren't commensurate with the risks, are standing on the sidelines. Foreign capital infinitely prefers situations where the upside potential is vast if risks must be taken to get in. By that measure, Russia or Brazil, Venezuela, Vietnam, or even China are much more attractive prospects than South Africa.

Whenever a young democracy encounters the challenge of hard economic problems, populism pops out of the wings. And sooner or later, without fail, economic populism translates into economic crisis and ultimately into a drop in real wages. That risk is increasingly apparent in South Africa. If it materializes, the prospects for economic emancipation

Originally published in *Business Week* (19 September 1994): 22. Reprinted with permission.

of the poor black population become slim. Unfortunately, the issue is not narrowly economic. Democracy is called on to come up with results that the economy cannot create.

Promises, Promises

On the home front, tensions are building around wage settlements and the budget. Workers equate democracy with the long-awaited opportunity to get economic benefits they have been flagrantly denied. And politicians are reluctant to say no, knowing that if the voters don't see economic progress reflected in their paychecks, there are plenty of politicians ready to promise the sky. That is the first step to increased spending, which soon is followed by inflation.

The next step, typically, is for inflation to be contained by allowing the currency to become overvalued. The obvious motivation is to stop a vicious circle of price inflation, wage inflation, and currency depreciation. But the overvalued currency contains the seeds of a currency crisis. That translates into shorter horizons and higher interest rates to persuade investors to stay on board. Those high interest rates in turn get borrowers into trouble—insolvency, then bankruptcy. Ultimately, the house of cards collapses. When the country runs out of foreign exchange, real wages plummet.

An economic collapse of South Africa is not around the corner, of course. One insidious aspect of populism is that at the outset, it is strikingly successful. More purchasing power does create jobs and prosperity—inflation comes later. Those who warn of the risks are loudly contradicted by the facts and lose credibility. And while the voices of moderation and prudence are relegated to the sidelines, populists gain in popularity and power. And because at first, populist policies pay off, they are carried far beyond the reasonable point—where they set the stage for collapse.

Latin Disease

This populist cycle is well known from countless examples in Latin America, always accompanied by the claim that "this economy is different." If wages can be raised, the argument runs, there will be growth; inflation is not a problem, and exchange rates do not matter. All this is true at the outset, but none of it for long. A memorable example of this cycle could be seen in Peru in the 1980s, when President Alan García thought he could create prosperity with the stroke of a pen. He had one great year, one good one, and then an awesome crash.

South Africa could catch the Latin American disease. Reminding Pretoria of the pending risks is useful, but the coalition's skillful crafting of a conservative strategy attests to its understanding of the risk. Attention of South Africa's policymakers and the outside world must focus on a few specific points:

• The world economic community must watch for populist challenges to the current economic plan and denounce them the moment they materialize.

• Public policy and international support must stress a massive investment effort in human capital—the only known source of sustained growth and prosperity. Here we are talking about an economy in which discrimination has kept the majority of the population out of fully productive lives.

• Open up the economy, which is riddled with protection, regulation, and inefficiency, freeing resources that can raise real wages without straining stability.

• Multilateral institutions must commit themselves to making South Africa's transition to a democratic, pluralistic society a showcase success, just as for security reasons they are marshaled to help achieve reform and stabilization in Eastern Europe.

37

Mexico Should Ditch the Peso for the Dollar

If Mexico wants to change, it should give up the peso and adopt the dollar as its currency. If that is done, an economic boom will result within the year, with 6 percent growth almost guaranteed.

Why give up the peso? Because each time Mexico makes economic progress, a currency crisis destroys it. Mexico's economy runs on a political cycle, with presidential elections coming every six years. By the third or fourth year, the economy is almost always growing, as it is now. Then election-year spending and borrowing lead to a peso crisis. This is the third year of the current political cycle, and Mexico has successfully emerged from the 1994–95 peso crisis. Unless Mexico changes its currency system, a replay of the crisis-collapse-recovery cycle will occur in 2000, the year of the next presidential election.

The seeds for trouble are already planted. There are grave political uncertainties as democracy catches up with a bankrupt official party and its hold on power. The congressional elections in July, when the National Action Party and the Revolutionary Democratic Party may increase their clout, will indicate what is to come. The financial system is in trouble, too. It continues to limp along with dilapidated balance sheets and daily infusions of government support.

Nations like to have their own money for many reasons. First and most prominent is nationalism. A country has its flag, its airline, and its money. They are part of its culture and identity. Printing money is also a source of funding for governments. They can pay out more to their

Originally published in *Business Week* (19 May 1997): 22. Reprinted with permission.

political constituencies by letting the printing presses run. Monetary policy, exercised through adjustments in interest and exchange rates, can also be valuable by providing flexibility to offset shocks to the economy.

Abused Policy

It is immediately clear that these traditional arguments are not compelling when it comes to Mexico. Every six years, Mexican government officials have abused just this flexibility, causing peso crises. They have overvalued the currency and printed money, even in the face of capital flight.

A dollar plan for Mexico could not be more simple. The country declares that the dollar is legal tender. The central bank uses its dollar reserves to retire large bills from circulation and replaces them with real dollar bills. Coins and small change in pesos can be left without risk. The banking system makes loans and takes deposits only in dollars.

The net effect would be to end currency volatility and inflation in Mexico. Prices and wages would no longer reflect the uncertainty that comes with regular peso crises and soaring inflation every six years. Wage growth would be limited to productivity increases. Prices would probably decline as people no longer worried about currency depreciation or inflation.

Argentina Prevailed

Can a plan like that work? Is it really that simple? Argentina has already declared parity with the dollar. No week passes without all of Argentina applauding that dramatic day in 1992 when the country made an irreversible commitment to the dollar. Growth has averaged an unprecedented 5 percent and now is running at near 7 percent. Stability was tested when capital flight after the last peso crisis threatened the Argentine economy. The dollar standard prevailed.

To avoid offending nationalist sensibilities, it would be better for Mexico to take the Argentine route and create a currency board that would manage a dollar-pegged peso. But Mexican presidential politicians have a record of manipulating the peso during election seasons. They simply can't be trusted not to interfere with a currency board. So the Mexican economy must become dollarized.

In the past, managing monetary and currency policy has led to disasters. It won't be any different in the future. The same people are in charge. They are well-intentioned, well-trained—and overwhelmed by the politics of the day. That costly insistence on trying to outsmart markets has destroyed progress for decades. The lesson surely is to ask whether it is worth retaining the peso as a national currency, and the answer is no.

Mexico has made extraordinary efforts in restructuring its economy and recognizing that integration with the world is a source of growth. NAFTA was a huge gamble and is now paying off. However, currency stability is an essential underpinning for flows of direct investment to Mexico. It is critical for obtaining low-risk interest rates on loans. These in turn are essential for a revival of investment and high growth. If Mexico wants social progress and political stability, the country must follow up the bold NAFTA move with one more downpayment for prosperity. It must move irreversibly on the dollar.

38
Brazil's Policy Options for the Second Term

Brazil is different, and always has been. Through the Mexican crisis, through the Asian crisis, and through the Russian crisis still underway—Brazil manages to hang on and hang in. Yet, Brazil remains one of the leading candidates on everybody's list: large budget deficits, large current account deficits, and lots of short-term debt are a giveaway to the crisis spotters, and Brazil has all of those. And yet it seemingly never happens. One reason Brazil enjoys more confidence than Russia or Venezuela is the firm expectation of a reelection for President Cardoso in the first turn and the resulting mandate for major reform in his second term. But there is also important private-sector progress in Brazil in the 1990s, which conveys the sense of a country that has all the makings of an important player in the world economy.

Brazil is different: without nuclear weapons, Russia would just be Africa and Venezuela, an inconsequential sideshow in a rapidly modernizing Latin America. Brazil, by contrast, is major league, but has not quite come through on its promise. With that promise, investors are not quite willing to give up. The government's well-trained interior decorators (Minister Malan the best of them—a true Pitanguy in his cosmetic attention to budgets, balance sheets, and investor egos) have been essential to the eternal youth of the notion that Brazil is the country of the future. All that is not enough once the election is past. The country has been living on the promise of things to come, but they do have to come some day, specifically in the next half a year. Without critical policy steps, lenders will lose confidence, and once that happens, the dike breaks.

What needs to be done? The key results to look for is the combination of reduced financial vulnerability and increased growth. The two goals are, of course, interrelated: higher growth improves fiscal performance and hence reduces financial vulnerability; less vulnerability lowers interest rates and hence raises growth. Reduced vulnerability is important because you cannot hold your breath forever, living with a near-state of siege defensive posture, where macroeconomics casts a shadow over everyday business life. Increased growth is essential because Brazil has been doing miserably in the past two decades, including the Cardoso years. From near 8 percent in 1960–80, growth fell to barely 2 percent in the 1980–98 period. That is just above the growth of population, meaning that the average person has not really gotten ahead, more so if we include the increased indebtedness and the fact that most government assets now are gone.

What role can exchange rates play in the return to financial stability and growth? Not much; there is no nifty trick that gets the country out of the box. A *maxi* devaluation is a terrible answer and has always been, at least since inflation and balance sheets have become an issue. A more aggressive crawling peg would have been a very good strategy early on in the Real plan, and it would have avoided the costly real appreciation that is now reflected in low growth, a large external deficit, sharply increased debt, and heightened vulnerability. Going the other way has had a payoff in lower inflation, but of course at a quite formidable price in terms of fragility and growth performance. Even if it is accepted, in hindsight, that the policy choice was bad, rewinding the tape years later just is not an option. Exchange-rate policy can at best help by increasing the commitment to a hard policy as Argentina has done and, in that way, reaping ultimately the rewards of confidence and interest-rate reduction.

Keeping the options open in the form of wider bands and an uncertain pace of crawl is a risky strategy for a country that has poor public finance and large external vulnerability; investors will charge a premium for the option. Keeping one's options is expensive in world finance. Therefore, if the policymakers are committed to low inflation, as surely is the case in Brazil, then they will surely resist a major move in the currency. And if that is their intention, they might as well go all the way in commitment and thus get rid of paying unnecessary premia to investors. The magic word here is *currency board*. Does it make sense for Brazil? Clearly, in Argentina it has been a decisive step to establish normality. In Brazil, as

President Cardoso becomes a lame duck and other possibly less promising policymakers appear on the horizon, institutionalization of financial stability is critical. Linking monetary policy rigidly to a fixed currency value is not at all plausible. It might be thought that this is a strategy for financially distressed economies and banana republics only, and not for a large and successful economy. Unfortunately, Brazil's status is damaged by two decades of mismanagement and hence does not have the luxury. The country has to show that independent of domestic politics of the day and personalities, there is a commitment to stability; that takes more than talk. That is surely even truer in emerging market finance, disillusioned by three years of crises.

The quest for financial stability, then, involves predominantly the virtuous circle of budget cuts inducing lower interest rates, lower deficits, and so on. If these cuts are lasting and not just provisional emergency measures, there is room here to make an important difference. But budget cuts will surely hurt growth, at least at the outset. The lower growth will improve the external balance, and that helps to foster some confidence. But investors understand that a Brazil without much growth is a risk. Hence more commitment on the exchange-rate front is an essential step to leverage the budget cuts into important interest-rate reductions.

If competitiveness cannot be achieved by exchange-rate movements, clearly labor market flexibility and productivity must be the means. Too little has happened here, in part because the government overly politicized *all* fronts of economic adjustment. The prospects of undoing a large overvaluation by this strategy can at best be limited; Argentina has gone that way with the greatest of energy. Wherever the government could find impediments to exports or unnecessary excess costs, from poor ports to cumbersome regulation in public finance, they have been all-out aggressive. There has been quite a bit of success, but clearly not enough to offset a high exchange rate. If Brazil wants to do well, it will have to at the very least match the Argentine enthusiasm for competitiveness. Labor-market flexibility is, of course, a key extra issue with links both to better employment prospects and reduced costs. Wages in local currency must come down and employment must go up. The two together, whether in Argentina or in Brazil, will only happen in far more flexible markets.

There is much hope that in the second term, President Cardoso can unwind much of what may have been done wrong, or not done, in the first. As a result, so the story goes, Brazil can then quickly move on to strong performance, with no more recurrent state of siege of near-currency crises and record interest rates. The expectations are excessively favorable. The central scenario is surely just 3 percent growth. The external environment is less benign than it has been in the past and the expectations of political support for radical reform too optimistic. Moreover, investors soon will look ahead beyond Cardoso and Lula, and they may see, unlike just now, much uncertainty and little comfort.

39

Brazil Beyond Tropical Illusions

Brazil is now in financial free-fall; in rapid succession, the country has gone from a failed mini devaluation (like Mexico in 1994) to a small exchange-rate band that collapsed within a day to a market-driven mega depreciation. Policymakers are shell-shocked by what is happening in the markets and so far unable to bring that major change of regime, which would justify renewed confidence in the country and its finances. True, its Congress has started passing the laws that might have been enough last year, but now they are way behind the curve. They look back to defend a record of interior decorating disguised as genuine progress. But prosperity is not measured by the stock market and privatization and all the money borrowed, but rather whether the economy's output per head is up and investment in the future has been high; after two decades of experimenting with bad money, unsurprisingly, they are not. The country got caught up in defending its overvalued currency and lost sight of the more basic question of growth and stability; they made a big bad debt, doubled and tripled the stakes, and now have been kicked out of the Casino. It is time for drastic reform.

Like so many stabilization attempts in its own history, and throughout Latin America, now the real plan has crashed. It lasted much longer than the others and looked a lot better, but that was because a gigantic amount of money was borrowed. On top, the revenues from privatization were made available to finance an appearance of stability and normality that everybody wanted to believe for their own reasons: the president to get another term of office, Brazilians because the pain of normality in a poor country with vast inequality is too stark. And investors were happy to join the fantasy because it was good business: agreed, Brazil is different. Yes, as always, until further notice; until then, let's deny reality. The Asian crisis had little to do with Brazil's collapse. It is all homemade, just as Mexico at the time, with an overvalued exchange rate and a huge budget deficit, vast short-term foreign obligations, and an explosive indexed domestic debt.

Brazil's claim to credit was that it stopped inflation but it did nothing to make it stick. The first phase of a stabilization without fiscal austerity, and with a strong currency, is always euphoria; inflation is low, money comes in from abroad, stock markets boom, consumption rises, growth is finally back. The second phase, once the doubts come and investors take their pound of flesh, means high interest rates and a shortening of maturities and indexing of the debt—one more helping of money please, just until the election and the IMF will help make it safe. And then comes the inevitable third chapter when investors want to get out while there is some money to leave, and that is when the house of cards collapses. Interest rates can't stay high forever, which means the currency won't hold, which means you have to get out, fast. Just like every other bubble.

The basic theorem of currency crises is this: they take a lot longer to come than you would think, and then they happen a lot faster than you would have thought. And then there is another theorem: of three crises predicted by economists, two never happen and the third is far worse than expected. Brazil confirms these truths. The amazing thing is this: after Mexico, after Asia, after Russia, just what were the Brazilians thinking? The investors are easy to understand—they know there is a brief window of reserve use and IMF money that allows them to jump ship and get off the boat with their feet dry. But how about those who hold the bag, in particular the government. Do they still believe in Santa Claus and "too large to fail"? And the IMF or the U.S. Treasury, should they not know better by now to be more skeptical when they see just promises and absolutely no reality? The answer that Brazil's government was unwilling to cooperate sounds absurd, is probably true, and just means that the IMF has now become an unconditional lender of last resort playing, promoting instability rather than sound finance. IMF chief

Camdessus has become the world's biggest croupier; Earth to Camdessus, get a grip.

There are three steps that have to be taken to create a stable and ultimately successful economy. First and most immediately, the country must adopt a currency board. The inflation and the exchange rate have been a perennial problem in the past twenty years, responsible for the fact of zero per capita growth in all that time! Basta, get rid of the central bank just as Argentina did. That is a difficult step for a large and proud inward-looking country. But it not just reflects an adaptation to a modern capital market that is trigger-happy and unforgiving. It is just common sense after the awful economic record of two decades. The traditional argument for a central bank comes in three parts: national pride, the ability to create money, and the flexibility gained from an ability to adjust the exchange rate rather than undergo painful domestic adjustments. A second's reflection shows that none of these apply to tropical situations where each and all have become a liability. To be proud of the fifth currency in just a few years is a joke, to print lots of money is a risk, and to adjust the exchange rate would be nice, but overvaluing it first and then having it collapse is perhaps not quite the idea. Currency boards in Hong Kong and Argentina are not a panacea, but they are an extraordinary pillar of stability in the midst of regional turmoil. They are the way to go.

The second step, unfortunate and inevitable, is a restructuring of the domestic debt. It is of extremely short maturity and indexed to the dollar or money market rates and accordingly growing at explosive rates; large interest payments on snowballing debt are a large part of the fiscal problem. Lengthening the maturity at preset, moderate, but indexed rates is not punitive and can solve the problem that otherwise, along the way, would simply become another write-off as Brazil did just a few years ago. The argument that nobody will lend to Brazil anymore is absurd; lenders come back in no time the moment that last debt is locked away or written off, as they always have.

The third step is to make a downpayment on structural reform and creditworthiness. Brazil should immediately put the remaining privatizations on the table and get them done, without corruption. Such a step will create confidence and help reduce the cost of capital as Brazil comes back to the world capital market. Getting the government out of business is half the story of reform. The other half is for the government to retreat from arbitrary rule making and interference with business life. A century of big, powerful, and unstable government has created a business life that seeks favors and privileges in exchange for support of bad government. Horizons are short and investment—as opposed to speculation and asset sales—is low and so is growth. Brazil is at a crossroads; it has run out of both money and *jeitinho*.

VII
The East Asian Miracle, Not Quite

40

Paper Tigers, the IMF, and the World Capital Market

First Japan's collapse came as a major surprise: a country that had lectured the United States for years on how to grow and get ahead suddenly showed itself fully on the ropes with bankrupt banks and a stock market that took a catastrophic nose dive. Next Asia's meltdown came as a surprise to most of us. Until only recently, Asian tigers and baby tigers were held out as the example of how to get ahead in emerging economies: stable public finance, high saving and investment, determined integration in the world economy. Thailand is in a deep mess; Korea is in a deeper mess; the Philippines are getting there, as are Malaysia and Indonesia, where political succession issues get on top of large external deficits and fragile banks. By now the only question is how much further they will fall and who is next: is Hong Kong about to tumble, will Singapore hold out, and just how ripe is China for major trouble? Any country with a large deficit is under suspicion, as is any country that pegs the dollar, any country that has a real estate boom, any country that has an overage dictator with succession trouble, and any country that has a very sick banking system. With criteria set so widely, few countries escape scrutiny.

Asia's bureaucracies—the architects of the miracle and the grandmasters of old-style repressed finance and modern high-leverage borrowing—are up in revolt. They claim a conspiracy of international speculator-rogues is bringing down perfectly sound economies. Their image is getting tarnished, and they are reaching out for exchange control and restrictions from financial trades; they make things worse by the day. And as Malaysia's irate prime minister Dr. Mahathir throws a tantrum and even slanders the IMF as a co-conspirator, he pushes the red button: these are bad guys, not reliable to lend to, bye-bye. Asset markets swell as investors look for more congenial places where the red carpet is rolled out with exquisite skill: Russia and Bulgaria, Brazil and Egypt.

The current crisis is neither an inevitable result of Asia's growth experience in the past two decades nor of international capital markets per se. Emerging market finance is an important development; the benefits for the world economy are dramatic in that it facilitates capital accumulation in backward economies and thus speeds up their advance in the standard of living by decades. Of course, borrowing abroad can only supplement, not substitute for, domestic saving. But Asia has no problem here; the saving rates have been high throughout. It is the investment rates that have been phenomenal. The core problem of Asian economies is their link to the international capital market: poorly regulated and overly leveraged banks, financial institutions, and large corporations. Their new-found ability to borrow offshore for little has translated into an investment boom that made them exceptionally vulnerable. At the core of every banking problem are bad loans of dead companies and red hot real estate that just crashed. Asia's financial crisis today is predominantly a crisis of domestic finance, not a currency crisis. The vulnerability of financial systems made it impossible for governments to have normal interest rates; their attempt to go below world rates then opened them to speculative attack. The unwise betting of all foreign exchange reserves (as in Italy and Britain in 1992) could only translate into one outcome: currency depreciation. And once that became clear, all lenders scrambled to get out, only to find that it was too late. The resulting mess became too large even for long-term investors to hang around: stock markets were selling off and a vicious circle of depreciation, asset collapses, and interest rate hikes is under way. The financial carnage is not over.

Asia's dictators (or quasi-dictators) have little sympathy for spoilers, whether they be democratic opposition parties or international investors. They spoil the appearance of peace and prosperity; they show the emperor without clothes. Asia's drama just now has as much to do with the illegitimacy of megalomaniac-corrupt government as it has with narrow financial issues. Don't blame the speculators. Their job has never been to lose money, they just risk it; they are paid by their investors to take risks in emerging opportunities and to pull out before the door closes. That is obviously very inconvenient for the finance minister, but it has been the rule of finance since day one. If a country goes into the game of international borrowing and seeking investors, it must check in all illusions at the front door. When Malaysia's prime minister calls the speculators "morons" and "racist," he is totally wrong: they are not stupid and they are not racist; in fact, they are color blind. But they do have a fine nose for trouble, and when they see it they rightly run.

It is surprising that Asia's borrowing, and especially that of Thailand, got as far as it did. It almost amounts to a reenactment of the 1980s debt crisis. The chief reason is that Japan neither had nor learned the lessons. Japanese banks, eager to restore their balance sheets by juicy premia in Asia, lent upward of $40 billion to Thailand. If anyone is to be blamed, it is the Japanese banks and their supervisors along with Thailand's financial authority, not the New York speculators who brought down the house of cards.

The IMF, too, is now coming under criticism. In the past, the IMF rarely commented on the *details* of budgets. They just watched the money supply and the deficit. But now their influence is vastly larger and so is their sense of responsibility. They now work with the leverage of capital markets. If the IMF gives its blessing, money pours into a country and removes all concerns about external finance. If the IMF frowns, all money stops. If the IMF says trouble, all money scrambles out in a chaotic flight. That new leverage makes the IMF the policeman of good finance. None of the large countries can or wants to play the role; the IMF is just right and is growing into its new role. The fund is totally justified in warning—at a time of intense systemic crisis in the region—that Malaysia's proclivity for megaprojects is perilous, that Thailand needs to pull its socks up, that Indonesia's deficit is too large. The whole world benefits if the IMF uses more force in its surveillance role. However irritated the finance minister who is chastised, three cheers to the IMF for speaking up loud and clear.

Asia is not the only place to look for unsound finance. South Africa is surely very fragile and has under way extremely perilous forward operations not unlike those of Thailand that caused the crash. Brazil is waiting for its crisis, hoping to push it beyond the next election; Russia is desperately and so far successfully pulling back from the brink. And more. Emerging maket finance will show high yields and, on occasion, very high risks; caveat emptor.

The new world of aggressively financing countries on the periphery means more uncertainty, more instability, and the occasional crisis. But crises are good: they do have an educational function in disciplining both lenders and borrowers to control risky exposures, limit vulnerability, and think of what can go wrong. There is a big need for that in emerging markets, and that is the silver lining in current clouds of crisis.

41

Why Is Japan Shooting Itself in the Foot?

A decade ago, Japan seemed all-powerful—and all set to play a dominant role in world trade and finance. Today, the yen is as almighty as the dollar was at the peak of its overvaluation in 1985, but its strength is illusory. The truth is that overly hard currencies cut first into profits and then into jobs, financial stability, and social cohesion.

The United States went down this road in the '80s. It has taken a decade to repair the damage from high real interest rates, bad balance sheets, overvaluation, and premature and excessive deindustrialization. Japan, for its part, has had deep pockets: losses were covered in home markets by shareholders and bankers who did not ask questions. Now, after many years of financial distress and no growth, the pockets are empty, and a serious battle is under way. Japanese companies know what to do—flee offshore and away from the strong yen, leaving behind broken lifetime contracts, broken banks, and broken public finance.

While the yen is going through the roof, Japan's economy is going through the floor. Companies are on the treadmill of currency appreciation and cost-cutting, banks are in trouble, and the government stands by wringing its hands. Japan is in a deadly spiral of overvaluation that is entirely self-inflicted: it madly pushes out goods and sucks in money. The Japanese save famously, but with profitability depressed, they invest little, and hence flood the world with goods. But as asset-holders, the Japanese insist on hard yen in their balance sheets and earnings flows, dumping surplus dollars around the world. The result, perversely, is a yen so hard that they can't afford to live on it.

Originally published in *Business Week* (8 May 1995): 26. Reprinted with permission.

Tired Model

In the past, there was Japan Inc.—a tight partnership of government and business that assured stability and growth. The goods and asset markets were kept repressed so companies could enjoy cheap finance from forced savings and high domestic prices to support battles for foreign market share. A rising yen was the rule—but never so fast that productivity growth couldn't pay for the strengthening of the currency. Today, the model is wearing thin: companies want to survive, and that means going offshore. Financial markets cannot cover up de facto bankruptcy forever, and that means credit is getting rationed. Government is straddling the fence between international commitments and the domestic conspiracy to keep markets sheltered. In policy and politics, the country is faring no better: old-timers are running the Ministry of International Trade & Industry, the Bank of Japan, and the Ministry of Finance as if nothing had happened. But with one-party rule shattered, politics is turning into a free-for-all.

For once, U.S. policies are not the reason for the strong yen. In comparison with Japan and Germany, the United States looks far sounder than it did in 1985, at the dollar's peak. The budget deficit is smaller than Germany's or Japan's, and the inflation rate has been moderate for a decade. True, budget-cutting would be desirable, and it would be a good idea to have a more concrete commitment from the Federal Reserve to moderate inflation, but even that would not make much difference to the yen.

Treadmill

Hot money funds might magnify the problem, but don't blame them—this is a problem of Japan Inc. malfunctioning. Over the past few years, Japanese monetary policy has been consistently supertight. True, interest rates were low, but prices were falling, and that meant real interest rates were high, especially considering the strained balance sheets and the absence of growth. Fiscal policy was also misaligned: there was stimulus, but it was always too little, too late. The righteousness of wrongheaded policymakers is reminiscent of the United States in 1928–32, when insistence on balanced budgets and tight monetary control precipitated the Great Depression. Japan needs prosperity policies, not more deflation.

Japan must also deal with its perennial trade problem. Until Japan offers an honest program of market opening instead of the empty promises of the past decade, financial markets will view Japan's trade surplus and yen shortage as reasons to push up the yen even more.

So far, the problem has mostly been one for Japan and for yen debtors. The trouble may not stay there, though: increasing fragility in Japan could cause worldwide instability. Until Tokyo grasps its own interests, the rest of us can do little to help Japan along.

To get off the treadmill, Japan must abandon the insularity of its trade and finance and come to grips with the incompetence of its policymakers. On the present course, the economy will hollow out at a rapid pace, and a society reared on consensus will become divided.

42

What's the Weakest Link in the World Economy? Japan

The Asian miracle is gone—and Japan may be feeling it worst of all. The country is on the ropes, pummeled by a collapse of asset prices and loss of confidence and by misgovernance, corruption, and political stalemate. Instead of solving the Asian crisis, Japan is increasingly the central problem for the entire world economy. Unless Japan grows, global prosperity and free trade will suffer. The situation in Japan has all the overtones of the United States in 1929: as the economy sinks, bureaucrats do little and claim that everything will work out in time.

Tokyo is deaf to advice from U.S. policymakers, who have been right all along. Even the International Monetary Fund, with characteristic convolution, has expressed skepticism. As an IMF deputy managing director recently said in Tokyo: "It will be important that no further withdrawal of fiscal stimulus take place in Japan, although further efforts are needed later on to make progress on fiscal consolidation." Let's be a bit more forceful here. Earth to Japan: get a grip! Get moving and do something big, because the economy is falling out of control.

All Gone

A decade ago, Japan was king of the world economy. The country was about to own all of America. A city block in Tokyo was worth more than all of California. Technology was tops. Quality was unrivaled. Public finance was exemplary. And stock market valuation reflected an

Originally published in *Business Week* (12 January 1998): 28. Reprinted with permission.

unlimited future of prosperity. None of that is left today. The United States has replaced Japan as the economic model, with strong growth, full employment, a balanced budget, and record asset prices.

Japan can't manage to take off into sustained growth. The budget deficit is huge and getting worse. Falling asset prices threaten bankruptcy throughout the financial system, from banks to insurance companies. The only growth is from an overly depreciated yen, as Japanese goods flood the U.S. market, hurting the rest of Asia. Undoubtedly, this is cheerful news to Representative Richard A. Gephardt (D-Mo.). There is nothing better for a protectionist would-be Presidential candidate than the deluge of imports starting to arrive.

Japan must urgently do three things. It must clean up its banks completely so that they can start lending rather than hiding their losses. The government's new package does not even begin to solve the problems at the banks, which hold bad loans adding up to nearly 15 percent of gross domestic product. The country must also introduce a major tax cut— amounting to at least 2 percent of GDP—to spur consumer spending. The $15 billion in tax cuts proposed by Prime Minister Ryutaru Hashimoto is much too small to boost the economy. Finally, to pay for all of this, Japan must deregulate dramatically. This will increase economic activity, create jobs, and generate the growth that will then provide the revenues to balance the budget.

Japan's bureaucrats are still mismanaging the world's second-largest economy. Disdainful of common sense and market economics, they hiked taxes, only to find that the economy fell like a rock. A recession will result, and will more likely be deeper than the previous three. In fact, the 1990s look increasingly like a single long recession briefly interrupted by aborted recoveries. Unless the tight fiscal policies are set aside, the economy will go down, taking the budget with it.

Much the same goes for the effort to clean up the banks. The Japanese bank cleanup is politicized, as it was in the United States. Populists hate the banks and conveniently forget that banks are a necessary part of the economy. The more prosperous they are, the more they lend. Bank cleanups are costly, but there is little choice. Without lending, there's no growth. Tokyo must bite the bullet and override the voters with some blunt truth about past mismanagement and current risks.

Deregulation is the third step Japan must take to get its economy going. It has been promised forever yet remains stalled. Because of restrictions to entry and a high cost of doing business, Japan's economy has too few people paying taxes. The nation desperately needs a Reagan-Thatcher revolution.

Japan is the weakest link in the world economy. It is rich beyond belief, mismanaged like no other place, stuck in a slump, and sinking fast. Without a vigorous economic expansion, Japan's fiscal problems cannot be solved, the Asian financial crisis cannot get better, and the open world trading system cannot operate smoothly. The United States should not and cannot bail out a rich trading partner that can't get its act together.

Hashimoto has said, characteristically: "We are different from the Asian economies. We are rich." True, but it seems increasingly that Japan would rather take its wealth to the grave than do what is necessary to change.

43

Mexico Learned Its Lesson. Now, Will East Asia?

In the latest round of high finance, Malaysia's Prime Minister Mahathir called speculators "unnecessary, unproductive, and immoral." One day, Mahathir is credibly talking of high-tech corridors to advance his country to First World status by 2020. The next, there is a serious question about the model, the future, and the man.

On the other side of the debate is George Soros, speculator-incarnate, announcing that Mahathir is a menace to his country, urging him to stop the verbal rampage lest investors get even more concerned about the viability of the Malaysian economic model. No question, Soros is right. Yet Asia finds it hard to accept the message and may reject the dominant role international capital is playing in emerging economies.

The Asian currency crisis that started in Thailand and has since taken its toll in the Philippines, Indonesia, and Malaysia is not unlike the Mexican crisis of just a few years ago. Mexico at the time had a large deficit and an overvalued currency. Devaluation—too late and too little —made matters worse because it revealed the terrible shape of banks and the vast and highly liquid debt exposure of companies and the government. Meltdown ensued until the U.S. rescue pulled Mexico out. All, except the last, applies to Thailand, which is suffering, in addition, from an overheated real estate market financed by cheap bank loans. Not surprisingly, once Thailand was found wanting, speculators asked who was next. The Philippines was an obvious case because the currency had appreciated quite a bit and the deficit had grown large. Indonesia and

Originally published in *Business Week* (13 October 1997): 18. Reprinted with permission.

Malaysia were not as obvious, but fell to speculators as evidence of their own parlous financial and trade situations became known.

Sanity in Indonesia

If a good set of policy responses to the Southeast Asian currency crisis was now put in place, it would assure investors that a period of austere management and investor-friendly policies lies ahead. But this is where the parallels between Mexico and Southeast Asia end. The aftermath of the crisis in Asia has seen quite different policy responses. In Thailand, the government is far from resolving the financial mess that has been created. Deep-seated and pervasive corruption plays a big role in it, and incompetence accounts for a lot. The liabilities are larger and due at short notice, and creditors won't roll their claims over unless they see positive action. The Thai authorities have not come up with much. The play is not over, and there may be more than one act to come. In Indonesia, the government tried for a while to fight off the attack by raising rates, as any government should. But they soon realized that speculators had laid a siege and were not short on stamina. The country intelligently drew the lesson, let the currency go, and moved to an impressive show of budget cutting. It restored confidence, and investors are already back.

Malaysia takes the prize for incompetence. The dictator-Prime Minister took the currency issue personally. Having become the incarnation of Malaysia's miracle, he could not accept that world capital markets could sink the currency with so much ease. And every time Mahathir gets off another tirade about the International Monetary Fund and Soros and the need to put them all out of business, more investors recognize his totalitarianism and want to get their money out. Every tantrum leads to another wave of selling and another round of stock market decline and currency depreciation.

Safety Zone?

The Soros-Mahathir shoot-out reflects a much wider problem than bruised egos. Simply put, Asia has a hard time accepting free-market economics. Its governments enjoy the access to external finance, technology, and applause, but do not readily accept the discipline that comes with it. When the going gets tough, the leaders revert to control mode, suspending economic freedom and closing the country to negative influences by suppressing the press or restricting investors. Latin America has accepted the IMF and international capital, but Asia has not really. It just can't get itself to embrace the new reality. One could imagine other Asian countries hunkering down with Japan and China to create a safety zone where international capital does not have the dominant vote. That might be attractive to Malaysia, Japan, China, and South Korea, which have been dragging their heels on opening up to capital flows. It is also a sure way to hold back Asian growth.

A currency crisis is a wake-up call to bring bad finance, budgets, and unreal projects under control. Mahathir and his cohorts better stop blaming the messenger and get the message.

44

A Bailout Won't Do the Trick in Korea

Korea is the most recent emerging market domino to tumble. No surprise that the country is asking the IMF for a giant $60 billion package to avoid defaulting on its external debt. It is yet another economy that had prudent public finance and a small public debt, high growth, and a good name. But under the surface there was a different reality: two decades of failure to promote deregulation, competition, strict credit policies, and clean government. Korea desperately tried to become like Japan and the bad news is, it succeeded. What went wrong and what to do about it?

Excessive liquidity in the world capital market encouraged indiscriminate lending in Asia. Just about any country, bank, or company could get loans at a slight premium over what the U.S. government pays. Reality was set aside, and testing the credit-worthiness of loan customers was abandoned. No one added up total loan exposures or the timing of cash flows to pay for loans falling due. There is an irony in all this. In the 1980s, we suffered an emerging-market debt crash in the context of a tightening of world liquidity. This time around, the problem is too much liquidity.

There are several fundamental problems of the Korean economy that lie behind the current banking and corporate crisis. Statism has become counterproductive. Even today, the government is central to the course of the economy in a way that is only matched by Japan. Statism was helpful decades ago at the threshold of development. But now, planning and interventionism must give way to markets and decentralization in order to solve the increasing complexity of economic decision making.

Originally published in *Business Week* (8 December 1997): 26. Reprinted with permission.

Clueless

The financial system has become dysfunctional. For decades, Seoul allocated credit, and the financial system was merely the cash register. Today, that system is plain bankrupt, with a cleanup cost estimated at 15 percent of gross domestic product.

The industrial structure of Korea is unbalanced. A handful of companies control 50 percent of GDP. These *chaebol*—large in terms of concentration and vast in their range of activities—operate under a centralized, bureaucratic leadership. They lack the agility to adapt to rapidly changing opportunities and needs. In fact, they have no clue as to their future.

Korea is caught between competition from low-wage economies such as China and Southeast Asia on one side, and Japan on the other. Korean manufacturing will find it increasingly difficult to compete in the world market. The competitive devaluations of Asian currencies are a further burden.

Korean democratization has changed the workplace. It has brought to an end a world where wages lagged productivity by years, where labor was patient beyond belief, and strikes only took place after work. Democratization has also brought to the surface vast political corruption, as pervasive as the bad debts in the banking system. In fact, they are twins.

Just as in Japan (or in Germany), everything in Korea functions with clockwork precision. The trouble with so much regimentation by government and corporate bureaucracies is that creativity is stifled. Despite impressive human capital, innovation hasn't caught on. Getting ahead is just not an engineering question.

Elbow Grease

Korea cannot get out of the crisis with quick fixes. Some extra devaluation, a little reform, more subsidies to bad businesses and banks, and an external aid package that shores up loans won't do. As this disgraced government is about to lose at the polls, the new leadership must make a dramatic break. Korea needs to open up its economy fully to outside participation. Foreign investors must take over and clean up the mess with a wave of uncompromising corporate and banking restructurings that are long overdue. Neither the government nor the Korean business community can do the job.

The almost daily call on the International Monetary Fund for new emergency loans is rapidly subverting that agency and the functioning of international capital markets. The IMF has become a lender of daily resort. A crisis such as the present one must be exploited to put in place a better-functioning economy. A minor attempt was made in Indonesia. In Korea there is a chance to go a great deal further. Foreign lenders, the IMF, the United States, and whoever else participates must settle for nothing less. Insisting only on a budget package that sets aside some money for bank cleanup won't cut it. But if Korea is unwilling, a moratorium on commercial debt service will teach both the country and its markets an overdue lesson.

45

An Achilles' Heel That Could Cripple China

When the 15th Congress of the Chinese Communist Party meets this fall, the appointment of new members in the leadership will draw much of the attention. But coming to grips with the huge and inefficient state-enterprise sector is at least as important. There will be a new commitment to reform, though, unfortunately, little else. The awful performance of state-owned enterprises (SOEs) and the growing potential of a financial disaster are surely the Achilles' heel of what now is called China's "primary stage of socialism," the euphemism for the current messy state of China's economy. Needless to say, the international implications are dramatic. If China gets stuck, Asia and the world need to worry.

China's extraordinary growth performance over the two decades since agricultural reform followed the catastrophic collapse of collectivism has been nothing short of remarkable. Over the past twenty years, China's per capita gross domestic product has quadrupled—a feat that has no counterpart in recorded world history. Savings and investment have been huge—too huge, in fact, in the sense that China could have developed with less inefficient public sector investment and more private consumption. Yet, China has grown faster than the other Asian superperformers. That success is mostly due to town- and village-owned enterprises (TVEs) and only in a smaller way to privately owned enterprise. SOEs contributed little.

Originally published in *Business Week* (15 September 1997): 24. Reprinted with permission.

Red Ink

Here is a sketch of China's economic landscape. According to the World Bank's "China's Management of Enterprise Assets: The State as Shareholder," there are about 7 million industrial companies. Of these, 5.7 million, all with fewer than seven employees, are individually owned, as are 60,000 that are either larger or have foreign participation. Another 1.5 million are the TVEs that have been the core of Chinese performance. Then there are the 118,000 SOEs that account for a third of industrial output, half of assets, two-thirds of urban employment, and 75 percent of investment. Half of them are incurring losses.

SOE reform has been on the agenda for years, with limited success. SOEs are being corporatized with bookkeeping and boards of directors making their appearance. In addition, economic performance is supposedly replacing the goal of simply meeting production targets regardless of cost or consumer demand. By and large, the process of reform is stuck. Indeed, the reform program itself is creating its own problems. Some attempts at change involve too much control, pitting the old Beijing ministries against the new boards. At other times there is too little control being exerted, allowing local managers to strip assets and raise wages endlessly.

Jobs Cut

As long as the bureaucrats in Beijing remain in place, we shouldn't be surprised when they interfere. A new script for reform means little unless the old controllers go and SOEs begin to operate more like the successful TVEs. Dismantling the centralized ministries must come first, but this is not even on the agenda. Second, SOEs are "small societies" in that they provide the whole range of social services for their employees—from housing, health, and schooling to pensions and funerals. Thus, reform must be accompanied by a new network of social services. Third, traditional SOEs, whether in France or China, are overstaffed, to provide both jobs for the masses and power and patronage to the administrators. A move to a profit-oriented mode of operation would mean a steep cut in jobs. Local governments and central authorities don't want the 110 million people employed by SOEs to join the floating population of migrants and unemployed.

Yet, reform must move into the fast lane or China's SOEs will bring down—not just slow down—the economic miracle. SOEs are a growing financial problem. They hurt healthy companies and banks by not paying their debts and they are a big drain on the budget. China's economy is already vulnerable, as in Thailand, to a real estate bubble. Beyond the financial factor, SOEs interfere with economywide efficiency. Their poor performance translates into protectionism, trouble in accepting World Trade Organization rules, limits to competition, and restrictions on internal trade. Everybody's playing field is tilted to keep the SOEs in the game.

China's political conundrum is this: it needs financial stability and rapid economic progress to legitimize the existing government. Yet it cannot get these without far more capitalism in the form of TVEs, joint ventures, and all-out private ownership. Perhaps the primary stage of socialism will be the last. Russia's move to raw capitalism scares the Chinese leadership. Yet they must do something. China is the coming big problem of the world economy.

46
Next, China?

Of late, pessimism has been a good rule of thumb in judging Asian financial prospects. Is China now under threat of losing stability and becoming part of the ever-widening Asian problem? Chinese devaluation is a possibility. But China does not need a devaluation. And its leaders would do well to reject the option squarely rather than use it as a blackmail tool in international poker.

The belief that China will devalue, sooner or later, rests on the fact that the country faces extraordinary restructuring challenges in the banking system and the state enterprise sector. These problems are hard to solve at the best of times, but without high growth the prospect strains political and social stability.

Unfortunately growth is down substantially, running somewhere between 5 and 7 percent. That compares unfavorably with the 10 percent average of the past fifteen years and is below the official target of 8 percent. The growth problem is, of course, largely a reflection of an export slump: Asian markets are vital to China; they have collapsed and so has export growth.

In the past decade, Chinese exports have often risen 20 percent a year; in the first half of 1998, they rose only 10 percent and by now growth may well have stopped. Because exports (in value-added terms) account for 10 percent of gross domestic product, going from 20 percent growth to zero costs 2 percent of GDP directly and, if you include knock-on effects, perhaps as much as 4 percent.

Originally published in the *Financial Times* (4 August 1998): 18. Reprinted with permission.

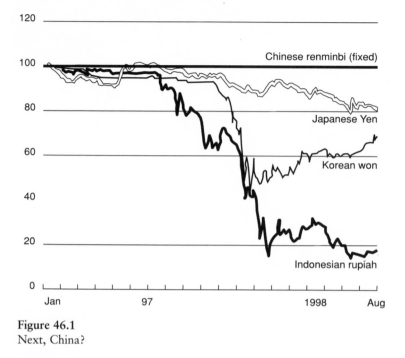

Figure 46.1
Next, China?

The problem is real and not about to disappear. Hence the conclusion: devaluation to get back to export growth is inevitable. All the same, the conclusion is wrong. China does not need to devalue, nor should it.

It does not need to because the country clearly has control of its exchange rate. True, all of Asia has undergone a competitive devaluation, leaving China with an overvalued currency and poor export performance. Even so, the external front is not under siege. Capital controls are quite tight (and getting tighter). There is a substantial current account surplus. And the country has sizeable foreign exchange reserves. This differs sharply from all the economies that have gone under. Moreover, if an extra buffer is needed, capital inflows can be increased by allowing more flexibility on joint ventures. That appears to have happened recently in telecommunications and might come about in other sectors. China is not hanging on to its last penny in reserves, nor is it about to call in the International Monetary Fund and the U.S. Treasury for an emergency package. On the contrary, it has the wherewithal to hang in and defend the present exchange rate if it wants to.

The real question is whether China should devalue, not whether it must. A small devaluation would do little for the country and a large devaluation might even do harm because it would surely set off a wave of financial instability, including currency depreciation throughout the region.

A small devaluation would do little because China must import about $1 for every $2 of exports. So a devaluation of 10 percent gains only 5 percent in competitiveness but highlights the prospects of further depreciation. A large devaluation would directly help competitiveness but, if it triggered repercussions (starting with a collapse in Hong Kong) and competitive devaluation everywhere, or higher interest rates to stem such an outcome, it would not help create better export opportunities. China is a big player. It cannot pretend not to be and get by with undercutting everybody else. In particular, China has a $50 billion trade surplus with the United States. This is already raising protectionist hackles in parts of the United States. If there were a devaluation, every opportunist in Congress would start complicating key policy objectives, such as Chinese entry into the World Trade Organisation. In sum, from the international point of view, devaluation is a bad idea.

So it would be on the domestic front. A large devaluation would tell every Chinese that the renminbi was not as good as the dollar. This could quickly lead to a black market in dollars and to bank runs, converting deposits into cash for exchange into dollars. China would face the choice of losing control of a shaky banking system under the pressure of devaluation or pushing ahead with banking reform over the next few years in the context of domestic financial stability.

The Chinese leadership abhors financial instability. They have long memories—remember that the Kuomintang lost China when they allowed extreme inflation. In the late 1980s, the authorities deliberately pushed down growth to fight inflation and the same happened in the past two years. Financial stability is politically even more important than high growth.

Still, the export slowdown is a fact. China needs to cope with it. It can do so through domestic expansion, rather than devaluation. The budget deficit is very small. So is the domestic public debt and inflation. There is absolutely no reason not to move ahead with fiscal expansion to shore up growth. Such spending need not take the form of more empty skyscrapers in Shanghai; it might just mean dealing with the pervasive bottlenecks in China's infrastructure. The substantial leeway for fiscal expansion offers some reassurance for faster growth and takes away some of the urgency of an export revival.

China's officials are talking out of both sides of their mouths. Threatening the prospect of devaluation, they have railroaded the United States into trying to save the yen. At the same time they say they are committed to being Asia's leading stable economy. China would do well to commit itself to the current exchange rate and hunker down for a few years with a focus on domestic growth and reform. Even if annual growth were "only" 6 percent, that should be enough both to raise the standard of living and deal with economic restructuring. If China gets too close to devaluation, what seems like a controlled event will become a catastrophic loss of control. Chinese leaders should get on with the WTO and get off flexing international financial muscle with the devaluation blackmail. Devaluation is a loser's game.

VIII

Good People and Bad Ideas

47

A Requiem for Chancellor Kohl

After the war, Churchill suffered a resounding defeat at the polls. In the long perspective of history, that is an inconsequential footnote. Much the same will be true of Chancellor Helmut Kohl, who just was ousted in no uncertain terms by the German electorate. He, too, has played an extraordinary role that will remain in the history books for centuries. The fleeting humiliation of electoral defeat is just a footnote that was by and large inevitable, since no great leader (and small ones even less) can let go before he is let go by the voters.

Kohl has accomplished two great deeds: unification and European Union. These deeds change the face of Europe forever, and for the good. Inserting an economically dominant Germany in a European Union meant heading off a hegemony quest that, just as in the past, could have gone badly wrong. Just the same can be said of unification: Kohl himself eagerly recounts a moment when, standing on a balcony in Berlin, he received an urgent message from Gorbachev: "If your tanks roll, so will ours." Tanks did not roll; the undoing of communist rule was unbelievably peaceful, even ultimately in Russia! Unification needed very cool heads at a time when people in the street were just grabbing freedom as if it was a foregone conclusion. Far from it; if it had not been for the special relationship Kohl had cultivated with Gorbachev, unification might not have happened and instead we could have had an uprising and suppression just as in the 1950s. Kohl gets the credit.

Whatever the quarrels about EMU and genuine questions about the costs of getting there or the benefits once there, there is no question that having a European Union is an extraordinary achievement. It surely is clear that Europe's move forward in a progressively strong integration, the internal market measures, and the common money are all for the good. Europe has major problems, but there are also the extraordinary advantages of an increasingly large and competitive market. It took stubborn insistence to hang in, fight for it, and make it happen. Kohl has delivered just that. Without his insistence, the world currency crisis would just now be knocking out Italy and perhaps even France. As it is, they are basking in the aftermath of interest rate cuts.

Much of the discontent expressed in Germany's election has to do with the here and now—someone that sets the European direction for the next century might well neglect the here and now of interest to the voters: jobs and feel-good rhetoric. Schroeder has filled the vacuum; it is always easy for a broad alliance focusing on the immediate—and promising what they cannot deliver—to oust someone who has been around too long and has lost the skill of being genuinely dishonest with the utmost sincerity. The red-green alliance will make the headlines much less with its accomplishments and much more with its quarrels, disagreements, and ultimate breakup.

Kohl might have engineered a soft landing, letting the next generation step in rather than his party being kicked out. He failed in that, but not necessarily for the worse. What has happened now is much better: the left gets a chance to discredit itself, the right can get a moment to rethink an agenda for the center, the next election will throw the weight to a group of genuine reformers on all sides. Mr. Schroeder is still flirting with a third way. Yes, there is one, but it is a dead-end street. The world economy holds out extraordinary promise, but also very substantial stress and tension. Europe now, more than ever, needs to take an active part in managing the world economy. Europe needs a leader to shape that role. Even before he has started, it is increasingly doubtful that Mr. Schroeder is a candidate for that job description.

48

Oskar Is Trouble

In Germany's election campaign, Schroeder offered the Blair promise: bright and young, fresh ideas and initiative, a compromise between social conscience and day-to-day business realism. He was the Trojan horse, used as the unthreatening face of a new approach—lacking convictions was his great asset, so that he could be everything to everybody. But inside every little problem, there is a big one trying to get out—Oskar Lafontaine, who took the center stage, staffed the top jobs, and set an activist agenda. Oskar Lafontaine is not center-left, or new-left; he is unreconstructed left. He is bright, he is a schemer, he is the winner in Germany's power struggle, and if he gets his way he will shape the future of Europe and not for the better. He is untouched by any notion of free market economics or sound finance, as if he had spent the past twenty years in some distant Gulag. In terms of sheer economic thinking and style, Lafontaine is to Greenspan and Rubin what Attila the Hun is to Western Civilization.

Europe has had its skirmishes with the center-left: Delors championed a Christian Democrat view of the market economy, and Jospin, and his activists, came from further left. But they all wound up in the middle, by and large compromising with the capital markets, which have little patience for the do-gooders and even less for architects of a *new social economy*. True, throughout Europe, even into the corporate boardroom, everyone leaves no doubt that they are unwilling to go to the U.S. extreme of "perform or perish"; they all want to keep some commitment to the welfare state, however expensive, unaffordable, and counterproductive.

Originally published in the *Wall Street Journal Europe* (25 November 1998): 10.

It was part of the culture and beyond narrow economic calculus. What is happening now, with Lafontaine's agenda, is going backward, as if the road to the competitive market economy, beyond the welfare state, had been a cul de sac.

Lafontaine can strengthen his hand by reaching for European support, by getting to the activists that have not gotten their way with Jospin and that have been in the wings (ostracized during EMU convergence under Prodi) in Italy. Surely, the ambition must be to turn Brussels into an instrument of pushing a new social agenda of sheltering labor from the market economy and taking from large corporations the front seat in the orchestra. While the free market economy had its heyday, until the world financial crisis revived skepticism about the benefits of unrestrained capitalism, all this would have been difficult. Now it is easy to speak of the need to control markets, social control of money, the need to create demand, and the State as a powerful way of achieving better economic outcomes.

What can Lafontaine accomplish? First and foremost, deregulation of labor markets and social benefits are going into reverse or, at least, into the slow lane. Second, Waigel pact budget discipline will come under attack not as a complement to supply-side reform but rather in a very crude spend-and-create-demand way. Fiscal reform is becoming anti-business taxation. Third, war will be declared on the ECB since cheap money is the easiest way to create jobs and take credit for it. All of this will be very counterproductive: stock prices might rise under the pressure of demand, but that won't last. Long-term interest rates will rise as savers perceive that discipline is lost; wage increases will be encouraged by pro-labor governments, and that means inflation will much sooner be an issue. In sum, an agenda of the past, and once thought dead, is having another life.

The demand-side rhetoric will take little time before we see references to the United States in the 1960s—bold fiscal expansion supported by monetary accommodation and fixed exchange rates, the way ahead. True, the United States then enjoyed a long period of expansion and record low unemployment; it also led to the great inflation of the 1970s. In Europe, the inflation will come much sooner because the encouragement for wage increases is already in the air.

Whatever Lafontaine may think, fixed exchange rates won't be part of his world economy. Britain surely will not sign up to a Europe that is going off the deep end intellectually, and the United States will most assuredly not link and fix currency rates unless things get bad enough and Gephardt becomes president. And even then, deep skepticism of European macroeconomics will make the United States want distance and independence from a plot to overthrow the market economy.

Europe is dying to have some growth, and Lafontaine promises just that, much as the Keynesian economists did for President Kennedy in the 1960s. But then it was an issue of real unemployment and not, as in Europe today, people being paid not to work. If this global economy is inflation-sensitive in the bond markets and wage-hungry in the labor market, it is too late to believe that big government, printing money, and borrowing from one's children are the way to get ahead.

49

The Crisis of Global Capitalism: Mixed Praise for Soros

There is no better time than now, with financial crises abounding and questions asked about just exactly what we think we are doing, to take a dramatic contrarian intellectual position. Markets are the enemy: regulate the beast, people first and down with unfettered capitalism! Soros writes, "I wonder if you would be reading this book if I had not gained a reputation as a financial wizard?" True, but even so, anyone who is looking for trading advice will be deeply disappointed; they will find more in the Bible or any how-to book. If you are thinking of a Christmas gift, this one would be for your mother-in-law.

A reader new to the writing of Soros will be baffled. The argument ranges freely and unconstrained by conventional discipline from the pathology of financial crises to a new role for the United Nations, from a closeup of the Russian collapse to the forthcoming demise of capitalism —very soon, somewhat later, or perhaps not—from a critique of economics and the need for liquidity at the periphery to an inquiry into the organizing principles of a moral society, including expanded powers for the European Commission in Brussels, as well as capital controls.

The basic theme is that financial crises and social dislocation everywhere are portending the very possibility of a collapse of market capitalism and the open society. The broad undercurrent is doom and alienation. "The institutions of representative democracy that for so long have functioned well in the United States, much of Europe, and elsewhere, have become endangered, and civic virtue, once lost, is difficult to

Originally published in the *Financial Times* (19 December 1998): 9, as a review of George Soros, *Open Society Endangered* (New York: Public Affairs, 1998).

recapture.... substitution of monetary values for all values is pushing society toward a dangerous disequilibrium ... market values cannot take the place of public spirit or to use an old-fashioned word, civic virtue." We are tearing *our* world apart, in finance and in politics; let good people stand up and get together to create a better society. This vast agenda is too much to chew on for anyone, let alone George Soros, who is not given the gifts of clear thought or a golden pen.

The book falls into three parts—a conceptual framework, a discussion of the current state of world finance, and an agenda for an open society. The first part is a retread of *The Alchemy of Finance*, and it has not improved since. The second part, which deals with the emerging market crisis, is by far the most interesting and well worth reading, in particular the incisive criticism of the IMF. The concluding part offers a sanctimonious elaboration of the notion that markets undermine intrinsic values and that societies had better deal both with finance and with a non-economic agenda.

The framework revisits Soros's concept of *reflexivity*—unlike in the objects of scientific study, economic reality does not exist in an independent fashion, beyond the influence of market participants' beliefs, perceptions, and expectations. On the contrary, unlike other facts like physics or the weather, they influence outcomes. Yes, it will rain, independent of my and everybody else's expectations; whether there is a boom or a bust is most surely influenced by what everybody thinks and how they act on it. I cannot imagine anyone disagreeing with this proposition, certainly not any undergraduate in economics. And then there is *fallibility* leading to the idea of an investment hypothesis as a *fertile fallacy*, as he calls it. The chief lesson is: "It is wise to always look for the fly in the ointment. When you know what it is, you are ahead of the game."

Like Einstein, who took pride in having failed high school, Soros makes much of not keeping up with financial economics. Accordingly, he tells us, his own financial success shows that financial economics is useless. Much of what he proposes is old hat in the economic interaction of expectations and outcomes, including the work of Nobel laureate Robert Lucas and much earlier work by Modigliani. The important work of Kahneman and Tversky—economic actors "framing" events in ways

difficult to square with a statistical evaluation—has long been standard reading in the economics of uncertainty and continues to be a fruitful line of research in experimental economics. His offensive comments about Nobel laureates Merton and Scholes—their failure at Long Term Capital Management documents the uselessness of financial economics—are plain mean and resonate poorly in a catechism of a better society. Enough said; he has no clue of what is done in financial economics research, and his ramblings in this part are at best an incoherent rendition of some common themes.

Soros's theory of boom/bust comes closest to a user guide on when to buy and when to run for cover. An elaborate dissection (p. 52) offers fully eight phases, from the early discovery of an investment hypothesis to its maturing, the challenge, the acceleration, the moment of truth, hanging on beyond belief, the downturn, and the crash. But "[N]ot every boom/bust process follows the same pattern. Every case is different and the curves have as many shapes as cases." Beware, in interpreting the current cycle, a few chapters and a few months later, a new model comes up that "differs from the original boom/bust model mainly in the complexity of its bust portion.... The length of the bust bears testimony to the complexity of the global capitalist system." And sometimes even that model is not enough, and we learn: "But when was the moment of truth? It may be best not to press the point. Models ought not to be taken too literally. There is nothing determinate about the course of history." So much for advice on when to sell and the creative use of hindsight.

Soros is most interesting in his analysis of the Asian crisis, the Russian collapse, and the failure of the IMF. His pictures of what went wrong and what are the flaws in the system is to the point, lively, and informative. He puts his finger keenly on the right spot: the IMF should have restructured the Russian debt rather than financing capital flight with inadequate funds, only to find soon a collapse of both debt and the currency. And he is right too in having argued for a currency board in Russia at the time. The IMF didn't have the guts and therefore failed. And what went wrong in Russia then is happening just now in Brazil all over again.

There is a short, blow-by-blow account of Soros's attempt to save Russia. Having sunk the boat with his letter to the *Financial Times* that called for devaluation, he reports how he followed up in trying to get the coast guard to rescue what was left. It is an endearing portrait of Soros as a crisis schemer, calling around with proposals and a rallying cry to save Russia if only to save capitalism. No question he was sincere; anyone who has seen him at work in the past decade knows his passion for being at the center of a financial crisis as a trader or, better yet, in his new persona as a mover and shaker.

The systemic reforms proposed here—an international credit insurance agency, capital controls, massive injections of liquidity at the world's periphery—are either grand or questionable. One is more inclined to favor the Bank for International Settlements suggestion that countries should negotiate debt covenants that include a contingency-based lengthening of maturities. It solves the problem of capital flight while maintaining a market-based orientation. It can be done tomorrow. Equally interesting is Argentina's solution of off-shore credit lines for their banks, which has the double advantage of a lender of last resort and agencies taking on the all-important issue of supervision.

The last half of the book is disappointing in its going round the bush on an open society—a society capable of infinite improvement—and the off-the-cuff proposals for reform of the world economic and political system. There is a plethora of suggestions, thrown out for discussion indiscriminately like chicken feed. It is not even clear which one Soros favors or why. Unfettered capitalism has many cutting-edge critics, while social improvement has many worthy champions. George Soros is not interesting on either theme. Thank God he is an unselfish, generous, and genuinely creative philanthropist, because otherwise he would just be another rich and self-important bore.

Index